Atmospheric Architectures

Atmospheric Architectures

The Aesthetics of Felt Spaces

GERNOT BÖHME

**EDITED AND TRANSLATED BY
A.-CHR. ENGELS-SCHWARZPAUL**

BLOOMSBURY VISUAL ARTS
LONDON · NEW YORK · OXFORD · NEW DELHI · SYDNEY

BLOOMSBURY VISUAL ARTS
Bloomsbury Publishing Plc
50 Bedford Square, London, WC1B 3DP, UK

BLOOMSBURY, BLOOMSBURY VISUAL ARTS and the Diana logo
are trademarks of Bloomsbury Publishing Plc

First published in English, 2017
Reprinted 2017
This edition published 2018

'Leibliche Anwesenheit im Raum'
'Atmosphären zwischenmenschlicher Kommunikation'
'Den Umgang mit Atmosphären lernen - eine neue ästhetische Erziehung des Menschen'
'Licht und Raum'
'Atmosphären kirchlicher Räume'

from Gernot Böhme, Architektur und Atmosphäre. © Wilhelm Fink GmbH & Co. KG,
Paderborn 2013.

'Atmosphäre als Grundbegriff einer neuen Ästhetik'
'Der Glanz des Materials'
'Die Kunst des Bühnenbildes als Paradigma einer Ästhetik der Atmosphären'
'Architektur: eine visuelle Kunst?'
'Die Stimme im leiblichen Raum'
'Das Ding und seine Ekstasen'
'Das große Konzert der Welt'

from: Gernot Böhme, Atmosphäre. Essays zur neuen Ästhetik. © Suhrkamp Verlag
Berlin 2013.

For legal purposes the Acknowledgements on p. xiii constitute an extension
of this copyright page.

Cover design: Eleanor Rose
Cover image © Hannah Hopewell

A catalogue record for this book is available from the British Library.

Library of Congress Cataloging-in-Publication Data
A catalog record for this book is available from the Library of Congress.

ISBN: HB: 978-1-3500-8970-9
ePDF: 978-1-4742-5810-4
ePub: 978-1-4742-5809-8

Typeset by Integra Software Services Pvt. Ltd.
Printed and bound in Great Britain

To find out more about our authors and books visit www.bloomsbury.com
and sign up for our newsletters.

Contents

Illustrations

List of Original Publications

'The art of staging as a paradigm for an aesthetics of atmospheres' originally published as 'Die Kunst des Bühnenbildes als Paradigma einer Ästhetik der Atmosphären' in (1995). *Atmosphäre: Essays zur neuen Ästhetik* (pp. 101–111). Frankfurt am Main: Suhrkamp Verlag. Reprinted in 2013 (7th revised edition).

'Atmosphere, a basic concept of a new aesthetic' originally published as 'Atmosphäre als Grundbegriff einer neuen Ästhetik' in (1995). *Atmosphäre: Essays zur neuen Ästhetik* (pp. 21–48). Frankfurt am Main: Suhrkamp Verlag. Reprinted 2013 (7th revised edition).

'Atmospheres in architecture' originally published as 'Atmosphären in der Architektur' in (2008). Metropole, pp. 52–67.

'Atmospheres of human communication' originally published as 'Atmosphären zwischenmenschlicher Kommunikation' in (2006). *Architektur und Atmosphäre* (pp. 32–42). München: Wilhelm Fink Verlag. Reprinted 2013 (2nd revised edition).

'Church atmospheres' originally published as 'Atmosphären kirchlicher Räume' in (2006). *Architektur und Atmosphäre* (pp. 139–150). München: Wilhelm Fink Verlag. Reprinted 2013 (2nd revised edition).

'The ecstasies of things: Ontology and aesthetics of thingness' originally published as 'Das Ding und seine Ekstasen' in (1995). *Atmosphäre: Essays zur neuen Ästhetik* (pp. 225–246). Frankfurt am Main: Suhrkamp Verlag. Reprinted 2013 (7th revised edition).

'The grand concert of the world' originally published as 'Das große Konzert der Welt' in (1995). *Atmosphäre: Essays zur neuen Ästhetik* (pp. 261–275). Frankfurt am Main: Suhrkamp Verlag. Reprinted in 2013 (7th revised edition).

'Learning to live with atmospheres: A new aesthetic humanist education' originally published as 'Den Umgang mit Atmosphären lernen – eine neue ästhetische Erziehung des Menschen' in (2006). *Architektur und Atmosphäre* (pp. 43–53). München: Wilhelm Fink Verlag. Reprinted 2013 (2nd revised edition).

'Light and space' originally published as 'Licht und Raum' in (2006). *Architektur und Atmosphäre* (pp. 91–103). München: Wilhelm Fink Verlag. Reprinted 2013 (2nd revised edition).

'Material Splendour' originally published as 'Der Glanz des Materials: Zur Kritik der ästhetischen Ökonomie' in (1995). *Atmosphäre: Essays zur neuen Ästhetik* (pp. 49–65). Frankfurt am Main: Suhrkamp Verlag. Reprinted in 2013 (7th revised edition).

'The presence of living bodies in space' originally published as 'Leibliche Anwesenheit im Raum' in (2006). *Architektur und Atmosphäre* (pp. 114–125). München: Wilhelm Fink Verlag. Reprinted 2013 (2nd revised edition).

'The voice in spaces of bodily presence' originally published as 'Die Stimme im leiblichen Raum' in (1995). *Atmosphäre: Essays zur neuen Ästhetik* (pp. 159–170). Frankfurt am Main: Suhrkamp Verlag. Reprinted in 2013 (7th revised edition).

Foreword

'Ecstasies'

In a comment on architectural drawing, the architect and educator John Hejduk once argued:

> What is important is that there is an ambience or an atmosphere that can be extracted in drawing that will give the same sensory aspect as being there, like going into a church and being overwhelmed by the Stations of the Cross… You can exude the sense of a situation by drawing, by model or by good form. (Hejduk, 1985: 58)

It is a statement that resonates with the richly articulated reflections of Gernot Böhme contained in this book, many of which appear here in English for the first time. In Hejduk's claim, the point is not about pictorial veracity, but rather about the construction of an atmosphere that the representation shares with its referent – although now, of course, neither of these terms, representation or referent, continue to hold. Instead they share a condition of co-presence, merging into one another, as the drawing itself can no longer be thought of as merely secondary. In addition, this entails a condition of complexity that goes beyond the visual parameters of the drawing. Certainly, qualities of composition, projection, form, line, tone and suchlike will be 'generators of atmosphere', as Böhme puts it, but we are now within a much more expansive field of sensory engagement, which entails the touch and scent (and thus even 'taste') of the drawing; its size and position in relation to our bodies; the non-intentional traces that it has come to bear; the luminescence of its material support and markings; and even, as Hejduk's brief text implies, its situation and the broader – let's say, cultural-material-environmental – conditions within which we encounter it.

Where Hejduk uses the word 'exudes', Böhme introduces his important idea of the 'ecstasies of things', which he mobilises against the conventional philosophical understanding of the closure and passivity of the object. Now, through their ecstasies – thought of as forms of presence – things extend beyond themselves to produce effects in complex relational interactions with other entities. The idea entails a 'principle of excitation', and it is an important notion for architecture – it gives us a way of articulating the effects of constellated things and, as Böhme would say, our atmospheric competence in interacting with them; it helps us to think about how even a small object of a certain kind placed in an empty room can seem to vivify and even 'fill' the space; and, at a larger scale, it prompts us to reconsider the way entire urban forms come to take shape and accrete within the sphere of influence of particular auratic objects (one thinks particularly here of religious relics here, sacred sites, etc.).

Shifting ideas of the affectivity of architecture have been central to how it has been conceptualised and to ideas of what its pursuit should be. Böhme's deeply stimulating texts give us important ways of thinking again about this history. At times the relations seem very close and correspondences spring to mind – whether it is Leon Battista Alberti's *concinnitas*; John Soane's 'poetry of architecture'; or László Moholy-Nagy's architectural spatialisations of light. But the reach of the ideas extends far beyond such examples, and suggests many interesting lines of inquiry. Moreover, with its reflections on the contemporary 'aesthetic economy', the book issues to us the critical challenge of thinking through the ubiquity of design in advanced capitalist society, in which manipulative and coercive uses of atmospheric production can seem all-too-evident and the emotions themselves are conscripted and animated by capital in the form of what has been called affective labour.

Professor Mark Dorrian,
Forbes Chair in Architecture,
Edinburgh College of Art,
The University of Edinburgh

Acknowledgements

I thank Gernot Böhme for extensive discussions over coffees and lunches, a remarkable lack of narcissistic investment, and a great generosity of spirit.

I also thank Ross Jenner for help with translation, advising on architectural and classics history, Greek terms and their spelling, Native English speakers' style, intelligence and humour, plain good sense, and companionship.

Kia ora to Carl Mika for locating a Novalis quote in English translation. The editors at Bloomsbury were helpful and supportive, particularly James Thompson and Claire Constable. I am grateful for their contribution.

Auckland University of Technology's School of Art and Design supported me with the grant of a sabbatical, which helped substantially to advance the translation and to discuss it with Gernot Böhme in Darmstadt.

Approaching Atmospheres

Translator's Introduction

When pressed for a definition of atmospheres, Gernot Böhme calls them *tuned spaces*. The term conjures up Jacob Böhme's writing about instruments and their character in *The Signature of All Things* (1651). Their attunement makes them sound with others in characteristic ways, reflecting the relationships of many elements in an enfolded, expansive space. Atmospheres, which are experienced through immersion and by the ways in which they affect our disposition, are impossible to locate precisely. They are dynamic, diffused and, as pre- and inter-subjective, spatial carriers of mood, suffused with emotional power (see pp. 69 and 20). Space, at least the space in which we are, is not something like an object. Rather, it provides a horizon, in which things and people appear and where their lives play out. Like much that is important about built spaces, atmosphere's enveloping nature as both void and totality is constitutively invisible but we can perceive it in other ways. Taking his lead here from Walter Benjamin and Hermann Schmitz, Böhme proposes that one of the best ways to access architecture as a spatial art is through bodily presence.

Architecture, so Benjamin, is experienced habitually and in a disposition of distraction – as much through haptic appropriation as through sight (1969: 239–240). His concept of aura (Greek αὔρα: breeze, Latin *aura*: breeze, breath) is a springboard for Böhme in conceptualizing atmosphere. Böhme emphasizes the relational role of aura, the 'indeterminate, spatially diffused quality of feeling' encompassing perceiver and perceived (2013: 27). Aura is a 'strange', connective 'tissue of space and time' (Benjamin, 2008: 23): as one breathes aura and absorbs it into one's body, body and environment invisibly and intangibly entwine (Takamura, 2011: 143). As self and world infuse and diffuse, sight and touch intersect; a perceptibility arises that corresponds to an other's attentiveness (Novalis, Kamnitzer, & Helmstatt, 1929).[1] Aura and atmospheres, then, suggest ways of relating to the world that are very different from those produced by the 'pervasive and dehabilitating split between subject and object' scarring modernity (Latham, 1999: 466). Indeed, to experience aura one must be able to transpose a common response in human relationships to relationships with inanimate or natural objects: to 'perceive the aura of an object we look at means to invest it with the ability to look at us in return' (Benjamin, 1969: 188). Like the Romantics, Benjamin links sensorial aspects of perception: sight, touch, and other senses – conjuring up a peripheral vision by which one feels one's way around a space (Latham, 1999: 463), rather than keeping it at a distance (as Alois Riegl thought typical of architecture since the Romans, 1985: 30). In the recognition of an Other, for which distance, however small, is necessary, objects transcend their boundaries; subject and object are part of the same world (Latham, 1999: 464).

Speculatively and through ephemeral experience, thought presses 'close to its object, as if through touching, smelling, tasting, it wanted to transform itself' (Adorno, 1982: 233). Perception is 'affective and merging participation', for Hermann Schmitz (whom Böhme considers to have first systematically introduced the term *atmosphere* into philosophy),[2] and atmospheres are 'moving emotional powers, spatial carriers of moods' (see p. 20). In bodily felt spaces, atmospheres can activate a kind of architectural engagement quite different from that triggered by Euclidean geometries. This difference reflects two contrasting European concepts of space, *topos* (τόπος, Aristotle) and *spatium* (Descartes). While *topos* is a place in which one finds oneself, a space of bodily presence whose dimensions and directions relate to the body (up/below, right/left, front/back), the geometrical proportions of *spatium* constitute space as a medium of representation for some-thing. *Topos* is characterized by tightness or expansion, movements or restrictions, brightness or darkness, lucidity or opacity, and so on, and the same characters, as Böhme calls them following Christian Cajus Lorenz Hirschfeld (see p. 58),[3] pertain to atmospheres as tuned spaces or spatially diffused quasi-objective feelings. A space can affect us as heavy or uplifting, serious and serene, festive, sublime, cool, or cosy, elegant, grand, medieval, and ancient. At least five types of characters: moods, synaesthesia, movement suggestions, and conventional and communicative characters participate in the perception and generation of

---

[1]See also p. 30.

[2]Other important precursors are Martin Heidegger (p. 41f), Otto Friedrich Bollnow (2010), Hubertus Tellenbach (p. 103f), und Christian Cajus Lorenz Hirschfeld (p. 25f).

[3]See also Rowe (1976).

atmospheres. In this area, Böhme significantly expands on Schmitz' elaboration of atmospheres. He identifies and analyses classical concerns, such as geometry, shape, proportions, dimensions, and also light, colour and sound, among the objective means by which atmospheres can be generated. Some material atmospheric aspects are conventional and depend on culture-specific values and judgements while, conversely, signs and symbols have not only conventional but also affective, atmospheric dimensions. Their embeddedness and continuity in a culture give them affective value. Atmospheres, then, arise between people and things; they are neither objective nor subjective but 'the shared reality of the perceiver and the perceived' (see p. 23). How this reality is conceived will impact on perception and spatial practices, in turn.

While acknowledging the overlap between an aesthetics of proximity and one of distance, as it were, Böhme takes issue with the dominance of semiotics in aesthetic theory in the 1990s (see, for instance, p. 15ff): semiotics wrongly privileges symbol-mediated communication over affective and corporeal modes of experience, reducing aesthetics to narrowly framed appreciation. Further, modern art left us with non-representational images, which are inaccessible to a semiotics-oriented aesthetic theory yet offer important experiences. An aesthetics of atmospheres, Böhme proposes, explicates experiences that, as in James Turell's works, no longer relate to tangible artefacts but to atmospherically tinctured spaces. Music, too, can be recognized as a spatio-emotional phenomenon and language for its ability to generate atmospheres. New media aesthetics and *aisthesis*, as a theory of perception, are two sides of the same cultural development in technical civilization.

Similarly, Böhme challenges the central importance of visual representation in architecture. The nature of most architectural work dictates that spaces that are, after all, designed for the bodily presence of people have to be presented in drawings, computer renderings, and models. This visual presentation further reinforces Euclidean notions of space. Yet, architecture is not a visual but a spatial art, which is best experienced in bodily sensing through which the spatial design enters directly into one's disposition. This immersive experience of architecture also includes the music deployed as ubiquitous acoustic furnishing in public spaces, department stores and malls, subway stations and trains, elevators, doctors' waiting rooms, and airports. An aesthetics of atmospheres develops a critical repertoire to analyse the emotional manipulation intended by these strategies. None of these aspects can be even approximated by a conception of architecture as a visual art – atmospheres are not visible; yet, so Böhme, they are vitally important.

Böhme's take on atmospheres is influenced by his personal and intellectual trajectory. Born in 1937 in Dessau, he studied mathematics, physics, and philosophy in Göttingen and Hamburg. Having completed his PhD thesis in Hamburg on the modes of time in 1966, he moved into philosophy, working particularly on Plato and Kant. His work at the Max-Planck-Institute in the 1970s investigated life conditions in the scientific-technological world. During that period, he also qualified as a professor with a dissertation on Plato, Aristotle, Leibnitz, and Kant's theories of time. In 1977, Böhme accepted a chair for philosophy at Darmstadt University of Technology, a position he held until his retirement in 2002. His research included classical and natural philosophy, philosophy of science, theories of time, aesthetics, ethics, technical civilization, philosophical anthropology, and Johann Wolfgang von Goethe. Böhme held professorships and guest professorships at Kyoto, Vienna, Graz, Rotterdam, and Linköping and conducted research at the University of Wisconsin, Australian National University, as well as Cambridge and Harvard Universities.

An active interest in the practical and social relevance of philosophy has always accompanied Böhme's academic and theoretical engagements. He co-initiated the 1984 *Darmstädter Verweigerungsformel*, a declaration signed by more than 100 scientists to refrain from participation in the development of weaponry and to make transparent the contribution of their disciplines to this sector. From 1997 to 2001, Böhme was *Sprecher* (speaker) at the Graduate School for *Technisierung und Gesellschaft* (Technification and Society), Darmstadt. With particular relevance for current global affairs, Böhme drafted the 1992 *Erklärung gegen Ausländerhaß, für Menschenrechte und Demokratie* (Declaration against the Hatred of Foreigners, for Human Rights and Democracy), at a time when violent attacks against migrants increased significantly in Germany. Whereas the majority of the population, as well as the state, seemed to tolerate if not condone such actions, 130 Darmstadt professors signed the declaration. A series of lectures during the summer of 1993 led to the publication of an edited collection, *Migration und Ausländerfeindlichkeit* (Migration and Xenophobia, co-edited with Rabindra Nath Chakraborty and Frank Weiler, G. Böhme, Chakraborty, & Weiler, 1994). Following his retirement from Darmstadt University of Technology, Böhme founded the Darmstadt *Institut für Praxis der Philosophie* (IPPh, a private institute for the practice of philosophy), which he has since directed.

Böhme's interest in the practice of philosophy has considerably influenced his approach to writing: typically, he works with a series of case studies, from which he develops and into which he embeds his theory. 'Scholastic' philosophizing, in the sense of an expert activity, or, in Schopenhauer's terms, a professorial philosophy for professors of philosophy (*Professorenphilosophie für Philosophieprofessoren*), is of little interest to Böhme. What matters to him is the realization of philosophy in personal and social life, a critical praxis complementing academic philosophy that engages with contemporary life. It is realized through participation and engagement, the ability to tolerate not-knowing and an involvement in life, as nature and with nature.

Until very recently, this aspect of Böhme's work was not apparent to Anglophone readers. The fact that an entire section (entitled *Das kritische Potential einer Ästhetik der Atmosphären*, The Critical Potential of an Aesthetics of Atmospheres) is missing in an English translation of *Atmosphäre als Grundbegriff einer neuen Ästhetik* ('Atmosphere as a Fundamental Concept of a New Aesthetics', 1993a)[4] would have further contributed to misunderstandings about his positions. In any event, only a few brief texts were available in English translation until 2000 (1993a, 1995c, 1998b, 2000a), and only six more (2003, 2004, 2005a, 2008b, 2009, 2010b) were published by 2010. Translations, in a wide variety of venues and often difficult to find, were undertaken by many different, often anonymous translators, using different terminologies and diverse approaches to the task of translation.

Perhaps not surprisingly, therefore, an impression arose with some writers that Böhme insufficiently considers *atmosphere* in its original meaning, namely as weather or climate. Most recently, Mădălina Diaconu (2014: 328) notes that 'the weather plays a role only as a subject of artistic representation' in the aesthetics of atmosphere.[5] Other critics consider Böhme's conception of atmosphere to lack temporality – either as quality (Morton, 2007: 166) or as history (implicitly, Boswell, 2014; explicitly, Riedel, 2015: 94. See, however, p. 70ff in this book).

Since 2010, with further English translations of Böhme's essays becoming available, there has been a fast-growing awareness of the role of atmospheres. The 'atmospheric turn', to which Böhme's work has contributed significantly, is of interest to contemporary philosophy, aesthetics and art criticism, music and visual arts, architectural practice and theory, performance, management and business studies, as well as education. This book now brings together Böhme's most seminal writings on the subject, providing a broad and systematic base for the further reception of his work and opening up opportunities for its extension in new directions.

In a recent publication, *Ästhetischer Kapitalismus* (Aesthetic Capitalism, 2016; to be published in English as *Critique of Aesthetic Capitalism*, 2017), Böhme takes up the topic of needs (*Bedürfnisse*) and desires (*Begehren*) again to explicate how aesthetic needs are neither needs nor desires, but *Begehrnisse* – a neologism condensing the German terms for *needs* and *desires*. *Begehrnisse* are not sated in their fulfilment like (basic) needs, but rather intensified, and therefore highly topical for practitioners of art, design, architecture, and many related fields. In a field of tensions concerning what

---

[4]Later published in a German collection of essays (Böhme, 1995a).
[5]However, see Böhme's essay, "'Mir läuft ein Schauer übern ganzen Leib' – das Wetter, die Witterungslehre und die Sprache der Gefühle' ('A Shudder Runs Through My Whole Body' – Weather, Meteorology and the Language of Feelings, 2007).

constitutes a good life in a precarious environmental present and future, it is crucial to come to terms with *Begehrnisse*. There is no point in differentiating between art and kitsch according to conventional aesthetic standards, and Böhme accordingly treats them equally: artists, designers, architects, artisans, cosmeticians, and florists are all aesthetic workers (see p. 65). They produce a *More* (Adorno, Adorno, Tiedemann, & Hullot-Kentor, 2002: 79) in artefacts, taking them beyond their thingness and traditional usefulness, which Böhme calls 'staging value' – a hybrid of use and exchange value. The qualities and meanings given to commodities for the purposes of exchange by branding and marketing experts may, if they serve to stage a personality or life style in the context of use, become their actual use value. Thus, the boundaries between architecture and the stage set blur when architecture acquires the staging value of a commodity. Under certain conditions, however, the intensification of everyday life can subvert all official intent in the production of environmental atmospheres. The aesthetization of the real, ubiquitous in developed capitalist economies, can be differently inflected. Böhme (2014) recounts the example of the Nordweststadt Centre, a shopping mall in a predominantly working-class quarter of Frankfurt (Germany), which has a higher than average proportion of migrants (Figure I.1). Like *flâneurs*, the residents of the Nordweststadt quarter have made the shopping centre their *urban village*: a place in which they spend their time at ease, meeting friends, participating in life, and, occasionally, also shopping.

To me, these cultural aspects of atmospheres are particularly interesting and relevant – now that Europe yet again faces the challenges Böhme and his colleagues addressed in the early 1990s. Rising figures of migrants seeking refuge and/or work challenge us to develop ethical and practical positions in response. Then as now, the actual increase in the numbers of migrants was probably less influential than the atmosphere of fear created by metaphors such as *marauders* and *swarms* or *floods* of migrants (Shariatmadari, 2015). In our age of comparison (Nietzsche), in which a fusion of horizons (Gadamer) is no longer a choice since none are left (as Joseph Campbell argued already some forty years ago, 1972: 221–222), collisions of people and ideologies are as unavoidable as they are commonplace. In his consideration of non-Western concepts that have affinity with his concept of atmospheres, Böhme has taken up this challenge.[6] Atmospheres' non-Euclidian and generative characteristics may offer alternatives to the prevailing zero-sum approaches to space and resources. They may change patterns of thinking, so that people no longer automatically assume that a gain for one side necessarily means loss for the other. If an atmosphere, a *More* transcending mere facticity, is produced between people in exchange, there is a possibility that it can create a common world with shared ways of thinking (Julmi, 2015: 55–56).

---

[6]See briefly in this collection, p. 103, and Böhme (1998c).

FIGURE I.1 Nordwest-Zentrum, Frankfurt (Apel, Beckert & Beckert, 1965–1968; extension: JSK, 2004) / © 2010 Gernot Böhme.

It seemed important to me to preserve Böhme's style, which locates him as a writer at a specific historical and sociocultural intersection, and I have therefore erred on the side of faithfulness in translation. Only sometimes, I followed Novalis' (1997: 28) maxim to act in the author's spirit by changing his diction. Only rarely, when an English translation rendered the German insufficiently, have I provided the original term in brackets.

One non-matching sphere of connotations between German and English warrants some discussion here in the beginning. The terms *Befindlichkeit* and *Befinden*, both derived from *sich befinden* (to be positioned, to find oneself, to feel), entail an ambiguity that matches them with the notion of bodily presence in space. When translated, the distinctions and affinities between the terms shift a little. First, efforts to make a clear distinction between *Befinden* (the actual condition one is in) and *Befindlichkeit* (the general term for such conditions, implying a reflexivity not inherent in *Befinden*) would sound awkward in English. Second, the double meaning referring both to location and to feeling is important to Böhme's use of the terms (this is discussed on p. 89f). Finally, *Befinden* and *Befindlichkeit* are, at least in the context of atmospheres, in some instances better translated as *disposition* and sometimes as *attunement*. Disposition remains closer to the subjective pole, perhaps, that is, to the dispositions a person brings to and maintains throughout a new situation (similar to Bourdieu's *habitus*). *Attunement* implies resonance and leans towards the totality of a situation, towards other persons, things or spaces and their respective ecstasies.

Böhme uses the term *ecstasy* in a literally spatial sense: it refers to the way in which a thing steps out of itself and into the surrounding space, where it becomes palpably present (Böhme, 2001a: 129) and, through its appearance as presence, generates an atmosphere. Objects, which are closed in their opposition to a subject, are not ecstatic as such. Yet thingness inheres as potentiality in every object (Brown, 2015: 5): what exceeds the object's mere materialization or utility, its force as vital, sensuous presence, is what makes a thing. Likewise, Böhme's differentiation of *atmosphere* and *the atmospheric* reveals (in contrast to what classical thing ontologies and the subject/object divide would suggest) stages of objectiveness. Following Schmitz (2002: 492, who calls them semi-things), Böhme draws attention to the quasi-objective qualities of the atmospheric: 'neither subject nor object – yet not nothing' (2013: 66). Paradigmatic examples are seasonal and diurnal phases (autumn, dusk, evening) and natural phenomena (wind, heat and mist), but also pain, voices, silence. The subject/object duality pertaining to Western thinking since Aristotle (see p. 39ff) affects the way we refer to our bodies in German: *Körper* designates in Böhme's terminology a body objectified in the gaze or (expert) discourse of others. *Leib*, by contrast, is the body directly given to our experience (see pp. 21 and 42ff). The body as *Leib*, our *Leiblichkeit*, makes us realize the *nature that we ourselves are* (see p. 61). In translation, I have endeavoured to preserve some of the distinction between *Körper* and *Leib* (and their cognates) by calling experiential and sensorially close phenomena *body* or *bodily* and more abstract, objective ones *corporeal* or *corporeality*.

The chapters in this collection have been selected from Böhme's classic books and influential articles to provide a theoretical framework for the discussion of atmospheres in architectural and urban spaces. They explore philosophical and aesthetic dimensions of atmospheres, examining them in different media (acoustics, light, and space) and spaces (corporeal and ephemeral, mundane and sacred). Combining philosophy with architecture, design, landscape design, scenography, music, and visual arts, the essays together provide a key to the concepts that motivate the work of some of the best contemporary architects, artists, and theorists: from Peter Zumthor, Herzog, & de Meuron and Juhani Pallasmaa to Olafur Eliasson and James Turrell. This systematic collection of important pieces – many of which were hitherto only available in German – offers various starting points and a range of reflective material to work with as we search for new approaches to sometimes urgent challenges. All chapters were newly translated to provide a coherent and consistent terminology and conceptual apparatus. They have gone through a process of discussion with and examination by Böhme himself, and footnotes were added where necessary to update references to social or aesthetic context.

As essays, the texts typically open up a field of engagement: Böhme welcomes the collaboration of writers with diverse ideas in trying to come to terms with pressing aesthetic and political problems – he considers systematic conclusions inappropriate at this stage (2013: 11). Initially, chapters recall and analyse life-world experiences, in which a familiarity with atmospheres is primarily receptive (they are experienced or suffered). They then identify connections of atmospheric experiences with everyday feelings. Gradually, the chapters move to explore atmospheres' origins, increasingly addressing generative aspects that make atmospheres such an important factor in the intensification of life. Addressing the role of atmospheres in both the work of professionals and the life of users, Böhme endeavours to cultivate an atmospheric competence that refrains from the kinds of judgement we are used to in aesthetic education. His intention is not to refine appreciation and distinction but to nurture, as a matter of course, an awareness of atmosphere. This would allow people to maintain a space for critical reflection vis-à-vis the persuasive as well as generative aspects of atmospheres.

'Atmosphere, a basic concept of a new aesthetic' explains why the introduction of the term *atmosphere* to aesthetics led to a fundamental turn. Classical aesthetics, from Immanuel Kant to Theodor W. Adorno, was essentially an aesthetics of judgement which increasingly focused on a theory of the work of art. By contrast, reviving Alexander Gottlieb Baumgarten's perspective, the new aesthetics is above all a theory of sensory experience. It is not simply an aesthetics of reception but equally concerned with the production of atmospheres. 'The ecstasies of things' takes the reader straight to the core of a theory of atmospheres. Whereas, traditionally, things were characterized by their qualities, that is, by what made them different from other things, ecstasies concern the ways in which things affect space, in other words, what they emanate. This will become central to a new understanding of architecture and design. 'Material splendour' empirically explores the role materiality currently plays in aesthetics and particularly in architecture. The chapter also shows that the theory of atmospheres has as much critical as phenomenologically descriptive potential. It is not simply a renewed appreciation of *what* things (and buildings) are made of but refers to the *how* of appearance, that is, their surfaces. 'Atmospheres in architecture' focuses on the turn brought about by the introduction of the term *atmosphere* in architecture. The use of various metaphors demonstrate how an understanding of architecture has, again and again, taken its bearings from music, sculpture, or painting. This chapter elaborates the proper of architecture: the art of space – not Euclidian space, though, but corporeal space, that is, the space in which we are.

Should, in previous chapters, readers have gained an impression that atmosphere primarily emanates from constellations of things, 'The presence of living bodies in space' revises this impression by looking at the historical and conceptual development of spaces of bodily presence. Even though the latter might sometimes seem superseded by forms of virtual presence, an appreciation of bodily existence obstinately persists and has given rise to a renewed interest in architecture where sensory experiences unfold as felt spaces of mood, action and perception. 'Atmospheres of human communication' extends the exploration of human presence in space from external atmospheres to the contribution of human participants. Atmospheres, the basis of communication, arise pre-linguistically wherever people meet. Atmosphere, as a *dispositif*, determines what is socially and communicatively possible.

'Learning to live with atmospheres: a new aesthetic humanist education' sketches the first practical consequences of these considerations: the ability to deal with atmospheres is a basic competence of human existence, and atmospheric proficiency an important element of 'education'. The engagement with Friedrich Schiller's classical work articulates a contemporary concept of an 'Aesthetic Education of Man'. Turning to an exposition of atmospheres in different media, 'The Grand Concert of the World' begins by discussing acoustic space: Murray Schafer's worldwide Soundscape project, on the one hand, and, on the other, John Cage's development of *musique concrète*. 'The voice in spaces of bodily presence' considers acoustic space in relation to the participating humans. Everybody co-determines atmosphere by producing sound. This goes usually unnoticed, but it becomes evident when the human voice takes on a decisive importance as, for instance, in some areas of new music.

'Light and space' deals with another crucial factor in the generation of atmospheres. A building's appearance is not solely determined by geometry and material: light is an essential moment of architecture. 'The art of the stage set as a paradigm for an aesthetics of atmospheres' explicitly addresses the question whether one can produce atmospheres consciously and at will. The ancient art of scenography demonstrates a long tradition of producing atmospheres. Its successes show that atmospheres are quasi-objective, spatially extended feelings – scenography would be pointless if every person in the audience felt the 'climate' on stage in a different way.

Böhme has always endeavoured to render his theories vivid and accessible by using concrete examples and, accordingly, the book concludes with a case study, 'Church Atmospheres'. Since the construction of early European temples, particular atmospheres were produced in sacred spaces. In Christian buildings, Böhme teases out the consequences of, on the one hand, the renunciation of traditional elements in 'modern' church construction (and the resulting production of an austere atmosphere). On the other hand, the secularization of old churches (used as hotels, night clubs, book shops, etc.) raises the question whether their architecture might transfer a sacred atmosphere into the new situation.

Professor Tina Engels-Schwarzpaul
School of Art and Design,
Auckland University of Technology – Te Wānanga
Aronui o Tāmaki Makau Rau, Aotearoa/New Zealand

1

Atmosphere, a Basic Concept of a New Aesthetic

The term *atmosphere* is not strange to aesthetic discourse; rather, it occurs frequently, even inevitably, in opening speeches at exhibitions, in art catalogues and celebratory orations. Mention may be made of the powerful atmosphere of a work, of an atmospheric effect or a rather atmospheric mode of representation. It seems as though atmosphere were tasked with designating something indefinite, something difficult to express, if only to conceal one's speechlessness. Atmosphere operates almost like Adorno's *More* (*Mehr*) in that it emphatically suggests a beyond of rational explanation, as though the proper, the aesthetically relevant began only there.

This deployment of the term *atmosphere* in aesthetic texts, oscillating between embarrassment and emphasis, corresponds with that in political discourse. Here, too, everything is said to depend on the atmosphere in which something takes place, and the improvement of the political atmosphere is a most important step. On the other hand, a report according to which negotiations took place *in a good atmosphere*, or the atmosphere was improved, is really only a euphemistic way of saying that nothing came out of the meeting. This vague use of the term atmosphere in aesthetic and political discourse rests upon an ordinary language use that is, in many ways, much more precise. Here, the term *atmosphere* is applied to humans, to spaces, and to nature. Thus, one speaks of the serene atmosphere of a spring morning or the ominous atmosphere of a stormy sky. One speaks of the delightful atmosphere of a valley or the homely atmosphere of a garden. On entering a room, one can immediately feel enveloped in a cosy atmosphere, but one can also end up in a tense atmosphere. Of a person one can say that he or she emanates an awe-inspiring atmosphere and of a man or a woman that an erotic atmosphere surrounds them. Here, too, atmosphere designates something indeterminate in a certain sense, something diffuse, but precisely not indeterminate with respect to what it is, its character. On the contrary, we obviously have a rich vocabulary at our disposal to characterize atmospheres, that is, as serene, melancholy, depressing, uplifting, imposing, inviting, and erotic. Atmospheres are indeterminate, above all, in regard to their ontological status. One does not quite know whether to attribute them to the objects or environments from which they emanate or to the subjects who experience them. One also does not quite know where they are. They seem to fill the space with a *Gefühlston* (feeling-tone), like a haze, as it were.

The frequent, rather embarrassed use of the term *atmosphere* in aesthetic discourse suggests that it refers to something that is aesthetically relevant but whose elaboration and articulation is still pending. An introduction of the term *atmosphere* into aesthetics should – as these introductory comments suggest – take up ordinary language distinctions between atmospheres of diverse character. Atmosphere, however, can only become a concept if one succeeds in accounting for the peculiar intermediate status of atmospheres, between subject and object. New Aesthetics, which was developed out of an ecological approach to questions of aesthetics, has done this successfully.

New aesthetics

Following Goethe, 'the mode in which [one] approach[es] a science or branch of knowledge; from which side, through which door [one] enter[s]' makes a significant difference (1840: xlvii). Accordingly, aesthetics opens up as an entirely different field when approached from the side of ecology, as something entirely different from its presentation in the tradition from Kant to Adorno and Lyotard. The endeavour to elaborate an aesthetics of nature as an aesthetic theory of nature, then, requires a principal revision of aesthetics as a field. The resulting new aesthetics is concerned with the relationship between environmental qualities and human states. This *And*, this in-between, through which environmental qualities and human states are related, is atmosphere. What is new about this new aesthetics can be articulated in three ways.

(a) Aesthetics has so far been an aesthetic of judgement; that is, it is not so much about experience, let alone sensuous experience – as the term's Greek origins (αἰσθητικός) might suggest. Rather, it is preoccupied with judgement, with speech, with conversation. Initially, someone's affective participation in something – in a work of art or in nature – may well have given rise to the theme of taste in aesthetics, under the heading of *approval capacity* (*Billigungsvermögen*). With Kant at the latest, however, it is about judgement, that is, the question of the right to participate in or reject something. Ever since, the social function of aesthetic theory has been to make the conversation about works of art possible. Aesthetic theory supplies the vocabulary for art history and art criticism, for the aforementioned speeches at exhibition openings and award ceremonies, and for essays in art catalogues. Thus, sensuousness and nature have all but disappeared from aesthetics.

(b) The centrality of judgement in aesthetics and its orientation towards communication has led to a dominance of language and, particularly in the late 1980s, to the dominance of semiotics in aesthetic theory. In this situation, literature is privileged over all other artistic genres, which are themselves interpreted within the same linguistic and communicative schemata. Aesthetics can take on the general title of *Languages of Art* (Goodman, 1968). However, it is not self-evident that an artist wants to communicate something to a potential recipient or viewer through his work. Equally, it cannot be taken for granted that a work of art is a sign, insofar as a sign always points to something it itself is not, namely to its meaning. Not every work of art has a meaning – on the contrary, one must insist that a work of art is in the first instance itself something, and that it possesses its own reality. This is evident in the contortions semiotics has to perform, with the term *iconic sign*, to subsume even images under the sign. Iconic signs are not meant to reproduce the object but, rather, 'some of the conditions of the perception of their referent' (Eco, 1972). Used in this way, an image of Mr. Miller is to be taken as a sign for Mr. Miller, even though it is Mr. Miller in a certain way: 'That's Mr. Miller', one replies to the question 'Who is that?'. In this way, Eco refers to the *Mona Lisa* as an iconic sign for Mona Lisa (Eco, 1968). However, quite apart from the fact that the reference of the painting *Mona Lisa* to a person called Mona Lisa is very much in doubt, as Ernst Gombrich showed in his essay about the portrait (1972: 15), nobody takes *Mona Lisa* to be the person Mona Lisa; rather, it is taken as an image, and it is with and through this image one gains experiences. The image does not refer to its meaning as a sign (which could at most be thought about) but in a certain sense it is itself what it represents, that is, the represented is present in and through the image. Of course, it is also possible to read such an image and to interpret it, but that would mean skipping over the experience of the presence of the represented, or even denying it.[1]

(c) *Aesthetic labour.* Abandoning its original and different orientation, aesthetics soon became a theory of art and of the work of art. This, combined with the social function of aesthetics as background knowledge for art criticism, led to a strongly normative orientation: aesthetics was not simply concerned with art but with genuine, true and great art, with the authentic work of art, the work of art of distinction. Although aestheticians were fully aware that aesthetic work is a much wider phenomenon, they registered this only peripherally and with contempt, as mere beautification, as arts and crafts, as kitsch, as commercial or applied art. All aesthetic production was thus regarded from the perspective of art and measured against its standards. This perspective began to change with Walter Benjamin's essay *The Work of Art in the Age of Mechanical Reproduction* (2008). On the one hand, Benjamin anticipated Pop Art here as a possibility before it actually existed; on the other, he took the aestheticization of the life world seriously and discussed this phenomenon under the heading of *Aestheticization of Politics.* To realize this perspectival change theoretically is now the remit of New Aesthetics. The primary task of aesthetics is no longer to determine what art or a work of art is and to provide the means for art criticism. Rather, the theme of aesthetics is now the full range of aesthetic work, which is generally defined as the production of atmospheres and extends in that sense from cosmetics to advertising, interior architecture, stage design and to art more narrowly defined. In this context, autonomous art is simply regarded as a special form of aesthetic work which, even as autonomous art, has a social function. In perceptual contexts that

---

[1]Such a denial is obvious in Eco's text when he discussed an advertisement featuring a beer glass:

Let us examine an advertisement. An outstretched hand offers me a glass foaming over with freshly poured beer, while over the outside of the glass extends a thin layer of vapor which immediately conveys a sensation of coldness. It would be interesting to see which of the properties of the object this picture contains. There is neither beer nor glass on the page, nor is there a damp and icy film. I feel certain visual stimuli, colors, spacial [*sic*] relationships, incidences of light and I coordinate them into a given perceptual structure. The same thing happens when I look at an actual glass of beer; I connect together some stimuli coming from an as yet unstructured field and I produce a *perceptum* based on a previously acquired experience. (Eco, 1976: 193)

In this analysis, sensory physiology clearly ruins the phenomenology of perception. After all, the effect of the advertisement is precisely that I actually feel its coolness when faced with the beer, and that I rely in no way on the support of a 'perceptual structure' to be able to think of 'icy film on the glass' (p. 193), as Eco puts it.

suspend action (*handlungsentlastende Situationen*), like museums and exhibitions, its task is to convey familiarity with atmospheres and mediate their engagement.

Concerning producers, then, New Aesthetics is a general theory of aesthetic work – understood as the production of atmospheres. Concerning recipients, it is a complete theory of perception, in which perception is understood as the experience of the presence of humans, objects, and environments.

Benjamin's aura

Though the expression *atmosphere* occurs frequently in aesthetic discourse, it is not yet a term in aesthetic theory. Nevertheless, there is another term, *aura*, which effectively acts as its placeholder in theory. In *The Work of Art*, Walter Benjamin introduced the term *aura* to designate that atmosphere of distance and awe which surrounds original works of art. He hoped to be able to indicate in this way the difference between an original and its reproductions. Benjamin also thought it possible to identify a general development in art caused by the loss of aura, which occurs automatically in the course of technical reproduction processes in art production. And indeed, the artistic avant-garde tried to shake off the aura of art by transferring art into everyday life. Duchamp's ready-mades, Brecht's disillusionment of the theatre, and the opening of art towards Pop Art are examples. They failed or, at least, the results are paradoxical. For precisely by declaring them to be works of art, Duchamp endowed his ready-mades with an aura, and now their presence in museums commands as much distance and respect as a sculpture by Veit Stoß. The avant-garde failed in stepping out of the holy halls of art and into life by jettisoning the aura. However, they undoubtedly succeeded in making the aura of works of art, their halo or atmosphere, a subject of discussion. And with that, it became clear that what makes a work a work of art cannot be grasped solely through its objective properties. However, the *More* that exceeds them, the aura, remained completely undetermined. *Aura* designates atmosphere in general, as it were, the empty characterless envelope of its presence.

Nevertheless, for the development of the term *atmosphere* as a basic concept of aesthetics, there is merit in recapping what Benjamin's concept of aura already established. Its genesis is paradoxical: Benjamin introduced it specifically to characterize works of art as such, yet he derived it from an experience of nature. I quote the entire passage here because of the special significance of this origin:

> What, then, is the aura? A strange tissue of space and time: the unique apparition of a distance, however near it may be. To follow with the eye – while resting on a summer afternoon – a mountain range on the horizon or a branch that casts its shadow on the beholder is to breathe the aura of those mountains, of that branch. In the light of this description, we can readily grasp the social basis of the aura's present decay. (Benjamin, 2008: 23)

When Walter Benjamin speaks of the 'apparition of a distance', he does not mean that distance appears; rather, he speaks of a phenomenon of remoteness that can also be sensed in things close by. It is an inaccessibility and distance that is palpable in works of art. Already here, he throws the term *unique* into the mix and thus commits a *petitio principii* (circular reasoning, begging the question), for the uniqueness of artworks is supposed to manifest precisely through aura. Aura itself is not unique but repeatable. But let us now return to the experience on which the concept of aura rests. The examples demonstrate that Benjamin assumes for the experience of aura, on the one hand, a certain mood in nature as a backdrop and, on the other, a certain mood in the viewer. Aura can appear in a situation of leisure, of work free, bodily relaxed contemplation. With Hermann Schmitz, one could say that 'summer afternoon' and 'rest' (Benjamin's example suggests that he contemplates mountain range and branch lying on his back) imply a bodily tendency of indefinite expansion. Aura can appear either in a distant mountain range, on the horizon or around a branch – that is, it appears in natural phenomena. It is from them that aura emanates, if the viewer lets them and himself be, that is, refrains from an active grasp on the world. The aura is obviously something spatially diffused, almost like a breath or a haze – an atmosphere, precisely. Benjamin says that one 'breathes' the aura. This breathing means that one absorbs aura bodily, lets it enter the bodily economy of tension and expansion, lets this atmosphere infuse the self. Precisely these dimensions of naturalness and corporeality in the experience of aura disappear in Benjamin's later use of the term. In this version, though, he presents his exemplary account of auratic experience almost as a definition.

To summarize: according to Benjamin, something like aura can be sensed not only in art products or even only in original works of art. To sense aura means to absorb it into one's own bodily disposition. What is sensed is an indeterminate, spatially diffused quality of feeling. With these definitions, we are now ready to elaborate the concept of atmosphere in the context of Hermann Schmitz's philosophy of the body.

The concept of atmosphere in Hermann Schmitz' philosophy

If I indicated at the beginning that *atmosphere* is an expression for something vague, this does not necessarily mean that the meaning of the term is itself vague. It is difficult, owing to the peculiar intermediary position of the phenomenon between subject and object, to define the status of atmospheres and thereby render discussion of atmospheres a legitimate concept. However, in advancing the term *atmosphere* as a basic concept of a new aesthetic, it is not necessary to provide original evidence for its legitimacy because Hermann Schmitz' philosophy of the body already provides an elaboration of the term *atmosphere*. Schmitz' concept of atmosphere, in turn, has a precursor in Ludwig Klages' talk of the 'reality of images'. Already in his early work, *Vom kosmogonischen Eros* (On the Cosmogonic Eros), Klages attempted to elaborate that appearances (images) possess a relatively autonomous reality and efficacy in relation to their carriers. The thesis of the relative autonomy of images rests, amongst other things, on a resigned attitude resulting from the experience that a person's physiognomy can carry a promise this person does not live up to (Klages, 2001: 93ff). Therefore, Klages conceives of an 'Eros of distance' that does not strive for closeness and possession, like the Platonic Eros, but keeps a distance and finds its fulfilment in the contemplative participation in the beautiful. Images possess actuality insofar as they are able, as such, to grasp the soul. Klages developed these insights not only in *Geist als Widersacher der Seele* (The Spirit as Adversary of the Soul, Klages & Schröder, 2000), but particularly systematically in *Grundlegung der Wissenschaft vom Ausdruck* (Fundamental Principles of a Science of Expression, Klages, 1970). What was called the actuality of images in *Vom kosmogonischen Eros*, he discusses here as expression, appearance, character, or essence. It is important in this context that these expressive qualities, particularly those of life, be accorded a kind of autonomy. 'The expression of a state of living is such that its appearance can cause the state [in question, G.B.] to appear' (Klages, 2001: 72). The appearances of expression are emotional powers and therefore sometimes called demons or even souls. By comparison, the perceiving soul is given a passive role: perception is affective and merging participation. Schmitz' concept of atmosphere takes up two aspects of Klages' ideas concerning the actuality of images, namely on the one hand, their relative autonomy in relation to things and, on the other, their role as active, externally pushing and pulling emotional entities.

In his concept of atmosphere, Schmitz detaches the phenomenon in question even more from things: since he no longer speaks of *images*, physiognomy no longer has a role either. Instead, Schmitz presents in detail the spatial character of atmosphere. Atmospheres are always spatially 'unbounded, poured out and placeless, that is, not locatable', they are moving emotional powers, spatial carriers of moods.

Schmitz introduces atmospheres by way of phenomenology, that is, not by definition but by building on the everyday experiences I mentioned early, that is, the experience of a tense atmosphere in a room, the oppressive mood before a thunderstorm, or the serene atmosphere of a garden. To legitimize a discourse on atmospheres, Schmitz draws on phenomenological method, according to which something is recognized as real if it intrudes irrefutably on experience, as well as on the philosophy of the body. The latter removes – at least partially – the uncertainty in the status of atmospheres that I noted above against the background of the subject/object dichotomy. For, according to this dichotomy, once the relative or absolute independence of atmospheres from objects is recognized, they have to be accounted for on the side of the subject. And this happens, in fact, when one regards the serenity of a valley or the melancholy of an evening as projections, namely as projection of moods that are themselves internal states of the soul. This view is certainly averse to the phenomenon, insofar as the serenity of a valley or the melancholy of an evening become noticeable precisely when one is in an entirely different mood at the moment one ends up in them and finds oneself seized and possibly *re-tuned* by them. Schmitz shows, in the context of an historical anthropology, that the projection hypothesis presupposes an introjection. He shows that early in our culture, during the Homeric era, feelings were experienced as something *outside*, as powers that intervene as stimuli into human bodily existence. That is, by the by, Schmitz' reconstruction of the Greek world of the gods. Against this background, something like a soul appears generally as a *counter-phenomenal construction*.[2] What is given phenomenally, that is, sensed, is the human body in its economy of tension and expansion and, further, in affective concern manifesting in bodily movements. Thus, Schmitz can define feelings as follows: they are 'spatial but placelessly diffused atmospheres, which visit the body they embed in the manner of [...] affective concern, which takes the form of emotion' (Schmitz, 1969: 343).

Obviously, a new aesthetics suggests itself here, which leaves behind not only the intellectualism of classical aesthetics but also its restriction to communicative phenomena and art. For atmospheres are obviously what is experienced in the bodily presence of humans and things, or in spaces. One can indeed find in Schmitz the beginnings of an aesthetics which claims the potential of the term *atmosphere*, if only hesitantly. This approach, in Volume III.4 of *System der Philosophie* (System of Philosophy), remains

---

[2]Schmitz constructs, nevertheless, complex phenomena from the basic elements of his *bodily alphabet*.

traditional insofar as it does not abandon the restriction of aesthetics to art. Aesthetics appears as a subparagraph in the section on art: the aesthetic sphere presupposes an 'aesthetic attitude', namely an attitude that permits the self to be affected by atmospheres from a distance. This attitude presupposes, on the one hand, the formation of an aesthetic subject and, on the other, the *art setting*, that is, perceptual contexts relieving subjects from the responsibility of acting (*handlungsentlastende Situationen*), such as museums and exhibitions. Schmitz' attempt suffers primarily from the fact that in a way he grants atmospheres too much autonomy in relation to things. They float freely like gods and, as such, have initially nothing to do with things – much less might they be produced by them. At most, objects can capture atmospheres, which then adhere to them like a nimbus. The autonomy of atmospheres is thus so great for Schmitz, and the thought that atmospheres might emanate from things so remote, that, on the contrary, he even regards things as aesthetic formations when they are characterized by atmospheres. He defines aesthetic formations as follows: 'I designate a manifest lower-level matter (e.g., a thing, sound, scent, colour) an *aesthetic formation* if it gathers into itself, in a quasi-corporeal way [...], atmospheres, which are objective feelings, and thus indicate bodily emotion' (Schmitz, 1969: 626). The characteristic tingeing of a thing by atmospheres must, so Schmitz, be interpreted according to the classical subjectivist *as-if* formula. Thus, we call a valley serene because it looks as if it were permeated with serenity.

Schmitz' approach is robust as an aesthetics of reception, which is able to render a complete account of perception as being affected by atmospheres. However, it is weak as an aesthetics of production. His theory of atmospheres almost militates against the possibility of their production through the qualities of things. Accordingly, this approach loses sight of the whole range of aesthetic work.

The ecstasies of things

To legitimize the discourse of atmospheres and to overcome their ontological placelessness, they must be unleashed from the objective/subjective dichotomy (see p. 22). Schmitz's philosophy of the body shows the far-reaching changes in thinking about the subject that are necessary to do this. The idea of a soul has to be abandoned, in order to reverse the 'introjection of emotions', and humans must principally be regarded as felt bodies (*Leiber*), that is, as in their self-givenness and self-experience as originally spatial beings. To sense oneself bodily is to sense concurrently one's being in an environment, one's feelings in this place.

The same must be performed for the side of the object. A claim that cannot be developed and analysed here at length is that the difficulty of forming a legitimate concept of atmospheres is caused by classical thing-ontology.[3] The decisive point here is that, in this way of thinking, the properties of a thing are considered *determinants*. Thus, a thing's form, colour, and even smell are thought to distinguish it from others, to delimit it to the outside and unify it internally; in short, the thing is generally conceived in its closure. Only very rarely does a philosopher emphasize, like Isaac Newton for example, that perceptibility pertains to the thing essentially. Ontological counterproposals, like that of Jakob Böhme who based his conception of things on the model of a musical instrument, exist as crypto-traditions only. Predominant is the view formulated by Kant, for instance, namely that one can *think* of a thing with all its determinants and then still ask whether this completely determined thing actually exists, whether it is there. Clearly, this way of thinking is an impediment and hostile to aesthetics. It presumes that a thing is what it is independently of its *Dasein*, and the latter is ultimately assigned to it by the thinking subject *positing* the thing. To give an example: When we say, for instance, that a cup is blue, we think of a thing that is determined by the colour blue, and thereby distinguished from others. This colour is something that the thing *possesses*. Further to its being blue, one could ask whether such a cup exists. Its *Dasein* would in that case be determined by a spatio-temporal localization. However, the being blue of the cup could also be thought in quite a different way, namely as the way or, better, a way in which the cup is present in space, how it makes its presence felt. The being blue of the cup is then no longer thought as something that is in some way limited to the cup and adheres to it but, quite to the contrary, as something that radiates out into the cup's surroundings and in a certain way colours and 'tinges' it, as Jacob Böhme would say. The cup's existence is already included in this view of the quality *blue*, for being blue is after all one mode of the cup's existence, an articulation of its visibility or its way of being present. Thus, the thing is no longer thought through its distinction from something other, through its delimitation and unity. Rather, it is thought through the ways in which it steps out of itself, which I propose to call 'the ecstasies of the thing'.

It should not be difficult to think colours, scents, and *the way a thing sounds* as ecstasies. This is already suggested by their designation as *secondary qualities* in the classical subject/object dichotomy, that is, qualities that do not belong to the thing as such, but rather only with reference to a subject. However, it is also important to think so-called primary qualities, for instance extension and form, as ecstasies. In classical thing-ontology, the

---

[3]See p. 37ff, for more detailed discussion.

form of a thing is conceived as something delimiting and enclosing, namely as that which encloses the thing's volume to the inside and delimits it to the outside. But a thing's form is also *effective* to the outside. It radiates into the surroundings, as it were, takes away the homogeneity of the surrounding space and fills it with tensions and movement suggestions. The same applies to the extension or the volume of a thing which, in classical thing-ontology, was thought as the thing's capacity to take up a certain amount of space, to occupy it, as it were, and resist the intrusion of other things into this space. A thing's extension and volume can, however, also be sensed outwardly; they give its space of presence weight and orientation. Volume, thought in terms of a thing's voluminosity, is the mightiness of its presence in space.

A thing-ontology modified thus makes it possible to think atmospheres in a meaningful way. Insofar as they are 'tinged' by the presences of things, of people or environmental constellations, that is, through their ecstasies, they are spaces. They are themselves spheres of presence of a something, its actuality in space. By contrast with Schmitz' approach, atmospheres are then not thought of as free floating but, on the contrary, as something emanating from and produced by things, people or their constellations. Accordingly, they are not conceived as something objective (i.e., as properties of things), and yet they are something thing-like, belonging to the thing – insofar as things articulate their spheres of presence through their qualities, conceived as ecstasies. But atmospheres are nothing subjective, like determinations of a state of mind, either. And yet, they are subject-like, they belong to subjects insofar as they are sensed by humans in bodily presence, and insofar as this sensing is simultaneously the subject's bodily being-located in space.

It is immediately clear that this modified thing-ontology favours aesthetic theory, even liberates it. Aesthetic work in its full spectrum comes into view. Even within the narrower sphere of art, for instance in visual arts, it becomes clear that, strictly speaking, the artist does not intend to endow a thing – be it a block of marble or a canvas – with particular properties (to be shaped and coloured in this or that way). Rather, it is about letting this thing step outside of itself in a certain way and thereby to let the presence of something become sensible.

Making atmospheres

Atmosphere simultaneously denotes the basic concept of a new aesthetic and its central object of knowledge. Atmosphere is the shared reality of the perceiver and the perceived. It is the reality of the perceived as the sphere of its presence and the reality of the perceiver insofar as he or she, in sensing the atmosphere, is bodily present in a particular way. At the same time, this synthetic function of atmosphere explains the peculiar turns of phrase according to which an evening is called melancholic, for example, and a garden serene. On closer examination, this way of putting it is no less legitimate than calling a leaf green. Not even a leaf has the objective property of being green. A leaf, too, can only be called green insofar as it shares an actuality with a perceiver. Strictly speaking, expressions like *serene* or *green* refer to this shared actuality, and they are simply named in one case more from the perspective of the object and in the other from the perspective of the perceiver. Thus, a valley is not called serene because it resembles in some way a serene human being but because the atmosphere it emits is serene, and because this can produce a serene mood in the perceiver.

This is just one example of how the term *atmosphere* can clarify connections and render intelligible manners of speech. But what is known about atmospheres? Classical aesthetics has only ever dealt with three or four atmospheres, namely the beautiful, the sublime (perhaps the Picturesque should be included), and finally the characterless atmosphere, or atmosphere *in general*, the aura. However, it was not at all clear that these topics were atmospheres, and many studies will need to be re-read or re-written. Above all, however, the extraordinary limitations of traditional aesthetics become apparent for there are, of course, many more atmospheres, not to say infinitely many: the serene atmosphere, the serious, the horrible, the oppressive atmosphere, the atmosphere of dread, the atmosphere of power, the atmosphere of the sacred and that of the depraved. The variety of available linguistic expressions indicates that there is a far more complex knowledge about atmosphere than aesthetic theory would suggest. Particularly, an extraordinary wealth of knowledge concerning atmospheres likely exists within the practical knowledge of aesthetic workers. This knowledge should be able to shed light on the correlation between the concrete properties of objects (objects of everyday use, works of art, natural elements) and the atmosphere they emanate. This question corresponds roughly to the question in classical aesthetics concerning the correlation of the concrete properties of a thing and its beauty. Except, now the concrete properties are read as ecstasies of the thing and beauty as its way of being present. Aesthetic work consists of endowing things, environments, or people themselves with properties that make something emanate from them. That is, it is about *making* atmospheres through work on the object. We find this kind of work everywhere. It is divided into many professional fields and as a whole furthers the increasing aestheticization of reality. In listing the branches of aesthetic work, one can see that it constitutes a large part of the work of society as a whole. These branches include design, scenography, advertising, the production of musical atmospheres (acoustic furnishing), cosmetics, interior architecture – and then, of course, the whole sphere of visual arts proper. When examining these areas in order to render their accumulated knowledge fertile for aesthetic theory, it becomes evident that this knowledge is usually implicit or tacit. This is of course partially due to the fact that it often involves artisanal skills that are rarely transmitted through words and much more by demonstration in teacher-student relationships. However, the lack of explicit knowledge is also in part ideologically motivated, namely by false aesthetic theories. Although actual practice looks quite different, it is still assumed in discussions that it is crucial to endow certain things and materials with certain properties. From time to time, however, one finds an explicit knowledge that aesthetic work consists in the production of atmospheres.

Since knowledge about the production of atmospheres is rarely made explicit and even then is still warped by the subject/object dichotomy, I want to return to a classical example once more. It is the theory of garden art (more precisely of the English landscape garden or park) as it is recorded in Hirschfeld's five volumes of the *Theorie der Gartenkunst* (translated as Theory of Garden Art, 1779–85, 2001). Here, the kind of selection of objects, colours, and sounds is made explicit by which 'scenes' of a particular emotional quality can be produced. Interestingly, Hirschfeld's language is close to scenography: he calls 'scenes' certain natural arrangements in which particular atmospheres, like serene, heroic, softly melancholic or serious, hold sway (Figures 1.1 and 1.2).

FIGURE 1.1 Branitz Park (Fürst Pückler), Cottbus / © 2007 Gernot Böhme.

FIGURE 1.2 Branitz Park with Fürst Pückler's tomb, Cottbus / © 2007 Gernot Bohme.

Following Hirschfeld, I would like to present a softly melancholic region in a way that shows how this atmosphere can be produced:

A softly melancholic region occurs in the absence of vistas; through depths and low areas, dense thickets and woodlands, often simply through groups of tall, closely spaced trees with thick foliage and a hollow sound wafting through their upper branches. It contains still or darkly murmuring water, nearly hidden from view; low-hanging, dark, or dusky green leaves and deep shadows spreading everywhere. It boasts nothing to signify life and activity. Sparse rays of light penetrate only to prevent the darkness from becoming mournful or terrible. Quiet and solitude are at home here. A solitary bird fluttering about, the indistinct buzzing of unknown creatures, a wood pigeon cooing from the hollow top of a leafless oak, a stray nightingale lamenting her lonely sorrows – these are enough to furnish the scene. (Hirschfeld, 2001: 187–188)

Hirschfeld lists various elements whose interplay apparently produces the softly melancholic atmosphere: seclusion and silence; water, provided it is still or darkly murmuring; the region must be shadowy; light present only sparingly to prevent the complete slipping away of the mood; colours dark – Hirschfeld speaks of a blackish green. In other parts of his work, which are more concerned with means, are even more explicit. Thus, in the chapter on water: 'darkness settling on ponds and other still bodies of water casts a mood of melancholy and sadness. Deep, silent water, obscured by reeds and overhanging vegetation, where even sunlight cannot penetrate, is an appropriate setting for benches dedicated to such feelings, to hermitages, urns, and monuments honouring the spirits of departed friends' (Hirschfeld, 2001: 180–181). Similarly, in the section on woodlands: 'When it consists of ancient, towering trees with thick and very dark foliage, its character will be grave and with a certain solemn dignity that exudes a kind of reverence. Feelings of peace run through the spirit and lead it, unmindfully, to drift away in serene contemplation, in fond amazement' (2001: 180). Thus, the landscape gardener's expertise consists, according to Hirschfeld, in knowing by which elements the character of a region is brought forth. Such elements are water, light and shadow, colour, woodlands, hills, stones and rocks, and finally also buildings. Thus, Hirschfeld recommends for the softly melancholic region the arrangement of urns, memorials, or hermitages.

One has to ask, of course, which role these elements play in the overall production of atmosphere. Obviously, the whole is more than its parts, but this is not sufficient. With garden art, one is in a sense within reality itself. However, the same atmospheres can also be generated by words or paintings. After all, the peculiar quality of a story one reads or listens to is that it not only tells us that a particular atmosphere prevailed somewhere else but that it summons this atmosphere itself, that it conjures it up. Similarly, pictures that represent a melancholic scene not only signify this scene but produce the scene itself. Consequently, one might surmise that the elements of a region listed by Hirschfeld do not somehow compose its character but that they, too, conjure up an atmosphere. I would like to illustrate this with a literary example, namely with Grimm's fairy tale *Jorinda and Joringel*, in which a softly melancholic scene is gradually condensed through apprehension into leaden heaviness.

Now, there was once a maiden who was called Jorinda, who was fairer than all other girls. She and a handsome youth named Joringel had promised to marry each other. They were still in the days of betrothal, and their greatest happiness was being together. One day in order that they might be able to talk together in peace they went for a walk in the forest. 'Take care', said Joringel, 'that you do not go too near the castle'. It was a beautiful evening. The sun shone brightly between the trunks of the trees into the dark green of the forest, and the turtle-doves sang mournfully upon the beech trees.

Jorinda wept now and then. She sat down in the sunshine and was sorrowful. Joringel was sorrowful too. They were as sad as if they were about to die. Then they looked around them, and were quite at a loss, for they did not know by which way they should go home. The sun was still half above the mountain and half under. Joringel looked through the bushes, and saw the old walls of the castle close at hand. He was horror-stricken and filled with deadly fear. Jorinda was singing,

'My little bird, with the necklace red,

Sings sorrow, sorrow, sorrow,

He sings that the dove must soon be dead,

Sings sorrow, sor – jug, jug, jug.'

Joringel looked for Jorinda. She was changed into a nightingale, and sang, jug, jug, jug. A screech-owl with glowing eyes flew three times round about her, and three times cried, to-whoo, to-whoo, to-whoo.

Joringel could not move. He stood there like a stone, and could neither weep nor speak, nor move hand or foot. The sun had now set. (Grimm Brothers, n.d.)[4]

On comparing this text with Hirschfeld's description of the softly melancholy region, related aspects emerge: the dark and shadowy green, which is barely and diminishingly illuminated by sunlight; the mournful sounds of the turtle-dove; old ruins in the background.

A comparison of two aesthetic workers as different as the landscape gardener and the writer clearly shows their highly developed awareness of the means by which to create particular atmospheres. A more comprehensive study of the practical knowledge held by the entire range of aesthetic workers, from stage designer to cosmetician, would throw a new light on aesthetic objects, including works of art. Their *properties* would then be understood as conditions of their atmospheric efficacy.

The critical potential of an aesthetics of atmospheres

A consideration of the widespread knowledge about the production of atmospheres, with its specific variations in many different professions, suggests that significant power adheres to this knowledge. It uses neither physical violence nor commanding speech but engages the affectivity of people; it affects their mind, manipulates moods, and evokes emotions. This power does not appear as such, it rather impacts the unconscious. Although it operates in the realm of the senses, it is nevertheless invisible and more difficult to grasp than any other power. Politics uses it as much as economics; it has traditionally been applied all along by religious communities and is today

---

[4]The Grimms drew on Heinrich Stilling, their contemporary. See, for instance, Jung (1979: 73ff).

applied by the culture industries to an unlimited field where they stage life and preform experience. With that, a serious critical task accrues to the aesthetic of atmospheres.

Critique has always been a task of aesthetics. One can even say that classical aesthetics *was* essentially critique. In Kant, aesthetics appears as a critique of judgement, for Moses Mendelssohn it was a critique of *Billigungsvermögen* (approval capacity). In each case, aesthetics sought to advance spontaneous acceptance and rejection, or approval and disapproval, through critical analysis to a point where these responses could be rationalized and justified. However, due to the restriction of aesthetics to a theory of art, its content was essentially an elaboration of the criteria for assessing works of art and their constant adjustment to actual developments in art. Aesthetics as critique was to distinguish the true, the genuine, the proper work of art from kitsch, craft, mere fabrication, commercial product, and advertisement. The criteria, then, were authenticity, proportion and necessity of the work, originality and significance of the product. The more art dissolved or passed over into life – an explicit demand of the avant-garde – the more aesthetics insisted on stabilizing the boundaries between *true art* and mere applied arts. This is quite clearly evident in Adorno's pejorative deployment of the expression 'artisanal'. Adorno calls the 'constructed, strictly objective artwork' the 'sworn enemy of everything artisanal' (Adorno et al., 2002: 58). The artisanal is for him the epitome of merely external, meaningless and vacuous 'beautification' of life (257–258). Adorno mistakes or disapproves of whatever might articulate itself in the artisanal as style and atmosphere of a way of life. The streamline design of chairs, for instance, is nothing but 'applied art': 'In applied arts, products are, for example, adapted to the streamlined form that serves to reduce air resistance, even though the chairs will not be meeting with this resistance' (217).

Another term by which traditional aesthetics sought to delimit and protect true art against the tide of an aestheticization of life and the world is *kitsch*. Kitsch was diagnosed particularly wherever aesthetic products had a use value and affected the mood. The painting in the bedroom was kitsch as much as the holiday postcard – not just the card, though, but also the sunset itself that people wistfully indulged in. Even artworks that were degraded to objects of everyday contemplation, like Dürer's hands, or came into the sphere of advertising, like the Venus de Milo, became kitsch. The statement by the Heidelberg art historian, Erik Forssman is characteristic: kitsch does not like true art seek 'to activate our judgement but captivate our heart' (Forssman, 1975: 9).

With these assessments, traditional aesthetics is unfit to deal with the increasing aestheticization of the world. Its rejection simply relies on the disgust of *Bildungsbürger* (middle-class intellectuals), its critique is a judgement of taste that looks down on all of design, arts and crafts, as well as the culture industries, as something neither true nor authentic, and thus below standard.

By contrast, the aesthetics of atmospheres suspends such quality assessments and damnations – at least temporarily. Provisionally, it demands the equal recognition of all products of aesthetic work, from cosmetics to stage design, from advertising to industrial design to so-called true art. That also means a rehabilitation of kitsch and the liberation of the aesthetic creation of the life world from the verdict of 'applied arts'. This rehabilitation relies, on the one hand, on the acknowledgement of a basic human need for aesthetics and, on the other, on the awareness that to show oneself, or to step out of oneself and *appear*, is an essential feature of nature.

Aesthetics is often deemed to be a province of elites, either estate-based elites or the aristocracy of money. This tradition goes back to the Greeks where the *aristoi* (ἄριστοι, the best) were also always the most beautiful. What was lost from the perspective of the *aristoi*, who looked at life as intensification, is the fact that aesthetics is a basic need of all humanity. Such need did not appear obvious in simple and bad people because, too preoccupied with survival in any case, they could not attend to the *way* of life. However, this basic need reappears within the frame of an aesthetics of atmospheres. For it shows how the environment and the qualities of their surroundings is responsible for people's well-being. Nobody is indifferent to his or her condition. At this point, the rehabilitation of applied art and the aestheticization of everyday life tip over into a critique of the conditions of life: it becomes clear that a humane existence includes an aesthetic dimension.

On the other hand, aesthetic work, and the aestheticization of everyday life, finds the basis for its legitimation in an essential feature of nature. For good reason, however, aesthetic work – and art in particular – has always been regarded as part of human *culture*. Against the backdrop of an aesthetics of atmospheres it becomes obvious that aesthetic culture is only the cultivation of something already embedded in nature. That is, as a theory of perception, aesthetics discovers an essential feature of nature that eludes the Natural Sciences, at least those of the modern period. In perception, we encounter nature as something perceptible; it is, to use a Greek term, *aistheton* (αἰθητόν, the perceived). According to this insight, nature does not simply appear as a context of reciprocal effects but as a communicative context, as the reciprocal effect of showing oneself and perceiving. Creatures of nature are not simply there, neither do they simply stand in a relationship of reciprocal effects, but they step outside themselves, they even grow, as Adolf Portmann puts it, organs of communication (1961: 77–97). Just think of the manifold patterns in fauna and flora, of flowers, bird songs, insect signals. The aesthetic work of human beings is a cultivation of this essential feature of nature, which is also effective in them. There is therefore not just an aesthetic basic need to live in a certain environment in which I feel happy but also a basic need to show myself and to co-determine through my presence the atmosphere of my surroundings. The phenomena of fashion, cosmetics, and self-staging at home and in public must be seen against this backdrop and not only against that of social critique.

The critical potential of an aesthetics of atmospheres is thus initially positioned against the condemnation of the *lower spheres* of the aesthetic and shows the legitimacy of an aestheticization of everyday life. It is in this way directed against aesthetics itself, it is a critique of aesthetic *hubris*. On the other hand, though, it is also a critique of the aestheticization of everyday life and the world, namely in all instances in which it becomes a law onto itself, and where its power has to be resisted.

First, this concerns the aestheticization of politics. The self-staging of power is as old as politics itself. The accoutrements of domination were intended to make distinctions from the dominated palpable, to impress them and demand their respect. What mattered in the architecture of palaces and castles was not only their utility as means of defence but the production of an atmosphere of sovereignty and superiority. That is to be taken as read and yet, already an understanding of these stagings would be a critique and could help the dominated to stand up to power. Aesthetics in the context of politics becomes problematic only when politics itself becomes a staging or pursues aestheticization in lieu of what really matters: the transformation of human conditions. Walter Benjamin was the first to note this point – significantly in the afterword to that essay in which he first elaborated the concept of the aura. 'The logical outcome of fascism', he writes, 'is an aestheticizing of political life' (Benjamin, 2008: 41). In the context of the aestheticization of political life, Walter Benjamin focused particularly on the second aspect, namely the replacement of a transformation of human conditions with their aestheticization: 'Fascism attempts to organize the newly proletarianized masses while leaving intact the property relations which they strive to abolish. It sees its salvation in granting expression to the masses – but on no account granting them rights' (Benjamin, 2008: 41). Expression in place of rights! That is the replacement of politics by aesthetics. On the other hand, his writing also embraces the first aspect, which is even more impressive and evident in fascism, namely the self-staging of power and the exercise of power through a conjuring of atmospheres. Today, it is perhaps easiest to comprehend what happened there by looking at Leni Riefenstahl's *Triumph of the Will* (1935). The film represents a general mobilization of the masses by aesthetic means, including the badges and uniforms worn even by children; campfires, marches, torchlight processions; at the meta level, the programmes Beauty of Labour (*Schönheit der Arbeit*) and Strength through

Joy (*Kraft durch Freude*); and, finally, the hero worship and pseudo-aristocratic self-stylization of the S.S. The aestheticization of politics culminated in theatrical mass celebrations like the party rallies and the Olympic Games of 1936. All that has been succinctly presented in a book by the Hamburg political scientist Peter Reichel, *Der schöne Schein des Dritten Reiches* (The Beautiful Appearance of the Third Reich, 1991). It provides, among other things, an account of the extent to which the National Socialists represented themselves in aesthetic terms. Thus, the *Völkische Beobachter* wrote about Hitler's propaganda flights:

> If mountains and oceans, the blue of the sky and the stars of the night could tell stories, they would have to herald the exaltation of the German people [...]. This unique symphony of enthusiasm, which surged towards the Führer wherever the huge bird touched the earth during his travels, was the most monumental and sublime Germany has ever seen and experienced. (Reichel, 1991: 120)

The exercise of power by aesthetic means has, without a doubt, so far found its most distinct expression during National Socialism. However, it would be wrong to think that the aestheticization of politics is specific to National Socialism. Rather, Italian fascism only slightly lags behind, and the Soviet system has used equivalent means, albeit with less success. Far more important, though, is the fact that politics is staged in democratic states, too, and that it happens more and more *on stage*. This observation leads to the conjecture that the aestheticization of politics is not specific to totalitarian states but is rather related to the existence of mass media and their potentials, on the one hand, and, on the other, to the necessity that confronts contemporary states, regardless of their organizational form, namely the necessity constantly to win the loyalty of the masses in order to remain capable of acting.

Earlier critics of the aestheticization of politics already noted this correlation with the existence of the mass media: aside from Benjamin, Horkheimer and Adorno, and also Ernst Cassirer. They posited therefore – which seems problematic to us today – a principal affinity between fascism and modern mass culture (the American Way of Life). It is certain that power is exerted by film and television, by the blending of information and advertising and by the staging of day-to-day life in general. However, in these cases, it is economic power and not political power that subjects individuals by stirring their emotions and stimulating their desires. Horkheimer and Adorno criticized this development, still insufficiently, under the heading 'culture industry' in which they observed a trivializing of art. On the basis of an aesthetics of atmospheres it is today possible to re-perform this critique as a *Critique of Aesthetic Economy*.

Aesthetic economy denotes a particular phase in the development of capitalism in which the advanced Western industrial nations currently find themselves. It is a condition in which aesthetic work counts for a large part of the work of society as a whole, that is, in which a large part of total work is no longer concerned with the production of commodities but with their staging – or with the production of commodities whose use value itself consists in their deployment *for* staging – of people, of the public sphere, of a corporate image, and so on. It is the phase of high-gloss capitalism, where people take holidays in malls and *center-parcs*; where advertisements no longer suggest commodities but lifestyles; in which the reference to reality is replaced increasingly by mediated imagination. Philosopher Wolfgang Fritz Haug engaged with this condition already in 1971, in his important book *Critique of Commodity Aesthetics* (1986). However, with concepts and means derived from political economy, he was unable to strike the decisive point. He used the Marxian distinction between use value and exchange value of commodities. The use value of a commodity is given in the qualities that make it useful in a particular context of life praxis. The exchange value of the commodity, in contrast, is given through those qualities by which it counts for something in the market and can be sold. Haug believed that he could characterize the development of late capitalism by the fact that the exchange value comes to dominate over the use value. Through design and packaging, he proposed, commodities were given qualities which made them highly marketable, independently and often almost contrary to their potential use value. Indeed, commodities became conceivable that would have no use value but only exchange value. Haug targeted critically those sales strategies and buyer behaviours that were no longer concerned with the use of commodities but only with their possession. The keyword *status symbol* is the most apt characterization: a commodity one has purchased serves no other purpose than demonstrating that one is able to purchase it. This analysis often turns out to be inadequate. It is indeed correct that design, advertising, the creation of entire environments, and the suggestion of lifestyles in which commodities fulfil an atmospheric function serve the sales of those commodities. However, setting the exchange value in opposition to the use value does not properly reflect actual conditions. Rather, what matters is a specific use value of commodities, which is in complete accord with their staging for the purpose of sales. The value of commodities, unless it is its utility for the performance of some life-world tasks, in no way has to consist exclusively in the representation of exchange value. Rather, they are *used* precisely in their scenic function, as components of a style, as elements for the production of atmospheres. Therefore, one could speak of a scenic value of commodities – alongside use and exchange value, or as a subform of use value – put positively, of their aesthetic value; put critically, of their illusory value. Commodities like that have always existed, as accessories or objects for the beautification of life. Characteristic of our time is that there are hardly any commodities left that do not also have a scenic value; that this value can outweigh the other kinds of value; and, finally, that the only value an object has for us can, under certain conditions, consist of its scenic function. The slogan 'design is everything' would have its place here. However, until the legitimate need of humans to produce certain atmospheres through the design of their surroundings and to stage themselves is acknowledged, criticism comes too early. The atmospheric is part of life and staging serves its intensification.

Once the legitimacy of self-staging is established, however, it is time for the critique of aesthetic economy. By comparison with the elementary needs of life and survival, and given that these needs cannot be met globally, capitalism in Western industrialized nations shows itself as an economy of waste. The production of aesthetic values – packaging, design, styling, of products that serve nothing but glamour and self-staging – is luxury production. It does not fulfil elementary needs but constantly stimulates a ravenousness for the intensification of life. That is a harsh criticism, a moral criticism and therefore in a certain sense an external one. What reaches further, because it remains within the aesthetic itself, is the critique of usurpation, of manipulation and the suggestion exercised by the production of atmospheres upon those who are exposed to them. This starts with acoustic furnishing to produce a friendly and relaxed shopping atmosphere and includes the fantastic illusionary realities of our malls and shopping centres, as well as the suggestion and immaterial sales of whole lifestyles. These are new phenomena of constraints, alienation and delusion that are produced. The critique of atmospheres becomes a necessity. It could already suffice to promulgate an understanding of their feasibility to break their suggestive power and to make a freer and more playful engagement with atmospheres possible. By their nature, atmospheres are touching and of an inconspicuous importunity. They are actualities posing as reality.

Without all educated middle-class conceit, a critique has to be performed that does not spoil the joy in splendour and intensification of life but nonetheless preserves freedom vis-à-vis the power of atmospheres.

Conclusion

The new aesthetics is, first of all, what its name suggests, a general theory of perception. It frees the concept of perception from its restriction to information processing, provision of data and recognition of situations. Part of perception is being emotionally affected by the percept, as are the *actuality of images* and bodily states. At bottom, perceiving is the mode in which one is bodily present with something or someone or in one's surroundings. The primary *object* of perception is atmospheres. What is perceived primarily and directly are neither emotions nor figures, nor objects or their constellations as was assumed in Gestalt psychology, but atmospheres – in front of which, by an analytical way of seeing, something like objects, forms, and colours, are then distinguished.

The new aesthetics confronts the progressive aestheticization of reality, a task for which aesthetics as a theory of art or the work of art is entirely insufficient. More, since the latter takes place among educated elites in contexts requiring neither responsibility nor action, it hides the fact that aesthetics constitutes real social power. There are aesthetic needs and there is an aesthetic supply. Of course, there is aesthetic lust, but there is also aesthetic manipulation. The aesthetics of the artwork is joined, on an equal footing, by everyday aesthetics, commodity aesthetics, and the aesthetics of politics. The general aesthetic is tasked with making this expansive area of aesthetic reality transparent and accessible to language.

2

The Ecstasies of Things

Ontology and Aesthetics of Thingness

Subjectivism in aesthetics

Nature in some way has always been a topic in modern aesthetics and art. As aesthetic theory, however, aesthetics has invariably been a theory of the subject, never one of nature. Nature was only of interest insofar as it was the subject of art; at most, insofar as an *aesthetic attitude* to nature was also conceivable. That is, one could behold real nature with the eyes of the visual artist, as it were, with a 'framing eye', as Hermann Schmitz puts it (1977: 621 u. § 218e, ß). The reason for this situation is to be found in the subjectivism of aesthetics itself.

To be sure, aesthetics is subjectivist only in general, not in each single instance. Accordingly, there is a chunk of a theory of nature contained in the aesthetics of Hegel, for whom, after all, aesthetics is part of the objective spirit. The stages of the organic are, as they approach the beautiful, steps in which the idea comes into itself. Kant's aesthetic, by comparison, is definitely subjectivistic through and through insofar as the judgement of the beautiful and sublime is founded on an inner condition. However, this condition is interpreted as the cognisance of a kind of pre-stabilized harmony between inner and outer, between the capacities of the mind, on the one hand, and the existence of things and their configuration, on the other. What Kant's theory does not admit is that aesthetic experience not only includes the self-experience of the subject but also a certain experience of nature. Quite effortlessly, poetry allows nature to speak and painting touches us in its representations of nature through colours, forms, and atmospheres. The characters that appear in nature are nevertheless understood as mere metaphors in theory, as anthropomorphisms, or as projections. Thus, Novalis writes in *The Novices of Sais*: 'Does the cliff not become a unique Thou, whenever I speak to it?' (2005: 89). When one speaks to it; the initiative, then, lies on the side of the lyrical subject. Consequently, the individual is consistently seen as 'the constitutive factor of landscape' in the theory of landscape painting (Eberle, 1980), according to which sprawling nature is first organized into landscape by a 'scenic eye', a reflecting subject. The aesthetic attitude towards nature is regarded as a modern achievement, only made possible through the release of the subject from a direct confrontation with nature and through the opposition of farm and country or city and country. This analysis is not in question here, nor is the proposition that a particular attitude is needed to recognize certain characters of nature as such, and then to be able to talk of the beauty and sublimity of nature. However, this does not mean that these characters are created by the 'aesthetic attitude' or somehow projected into nature. They can indeed belong to nature itself and also always be experienced, even if not explicitly and in a laborious struggle with nature – perhaps more in the background and most effectively as a mood component. Neither is it in question that everything experienced by the subject is co-determined by it. However, *that* something is experienced is not in the subject's control. Rather, just as one has to assume a sensibility on the side of the subject, so one has to assume characters on the side of nature that address the subject. Further, the form-giving moment that already takes effect in each instance of the perception of nature is nothing like an arbitrary design process. It is much more like a co-design, a co-operation, or an interplay (of the subject's intention) with the object's emanations. Finally, we have to add today that the subject as a bodily being is endowed with senses that must correspond to the realms or *dimensions* of nature. Since humans as living beings are a product of evolution *in* nature, the old saying of the likeness between eye and sun – 'If the eye were not sunny, how could we perceive light?' (von Goethe, 1840: xxxix) – makes sense to us again today. Human sense organs, like all sense organs, must be understood as successful adaptations to the facts of nature; they are, as it were, the organism's responses to nature's address. This relationship – namely, of the perceptible preceding perception – is impressively demonstrated in the formation of analogous organs in different evolutionary strands. The eye was in a sense invented several times over during the course of evolution.

Whether one wants to argue using the phenomenology of perception or naturalistically using the theory of evolution, in either case an orientation towards perceptibility is shown to be a basic character of nature. A showing itself on the side of nature, or a stepping-outside-of-themselves of natural things, corresponds with receptivity on the side of the subject.

Terminological differentiations

To proceed with the exploration of this stepping-outside-of-themselves of things, it is first necessary to delimit the thematic area. A thing, in our context, is a physical, sensually given being. Both the German expression *Ding* (thing) and the Latin term *res* are of course often also used in a more general sense. Thus, *Ding* frequently designates indexically something that one cannot or does not want to name at that moment, or more generally the object of discussion or contemplation. When we concentrate on things as sensually given, physical beings, we do include products of the visual arts and nature, but we exclude entities like wind or night, or media like air or water. It goes without saying that this exclusion can only be a temporary measure: an aesthetics of nature, particularly, cannot apply to things only. However, aesthetics as a theory of visual arts cannot be limited to corporeally sensual givens either. It must be able to embrace laser sculptures, computer graphics, and other immaterial objects. In either case, a focus on the thing can therefore be only provisional; it is justified by the fact that classical ontology itself has taken shape principally as an ontology of the thing.

The prevalence of the thing in ontology

That ontology, at various points in the history of philosophy, has developed using the example of the thing is particularly significant from the perspective of aesthetics. For other entities – qualities, characters, physiognomic traits, atmospheres – were in the course of this development relegated to the realm of minority, of the ephemeral, indeterminate, merely subjective. Though it would be wrong to say that Plato defined *being* as a thing (quite the opposite!), his examples (bed, bridle) could indeed mislead one into thinking that the idea makes a thing a being. Aristotle, of course, then followed him in that direction as the original meaning of *eidos* and *idea* already suggests. *Eidos* (εἶδος) and *idea* (ἰδέα) mean appearance – but appearance of what? Of a thing, presumably. It would already be unusual to use *eidos* to mean the appearance of the sea, and the appearance of a person, in the sense of his or her physiognomy, would not usually be called *eidos* either. If *eidos* had been associated with physiognomy or character traits, ontology would have taken an entirely different direction already with Plato. *Eidos* is, after all, not an index or a symptom but the appearing matter itself. The Platonic theory of ideas certainly contains remnants of archaic Greek thought, according to which the Gods are Being proper: one is just through the Just, beautiful through participation in Beauty. Plato's concrete analyses, however, are already oriented towards the thing as individual being.

With Aristotle, the question of *on he on* (ὄν ᾗ ὄν, Being as such) then turns consistently into the question of the constitution of the thing. Being proper is, according to Aristotle, *tode ti* (τόδε τι, this particular something). Of course, one could take *tode ti* to mean something like *the air* and, for Aristotle, *hapla somata* (ἅπλα σώματα, simple bodies) like fire, water, earth, and air are definitely not bodies in our sense. Nevertheless, it is difficult to take *ti* in *tode ti* to mean something like air since *ti* means something particular, while air as a medium is *ahoriston* (αόϱιστον, unlimited). Simple bodies are, consequently, only the lowest stage of being. Degrees of being increase in different stages, according to the measure of internal unity – from simple bodies to organs to organisms. That Aristotle assigns organic beings the highest rank among beings proper could contradict the thesis that the thing was his prototype of being. After all, according to Aristotle, life and the principle of life, the soul, are ecstatic as such. The living as a perceiving being is beside itself. As subsisting being it lives in the passage of elements and as generating being it is part of a chain. And yet, Aristotle defines being also, via its autonomy, as *substance* and as constituted by the four causes.

There is no unambiguous equivalence for the expression *substance* in Aristotle's texts. However, Aristotle certainly attributes to *ousia* (ουσία, the true being), the autonomy that will later be characteristic of substance, that is, autonomy in a logical and perseverance in a temporal sense. Being is, according to Aristotle, that *of* which one predicates something but which does not appear as a predicate itself. Further, it perseveres in the face of changing terms (of place, quality, or quantity) and thereby makes movement possible. In itself, it can only come-to-be or pass away. The doctrine of the four causes, finally, shows that Aristotle was not only oriented towards the thing in his analysis of being but, more precisely, even towards the thing produced through craft. Being, in his sense, is determined by the four possible answers to the question *dia ti* (διὰ τι, for what reason?). It is composed of matter, it has a form, it has an efficient cause, and it is aligned with a purpose. A frequently used example of the constitution of being through form and material is the statue: a material (marble, bronze) is given a form (Hercules). However, Aristotle does not even take account of the double function of form here, namely as the form of matter and as the form presenting Hercules. (This double relationship is much more clearly articulated in Plato's analysis of images in the dialogue of the *Sophist*.)

Certainly, the form's efficacy is more profound in the case of living beings than it is in the work of artisans, but the model also applies in the realm of the organic: matter is shaped by form. Indeed, to impute an efficient cause as another constituent of each individual being only makes sense in the case of a type of being that does not have the principle of its motion within itself, that is, in the case of technical being. In the same way, the determination of the final cause for each being's end results precisely from a type of being whose end lies outside of itself, in an instrumental use. One can say that the practical analysis of a being as it is conducted in a technical context, namely the analysis according to producer, material, form, and purpose of the thing, has guided the theoretical analysis of being as such. Aristotle accordingly regarded the supreme being, organic essence, already as an automaton.

Similarly, the thing evidently prevails in Cartesian ontology. This cannot be shown quite as directly, though, as the use of *res* for both extended and thinking substance might suggest. In part, it only becomes apparent via Kant's retrospective analysis of the paralogisms of pure reason, in which he shows that the supposed determinations of the self are unwarranted transferences from thing-ontology; in part, it depends on the concept of substance itself: substance is, according to Descartes (1985: § 51), a being that is independent in its being (only relatively independent, though, since only God is truly independent). Furthermore, it is a being that is thought to carry determinacies. Clearly, then, something like free-floating qualities cannot exist, and relations must have a *fundamentum in re*, be founded in the thing.

The prevalence of the thing in ontology is very clear again in Kant: the object in experience is the actual being. Something like the night could, of course, be an object in experience, or the air or atmospheres. However, the object in experience is, according to Kant, first of all a substance carrying accidents, that is, it is conceived within the schema thing-property. In addition, the further analysis in the *Metaphysical Foundations of Natural Science* (1768) shows that substance is thought of as matter, and that in external perception the object is enclosed within finite limits, that it is therefore a body (see G. Böhme, 1986). Very much to Kant's credit, he does show that a self is not a being of this nature, but this leads him to the conclusion that the self is merely a *noumenon*.

Heidegger, finally, accords an ecstatic mode of being to the *human* being but, precisely because of this, not to the rest of being. The main types of non-human being are the present-to-hand and the ready-to-hand – the first a mere physical thing with its properties, the latter equipment with its suitabilities. In the realm of non-human ontology, the thing thus retains its prototypical character for being in general.

Life within the world of things

The thing's prevalence in ontology is astonishing. Why is the question, of what being is as such, not rather oriented towards powers, appearances, or figures? Whatever is to be considered as being must always be reified. Quite likely, the prevalence of the thing is closely linked with the fact that practical human life is primarily a life in a world of things. What that means, however, is not easy to say. It might simply mean that humans lead a bodily existence. In that case, other being would be something like a *body*, but in a certain sense precisely also the other of the body. However, perceiving bodily existence in movement, nourishment, and physical togetherness with others does not directly lead to privileging thing-ness. Bodily self-experience does not map onto thing-categories; that is, the way in which things are experienced cannot be understood as a projected experience of the body. Perhaps the reverse is correct: the engagement with other beings enables the experience of one's body primarily as a solid. One experiences its surface and thereby the boundary between inside and outside, one experiences touchability and localization, the competition with other bodies for space, one seeks and creates distance, and one experiences that *handling* is crucial for getting on. Bodily existence is certainly poured out in space, atmospherically affected and in bodily communication with other beings.[1] However, the will to self-assertion creates a distance and thereby a relative localization among bodies, it grapples with the impermeability and inertia of other beings and uses their temporal constancy, certainty, finiteness, and thereby manageability, for its own persistence. The thing becomes prototypical of all being because it is the most reliable support available to humans in their care for self-preservation. With Sartre, one could also say that being-for-itself, permanently imperilled, chooses being-in-itself as an ideal.

The closure of the thing within the main ontological models

Newton once said in his dispute with Descartes that it was possible to abstract all determinations from a body, save expansion and perceptibility, without taking away anything of its essence, that is, to be a body ('*De Gravitatione et aequipondio fluidorum*' in Newton, Hall, & Hall, 1962: 122, 139–140). This determination of perceptibility as an essential predicate of the body or the thing in general is extraordinarily rare. A thing is usually characterized *in itself*, without regard for the possibility of being for others or for something other,

---

[1] See Schmitz, *System der Philosophie*, particularly *Vol. II 1 Der Leib* (1965).

without consideration of whether such being-for-others might even be part of its essence. Within thing-ontology, therefore, the basic determinations of being as such portray the thing generally as enclosed-in-itself. There are significant exceptions to this rule, though, which will be treated in the next section. First, however, let us turn to models in which the thing is something closed and enclosed-in-itself.

Through *eidos* (appearance) Plato had still characterized being as appearing. For him, a being's being is exactly its emergence in a specific manner. The sun is therefore the most suitable analogue by which to study what makes an idea an idea. It is astonishing to see how the same expression *eidos* (εἶδος, idea) subsequently turns inward, as it were, in (the writing of) his student Aristotle. The *eidos* or form of a thing has its essential function, according to Aristotle, not in an external relationship but in an interior one: it is the way in which something is a something. *Eidos* as *eidos* of a matter is its organizational form. As the integration of internal components, the *eidos* is simultaneously the principle of demarcation towards the outside and of autonomy. In higher beings, that is, in organic beings, *eidos* determines the difference between self and other and provides the being in its forms of movement with independence from external stimuli: nature-like, the being contains the principle of its own movement. This inward turn of *eidos* already amounts to the possibility that a thing's essence cannot be directly perceived, that is, that the correspondence between essence and its appearance is not without problems.

As with *eidos*, the *property* of a thing can be conceived turning both outward and inward, and as something by which a thing shows and makes itself present. This, however, is not the case in the classical ontology of thing and property, substance and accident. Properties are what a thing *has*. All determinations of substance *determine* the substance. In saying, for instance, that a table is blue, this blue is condensed into the table, as it were, it is merely something that adheres to the table. Blueness is not understood as a form of the table's spatio-corporeal presence. This is particularly obvious in the case of properties such as *heavy*. The weight of a body is understood as a property of this body, which is *in* it or *on* it, even though one knows, of course, that it is only its relative relatedness with other bodies, in particular, the earth. In reality, heaviness describes a mutual exposure of bodies resulting from their simultaneous presence in space. Nevertheless, heaviness is understood as a kind of possession of the body that it carries around.

The self-closure of the thing becomes particularly apparent in thing models that presume a differentiation of primary and secondary qualities. For in that instance, the properties that a thing *truly* has are distinguished from those that belong to it, or are ascribed to it, only in relation to a thinking subject. The will to objectivity prevailing in the distinction or enforcement of primary and secondary qualities assumes that the thing is essentially what it is in itself, and that it can then be additionally discovered. Heidegger called this form of being quite accurately presence at hand (*Vorhandenheit*). The present at hand just lies there, almost dead; it does not show itself, one can only chance upon it. The extreme example of such an ontology is Descartes' *res extensa* (corporeal substance). Here, a thing is basically characterized by nothing but its closure and self-enclosure. It is inactive and limited.

Alternative thing models

The thing's closure in itself is not typical of the history of ontology in general. However, it seems to designate the dominant line in this history, or that which, looking at it in retrospect from the point of view of modern ontology, appears to be the dominant line. Even though the first model of a closed thing derives from the inward orientation of Aristotle's *eidos*, it is he, in particular, who determines the principal substances of everything, the simple bodies of fire, water, earth, and air, ecstatically. Simple bodies are perceptible as such and therefore characterized by sensitive qualities. Moist/dry, cold/warm are, as constitutive aspects of simple bodies, the modes in which they are sensibly present. Characteristically, when faced with such determination, one gains the impression that the simple bodies are almost dissolved or volatilized in this way, or that one has to assume an entity about the qualities warm or cold, moist or dry that is, while it shows itself in this way, nevertheless also determined in itself. Aristotle, in talking about a first matter (*prima materia*), takes account of such speculations, while at the same time closing the door on them by stating that first matter exists never in itself but in each case in the appearance of one of the four elements only.

A truly impressive counter model to the main line of European ontology can be found in Jakob Böhme's conception of a thing (see G. Böhme, 1989). This is evident already in his theory of the constitution of each thing through the seven forces or seven ghosts of God. On the one hand, these forces are themselves qualities such as tart, bitter, and sweet, on the other, *sound* belongs to thingness as the sixth constitutive moment. Rather than sound, Böhme might occasionally also say whiff or smell or taste – what is clear is that he includes stepping-out-of-oneself or revealing-oneself in thingness. In the context of creation theology, Böhme is in any event able to take the world as a whole, as well as every single thing, as a revelation by God, as a word that is spoken. Böhme's basic model of a thing is a musical instrument, as his text *De Signatura Rerum* (The signature of things, 1651) shows. A thing has a nature or an essence which is, however, not perceptible of itself nor as such. On the other hand, the thing's whole structure is oriented towards the revelation of its essence. The body is a sounding board, and it has an *attunement* resulting from its cut, covering, or cavities. Böhme calls this attunement a signature. The signature is restraint, as it were, or the form of articulation by which a thing can express itself. The expression – now called tune or reverberation – originates with the excitation of essence by the *spirit*. This is, on the whole, the spirit of God, but single beings, particularly animate beings, also have their own *spirit of volition* (*Willensgeist*).

Important about Böhme's thing model is, on the one hand, the strict distinction between inside and outside, that is, the principal imputation of a hidden essence, and, on the other hand, the fact that the thing is on the whole oriented towards revelation: 'and there is nothing that is created or born in Nature, but it also manifesteth its internal form externally, for the internal doth continually labour or work it self forth to manifestation' (J. Böhme, 1651).

Among the so-called thing models above, Aristotle's with its final cause and Heidegger's concept of the ready-to-hand's mode of being with its referential structure contain, of course, elements by which the thing points beyond itself and thus can be thought of or experienced as stepping-out-of-itself. This potentiality is given particularly with expressly social things, such as symbols like marriage rings, valuables like wares or particularly with signs (see Heidegger's analysis of the arrow in § 17 of *Being and Time*, 2010: 77f). Technical things, by comparison, become increasingly systemic, that is, they are what they are as components of larger systems. Therefore, they can be differentiated only with difficulty and defined in their essence only through relationships. Even if one can almost speak of a tendency towards the thing's dissolution, this systemic character of thingness still does not mean the same as what I want to elaborate under the heading of the ecstatic here. For the relational and systemic character of things can also be enclosed and does not necessarily have to manifest. Thus, the description of a telephone is not likely to include the systemic character of this object, while an attempt at definition will always come across it very quickly. It is quite possible that things close up in very particular ways as they become technical. On the other hand, final cause, suitability, value, or system function can be connected to a whole spectrum of ways in which these essential forms of being-beyond-oneself manifest. This will be explored later. For now, let me mention just a few examples that indicate the gist of the argument: a tool can suggest its utility through its form; a commodity its value through its presentation; and a technical object its function and manner of use through labels.

The thing

From various perspectives, it might seem that a thing-ontology is obsolete today, and therefore a correction of the existing one is superfluous. However, if it is correct that traditional basic concepts in ontology may obstruct the project of an aesthetics of nature, then it is important to break those barriers, as it were, from within this ontology. As the above considerations have shown, European ontology has essentially been a thing-ontology, and within it the thing has been thought of at important points as closed in on itself. It further transpired that the different conceptions of the thing have their origin in different contexts of practice: tools of trade, crafts products, and musical instruments all represent thing models. Such practice contexts are characteristically determined by *manipulation* and *keeping at arm's length*. In that regard, an important question is how a thing must be thought when it is seen more openly in its ecstasies. From there, the question arises whether consequentially the privilege of the thing in ontology must generally be jettisoned.

Developments in the natural sciences allow us today to see nature no longer simply as a context of reciprocal effects between things. For a long time, it was thought that cognition and communication as modes of being were to be reserved for the human being. To impute an address on the part of nature to the human feeling of being addressed by nature seemed an anthropomorphism; to impute expression to nature, to ascribe a language to it, was better left to the Romantics. The advent of the concept of information in the natural sciences, as well as the systems view of nature, has changed matters significantly. If the natural sciences demonstrate something akin to cognition already at the level of molecules, notions of appearing and response will also be acceptable again at the phenomenological level. The Greek term *physis* (φύσις, nature) took arising and flowering as its central characteristics; the Latin term *natura* centres on giving birth. Both imply coming-forth, appearing, and the difference between closure and openness. Why should we not accept the ecstatic as an essential feature of nature, in its entirety as much as in every single thing? Is not every flower proof that natural things present themselves, out of themselves and for others?

Thus, we must characterize things according to the forms of their presence. I deliberately do not say *determine*, since this traditionally means isolating and excluding. Forms of presence, by contrast, are modes in which a thing characteristically steps out of itself. I call these ecstasies. Of course, one could also speak of forms of givenness since we, as exploring humans, experience these forms of the presence of things as forms in which things are present *to us*. Since we have learned to understand ourselves as nature, however, and since the presence of things no longer means their givenness for a worldless and bodiless subject but an interference with one's own bodily presence, we can conjecture that forms of self-presencing can simultaneously be discerned in the forms of the givenness of things.

So, what are the ecstasies of things? How should they be named? One method is certainly to reinterpret the existing categories of things as such as ecstasies, or to show them to be *reified* ecstasies.

Spatiality lends itself primarily to this purpose. The spatiality of things has been understood as locatability (occupying a *topos*) and as the encompassing of a volume. But how does a thing show that it is emplaced or that it is voluminous? There is no short answer to these questions, especially when one considers that this way of thinking about the thing implies always, after all, a particular relationship between appearance and self-closure. To be emplaced or voluminous may exactly not be visible. Provisionally, one could say, however, that locality appears in the constellation between things, through the formation of gaps and interstices, and thereby tightness and expanse. Potentially implying both impenetrability and opaqueness, volume appears as opacity, namely through the formation of an enveloping surface.

The Platonic *eidos* can be interpreted as the second form of presence, a manifestation of *what* a thing is. When questioning what the ecstasies of a thing are, it is most astonishing indeed that Plato considers appearance as an answer to the question concerning the being of Being and, for each being, concerning its essence. What we miss ontologically about most occidental thing-conceptions is the explicit indication of a thing's dimension, along which it brings itself into appearance. Yet, here, this dimension of appearance seems to have completely absorbed the question concerning the thing itself: the thing is identical with its making an appearance or, better, its having made an appearance. On the one hand, this testified to a great trust in the openness of things: they do not hide anything, they do not deceive, and the face they show us is not just a symptom; on the other hand, this conception assumes that the being of things is altogether emergence. This, of course, presupposes that a general recipient can be imputed for this emergence, be it a world-soul or reason. For us, *eidos* can only be one, if prominent ecstasy among others. The classical work of art, specifically the statue, seems to me the basic model for things that are ecstatic in this way: in a certain way, they are what they show. Their essence and meaning is, after all, to render something or someone evident and present. In the case of a statue, one can ask who or what it is, and the answer will be, that is Socrates, or that is a *herma* (ἕρμα). Curiously, one can designate precisely these things, which always appear as prototypes of things whose being is exhausted in presentation, also as things that are precisely not what they are. After all, an image of Socrates is properly an image and not Socrates. Therefore, the idea of being as selfhood arises, as a reaction against being as presentation, and that in two ways: on the one hand, there is *eidos itself*, that which only *presents* a thing (the table as such, as opposed to the concrete table), on the other hand Socrates himself, for whom being-Socrates is only one manifestation of himself. The generalization of this way of being ecstatic is of course intimately connected with an aristocratic, free culture; with an identification of the good and the beautiful, the aesthetic and the ethic; with the belief that the Gods are present in their statues. Today, ecstasy as the direct manifestation of essence appears to us only as a special stroke of luck or as an ideal, which normally cannot be realized. It was a pursuit of Bauhaus-Design, for instance, where form was to express function and nothing else.

Another form of being ecstatic is physiognomy, of which two modes evidently need further differentiation. One is given in Böhme's concept of the signature, according to which the physiognomy of a thing is, as it were, the screen through which its essence comes into appearance; that is, it is the restriction placed on the thing's expression by its material constitution. The other conception of physiognomy (or, the thing's being-physiognomic) considers the thing's manifest forms as traces, as the routes taken towards its manifestation, as it were. In yet another conception of physiognomy, a thing's traits themselves constitute the way in which the thing shows itself. This threefold way of understanding the physiognomy of the thing as ecstasies needs further explanation.

Physiognomy, in any case, is not the same as *eidos*. To say that a thing has or shows a physiognomy always implies the difference between inside and outside, between (more or less hidden) essence and expression. Where the three conceptions differ is in the role the physiognomic traits themselves are given in the expression of the thing.

In the first case, as in the second, expression proper is still distinguished from physiognomic traits. That attention is paid to the traits at all, instead of exposing or opening oneself to the expressions themselves, springs partially from a distancing and analytic comportment and partially from the fact that the thing sometimes indeed does not express itself, that is, sleeps or is dead. One wants to determine from the traits how the thing might principally express itself or has expressed itself as a rule. This is particularly evident in physiognomic characterology, where Kretschmar's constitutional theory tends towards the first type (physiognomy proper, that is, the reading of facial traits) and graphology tends towards the second. In the first case, it is not necessary to impute a *particular* essence that freely expresses itself. This essence can also be simply *free* or an as yet undetermined potency. Physiognomy *qua* signature first gives the expression articulation and contour. In that way, the signature is something that is also expressed in each expression but is neither the act of expression itself nor its content. It is, rather, a style, a tonality, an attunement. Thus, to identify the signature as such is not to recognize the essence of something but only the limits of its expressive capacity.

The second conception of physiognomy assumes a more or less determined essence that leaves permanent traces in the flow of its expression. A person's facial features, like laughter lines, give evidence of a cheerful nature; hand writing retains the trace of lively movement – in the same way as a tree's movement of growth is contained in the patterns of its bark, or the blossoming

FIGURE 2.1 Orchard Rosenhöhe, Darmstadt / © 2005 Gernot Bohme.

of a flower is preserved in the sway of its stem and the gesture of its petals. In that way, physiognomic traits are themselves revelation, even if a deposited, dead one. However, they also always point beyond themselves, or can be read and experienced as traces, and thereby suggest the experience of an expression whose result they merely are.

This leads us to the third conception of physiognomy which does not require the imputation of an inner essence that manifests through *traits*, or in them as a result of facial expressions. Rather, the traits themselves are taken as the mode in which a thing presents itself. There is no need to read them as traces of movement, rather, they themselves invite movement. Schmitz very aptly spoke of 'movement impressions' (*Bewegungsanmutungen*) here. The forms a thing can take provide a feeling for the ways in which one may embrace and handle it; the lines of a mountain range invite the eyes to follow them. Thus, the thing ecstatically reaches, through its forms and character, into a space of potential movements (Figure 2.2).

Colour is a special ecstasy. It has mostly been regarded as the property of a thing and insofar limited to it – or as a mere perception of the subject, a subjective reaction to certain objective properties of the thing, to primary qualities. This dichotomization, however, overlooks a third possibility, namely that one ecstasy of things might consist in being-colourful. Certainly, *being blue* is something that belongs to the side of the thing, not to the side of

FIGURE 2.2 Jugendstil candelabra / © 2016 Gernot Bohme.

the subject. Being blue on the side of the thing corresponds to seeing blue on the side of the subject. It does not follow, of course, that being blue is something that determines the thing in and of itself – it is, though, the colour of its presence: colour is the visible presence of a thing. As such, it is also simultaneously always spatial. Through colour, the thing asserts its presence in space and radiates into it. Through its colourfulness, the individual thing organizes space as a whole, that is, it enters into constellations with other things or it centres the space if its colour is overwhelming, at the same time tinging and tinting all other things. As present, the colourful thing can be localized yet, in a certain way, its colourfulness is everywhere.

The other sensitive qualities should likewise be interpreted as forms of presence or ecstasies of things. This should be all the easier since sound or voice or smell are, after all, energetic or material emanations by which things fill a space and thereby evidence their presence. These ecstasies are used explicitly by some natural beings, humans included, to mark their presence and to indicate who or what is present. One can see, then, that something like language rests upon the ecstasies of things: seen in this way, language is primarily expression and self-marking and communication only secondarily.

An interpretation of sensitive qualities as ecstasies could lead one to assume, as psychologists do, a visual, or aural, or olfactory space. However, the legitimacy of this assumption is very doubtful; already Aristotle in his theory of the four elements had great difficulty justifying the existence of separate realms. Precisely when looking for the origin of qualities in the thing, one would hardly assume manifold spaces in which the thing is present simultaneously. This will become particularly evident when analysing so-called synaesthesia. These are always taken to mean that the subject shifts associatively from one sensory realm to another on the basis of experience. A red hue, for instance, is perceived as warm because the colour usually coincides with a sensation of warmth. More to the point, however, synaesthesia seem to indicate that the parametrization of experience can always only unsatisfactorily render the experienced presence of the thing.

Conclusion: Ontology and aesthetics

With the possible exception of Hegel's work, ontology and aesthetics have hardly been seen together in philosophy so far. De facto, ontology – at least in its main stream version – has obstructed aesthetics by interpreting being according to thing-schemata. Ontology also assumed that the thing is what it is, and that it can then somehow also be aesthetically effective or be grasped subjectively. In sum, classical ontology's obstruction was its failure to conceive the thing essentially as *aistheton* (αἰσθητόν, sensible). This is most clearly expressed in the sentence, otherwise so true, 'existence is not a predicate'. According to this ontology, one can endow the thing with all its predicates and then still ask whether it exists or not. That is, of course, also the case when predicates are taken to be determinations and thereby constraints on something. If, however, one understands what is designated by these predicates as ecstasies, or appreciates it in its being ecstatic, then such a statement makes no sense. The sun shines, the dog barks, the stone is warm – yes, but then also the flower is blue – all these phrases designate things in their being-there.

Classical ontology determines thingness through essence, unity, autarchy. These are, of course, important and even indispensable determinations of the thing. From the perspective of aesthetics, though, these ontological determinations are one-sided and not properly understood in what they designate and achieve. Granted, a thing has to be something determinate, have unity, and be, in what it is, in some way independent. Otherwise, it would not be a particular, individually nameable, locatable thing. It would dissolve, merge with its environment and perhaps only shine forth briefly. Only once these tendencies are included in the thing's ontology does it become apparent that there must be something that holds a thing together and makes it individually nameable. After all, classical ontology has designated space as something external to things. Granted, they can be in a place and, via their placement, enter into positional relationships with other things. However, that almost assumes that they could also be taken out of space, that they are what they are even without being in space. At best, the fact that they fill a space and have volume, that is, their expansion, still indicates that spatiality essentially belongs to them. However, these determinations, and particularly the Cartesian one that defines them as *res extensa*, still suggest that the spatiality in things is the limited interior space they enclose, as if space as a whole did not concern them. That, indeed, prevents the apperception of their ecstatic being – for, as ecstatic, they almost essentially step outside of themselves. But where? In any case outside, into space.

To sum up retrospectively what is needed to grasp a thing as an ecstatic being: first, there are principles of self-containment. Basically, these will be the classical principles of unity, essence, autarchy, and perhaps identity – but newly interpreted. Second, being needs to be principally understood in its polarity, that is, through the tension of openness and closure. If being is something *rising up*, a coming forth, it can neither be determined solely according to its having-come-forth nor thought of as entirely closed in on itself. Third, the principles of ecstatic being will have to include the contrast of *sleeping* and *waking*. This is a revival of the Aristotelian contrast between *dynamis* (δύναμις, potential) and *energeia* (ἐνέργεια, actuality). If coming forth is part of being, then coming forth itself is a performance of actuality. However, this implies simultaneously that what comes forth does not always have to come forth at the current moment, that is, it can also remain latent, or remain latent for a while. Thus, one could also say that a principle of *excitation* belongs to ecstatic being. On the other hand, one will have to assume that things – unlike mere *appearances* – have at least a permanent basic presence – and this, then, may indeed be related to their *essence*.

The individual ecstasies of the thing are, as already shown, not really predicates but more properly modes of being, forms of presence. That means, however, that things are not actually *determined* by ecstasies. The very fact that they transcend themselves in them renders them indeterminate. It follows that talk about being can no longer consist of definitions. A definition determines things in their essence and, as the word already indicates, delimits them. A report about the mode in which it is experienced is more appropriate for ecstatic being, or a description of this being, that is, a description of being in its rising up. The thing as ecstatic being is radically understood as *tode ti*, as 'this here'. It can only be experienced genuinely in its separate actual presence. According to classical ontology and logic, this should mean that it cannot be grasped linguistically at all. That, however, is not at all the case: to start with, it can be named. In a description, in contrast to the traditional sentence logic going back to Aristotle's *De Interpretatione*, even the utterance of a single expression is significant. When one says *the sun*, this means as much as the sun rises up, the sun is here. While the mode of this rising up and coming forth is left undetermined, the individual thing is designated as coming forth, or even called forth. Further, as described above, characteristically descriptive sentences: *the sun shines*, *the dog barks*, specify or designate the modes of coming forth. This process of verbalization is not at all impossible, as traditional logic following the principle *individuum est ineffabile* would have it. This follows from the fact that description does not start from the general, trying to make being more and more specific, but rather names the individual and calls it forth. The naming of things addresses them not only as something that has come forth but also as sources of coming forth. Therefore, the individuality of things thus named is not grounded in their specific way of coming forth but in the darkness and inexhaustibility of the ground from which they emerge.

A description is something principally different from a definition. It is for this reason that there are things or, better put, modes of addressing things by particular expressions that can only be defined and not described and, in the reverse, only be described and not defined. A flower, for example, cannot be defined but certainly described. A telephone could perhaps still be described but whatever one would say would remain rather external to what one means by *telephone* – one can really only define a telephone. To describe a thing – and by that I now mean strictly to describe a thing in its presence (i.e., not to provide, for instance, a description of a function or a machine, which would be more like a definition) – means to enter a relationship with this thing in the presence. Therefore, the description one supplies of a thing always stands, itself, in an ontic relationship with that thing. It is something like a picture. Both description and pictorial representation of a thing are not the thing itself, but they are meant to mediate the presence of the thing for someone. In their description or pictorial representation, things are *withdrawn* from their ecstasies. In *De Anima*, Aristotle determined this withdrawal very nicely by saying that a perceiver takes in the *eidos* without matter. Indeed, a thing's ecstasies are lifted off in description or pictorial representation, that is, off their source and are only mediated as such. Thus, description or pictorial representation themselves belong to the having-come-forth of the thing; they are lifted off (i.e., further articulated and marked but, on the other hand, also isolated and immobilized) ecstasies. Accordingly, the elements of a description or picture can certainly be heterogeneous to the thing. All that matters is that they allow – like the ecstasies of the thing itself – the thing to come forth and to be present. The relative autonomy accruing to phantasms vis-à-vis things and the free miscibility of their characters are, however, something quite different from the connection of concepts, whose objective reality, that is, their correspondence to things, could still be queried. Things themselves already step out of themselves and constitute the stage of fantastic events. In this way, aesthetics is set free by ontology itself and no longer remains bound to its serious rules.

3

Material Splendour

A Contribution to the Critique of Aesthetic Economy

A golden ladle

In his dialogue *Hippias Major*, Plato shows us Socrates in a discussion concerning beauty with the Sophist Hippias. To Socrates' question as to what the Beautiful is, Hippias had initially answered: 'a beautiful maiden is beautiful'. As we would expect, Socrates then clarifies that he is not concerned with a singular case, nor with a list – apart from maidens, one also calls flowers, horses or pots beautiful – but with beauty itself, with what makes the beautiful beautiful. To that, Hippias gives a second answer:

> Hippias: This that you ask about, the beautiful, is nothing else but gold [...] For we all know, I fancy, that wherever this is added, even what before appears ugly will appear beautiful when adorned with gold. (Plato, n.d.: 289d)

But Socrates is not content with this reply, either. He draws attention to the fact that other materials, like ivory for example, are also considered beautiful and adds:

> Socrates: [...] is beautiful stone also beautiful? Shall we say that it is, Hippias?

Hippias: Surely we shall say so, that is, where it is appropriate.

Socrates: But ugly when not appropriate? Shall I agree, or not?

Hippias: Agree, that is, when it is not appropriate.

Socrates: What then? Do not gold and ivory [...] when they are
appropriate, make things beautiful, and when they are not appropriate,
ugly? Shall we deny that [...]?

Hippias: We shall agree to this, at any rate, that whatever is appropriate to
any particular thing makes that thing beautiful.

Socrates: Well, then, [...] when some one has boiled the pot of which we
were speaking just now, the beautiful one, full of beautiful soup, is a
golden ladle appropriate to it, or one made of fig wood?

[...]

Socrates: [...] Which of the two ladles shall we say is appropriate to
the soup and the pot? Is it not evidently the one of fig wood? For
it is likely to make the soup smell better, and besides, my friend, it
would not break the pot, thereby spilling the soup, putting out the
fire, and making those who are to be entertained go without their
splendid soup; whereas the golden ladle would do all those things, so
that it seems to me that we must say that the wooden ladle is more
appropriate than the golden one, unless you disagree.

Hippias: No, for it is more appropriate, Socrates [...]. (Plato, n.d.:
290c–291a)

In this 2,400-years-old text, basic design problems are already clearly stated
– moreover, certain basic concepts are shaped that would determine all
subsequent discussion. It is from the process of craft production that the
nature of a thing is grasped, and what is given to that process is material
(Greek: ὕλη and Latin: *materia* both originally mean wood, or timber). Human
activity gives the material a form according to the function of the thing, and
this makes the thing what it is. This model of the thing, as a whole made
of form and matter, already holds the potential for form and matter to enter
into a relationship full of tension, to be in harmony with, or to be indifferent
to each other. Socrates' plea here is that the material of things must also
correspond to their function. Gold is not appropriate for a ladle; the Greek
expression here is *to prepon* (τὸ πρέπον, the appropriate. In more recent
design discussions, likewise, a quasi-moral term was chosen in discussing
'the truth to material'.

Along with this tension, that is, between matter and the form determined
by a thing's function, another one appears: between functionality and
aesthetics. According to the Sophist Hippias, these two dimensions have
nothing to do with each other. All that glitters is beautiful. In which case,
argues Socrates, a ladle must also be made from gold to be beautiful. Via a

detour, namely that other materials are also considered beautiful as long as they are 'appropriate', Socrates then inveigles Hippias into identifying the proper with the beautiful. For that is his opinion: beautiful is that which is, in form and matter, entirely functional. A golden ladle, therefore, cannot be beautiful.

Apart from these well-known dichotomies of form and matter, function and aesthetics (which are nevertheless formulated here for the first time in cultural history), something we may not have thought of also shows up. In his plea for fig wood as the most appropriate and therefore most beautiful material for a ladle, Socrates not only cites practical aspects but points out that the ladle made from fig wood 'make[s] the soup smell better'. These words articulate an everyday sensuousness from which we, in our distanced dealings with things, are worlds apart. Yet, if one remains faithful to the Greek word *aisthesis*, aesthetics is all about this sensuousness. *Aisthesis* means the sensuous-affective attendance to things.

Material aesthetics

The aestheticization of reality is essentially a matter of material aesthetics. Materiality, in this context, does not refer to an ahistorical or global reality but to our own; that is, it refers to the reality of advanced, usually Western, industrial nations, which, despite all crises and catastrophes, unfold a Babylonian splendour in their metropolises. Marble and stainless steel even in some subway stations; gold, silver, and precious timber panelling in restaurants, department stores, and airports. In addition, the colourfulness of flowers, the elegance of fabrics – and above all the flickering and glitter of light emitted by spots or halogen lamps bounding up and down, hither and thither, between mirrors and glass panes and marble floors. To guess the archetype of these staged settings is not difficult: it is the royal castle that has, by the splendour of its lights, lent its aesthetics to late capitalism (which is still capable of intensification).

The aestheticization of our reality consists in the first instance of an extensive presentation of materiality. Neither form nor style determines contemporary aesthetics. More likely, it is light, or perhaps indeterminacy, or space – the atmospheric as I would call it. In any case, it is materiality as it emerges and shows itself. There are astonishing parallels in the visual arts, where one could almost speak of a return of materiality or about the fact that, in many works, art turns into the presentation of materiality as such. Think of the works of Nicholas Lang, Gloria Friedmann, Magdalena Jetilová, or Stefan Huber: wood, little coloured sand piles, pollen, beeswax – or, not to forget Beuys, fat and felt. The aesthetics of the commodity world differs from the presentation of

FIGURE 3.1 Airport Terminal 2 (Ungers/Joos), Frankfurt / © 2010 A.-Chr. Engels-Schwarzpaul.

materiality in art, in the first instance, only because it holds on to the trivial identification of the aesthetic and the beautiful.

> What does this aesthetics of materiality have to tell us? What does it radiate to us? Splendour, solidity, wealth, nature?
> Splendour: We are attending a great festival, the festival of capitalism.
> Solidity: Everything is reputable, reliable and secure.
> Wealth: This is ours, we participate.
> Nature: This here is life.

Only by taking a step back does one fully realize the fascination that is exerted by this festive atmosphere of arcades, shopping malls, airports and railway stations, restaurants, hotels, and, of course, derivatively, also private interiors. For example, when remembering the atmosphere of the German Democratic Republic and its beautiful *Einheits-Design*,[1] one realizes that the capitalist system's victory was, *inter alia*, also a victory of design. Perhaps

---

[1] *Einheits-Design* (standardized design) refers to design from the ex-GDR (see Bertsch, Hedler, & Dietz, 1994).

FIGURE 3.2 Men's toilet, Café Reichard, Cologne / © 2015 Gernot Bohme.

even not just *inter alia*: when it comes to motivations, wishes, and desires, what matters most is not what capitalism achieves, but what splendour it unfurls.

Material beauty

In what sense is material beautiful? In trying to answer this question, established aesthetic theories forsake us. Ever since antiquity, but also in modern aesthetics from Kant to Adorno, the question of beauty has been posed as a question of form: of proportion, harmony or symmetry. Even where, as in Kant, attention is directed to the free play of the imagination, its occasion is sought in form. Even today when, invigorated by new mathematics like chaos theory and fractal geometry, old questions are posed again, beauty is still identified with form.[2] In the process, materiality is usually overlooked, or it is even denied the honorific of beauty. For materiality is not form but 'amorphic' – that which has no form as such. For Kant, it belongs to the agreeable rather than the beautiful and, at most, generates appeal and emotion – materiality does not admit aesthetic judgement (Kant & Walker, 2007).

[2]See Cramer (1992) and Küppers (1993).

Contemporary aesthetics is dominated by semiotics, that is, by the theory of signs.[3] Signs need to be understood, they mean something or refer to something, and both reference and understanding are possible only insofar they are embedded in culture: signs are conventional. The semiotic dominance in aesthetics implies an orientation towards language and, to a certain extent, this orientation indeed helps one understand the aesthetic role of material. Splendour, solidity, wealth, nature: one can speak of a language in which material speaks to us. However, the linguistic paradigm is deficient even for conventional aspects of material aesthetics. While a golden ladle signals: 'I am gold, I am valuable', the material's aesthetic effect would be inadequately apprehended simply by understanding what there is to understand. This is drastically evident in the purely symbolic stage sets from the period of disillusionment in Brechtian theatre: one will indeed understand the messages *tree* or *lantern* written on cardboard signs; however, they are worlds apart from the look and feel that emanates from a tree silhouette, however poorly painted, or from an ever so dim lantern. Therefore, I propose speaking of a material's *social characteristics* and distinguishing them from its *synaesthetic characteristics*.

The term *character* here is taken from the tradition of physiognomy.[4] However, diverging from physiognomy, the *character traits* someone or something possesses are understood as impressive, rather than as expressive qualities. Here, in the realm of the aesthetics of matter, those qualities are to be called characters through which a substance makes a particular impression on someone who deals with it or is in its presence. It is actually definitive for material aesthetics that the impression we get from a material in no way comes about through an investigation of it, or through any dealings with it as an object. Rather, it is sensed atmospherically. It may well be true that the potential of this atmospheric sensing (and the correlative estimation of material in its concreteness) is initially formed through much more intimate, bodily experiences in childhood. This is why pedagogical reformers have always set great store by imparting a diversity of direct experiences of materiality. Today, in our distanced forms of life, the presence of materials is by contrast *only* felt atmospherically. *Only* in italics because, strictly speaking, it is not simply a question of a weaker feeling but of a different one. We sense a material

---

[3]When this essay was first published in the 1990s, aesthetic discourse was strongly focused by questions concerning signs and signification and impacted by linguistic models. While art and aesthetic discourses are more varied today, mediation through language, and thereby necessarily semiotics, continues to be an important practice in art commentary, as, for instance, in catalogues, museum tours, and art criticism.

[4]*Character* also refers implicitly to Hirschfeld's theatrical terminology. In his work *Theorie der Gartenkunst* (2001), Hirschfeld used very specific means to create *scenes* in a park or garden, and his frequent use of the expression *character* has the inflection of characters appearing in a scenographic setting. See p. 26ff, above.

insofar as the atmosphere it radiates enters into our disposition. We sense the presence of materials today by finding ourselves to be in a particular way, in response to their being present. The decision to call the characteristics that are relevant in this context *synaesthetic* indicates that this mode of experience differs from that of direct bodily or, more precisely, corporeal engagement.[5]

To give a few examples of expressions that indicate the character of a material: a material can be hard, soft, rough, warm, cold, moist, dry, light, or dark. Those are extremely general characterizations, of course, but they nevertheless demonstrate the decisive point, namely that we are dealing properly here with synesthetic, or intermodal qualities as psychologists call them. synaesthetic are qualities that occur in more than one sensory field. Thus, a tone is also referred to as high or sharp, a colour as warm, or a voice as course. Many people regard these phrases as metaphorical, in the sense that the expression *rough*, originating from the sensory field of touch, is transferred to the field of sound, for example. However, this is at most related to sequences of familiarization in early childhood, which could of course be quite different from person to person.

Decisive here, and particularly so for material aesthetics, is the fact that atmospheric sensing involves characteristics of atmospheres, which emanate from things and can be produced by quite different qualities in a thing. This can be demonstrated particularly nicely in the case of a material's *coldness* or *warmth*. Strictly speaking, of course, these expressions cannot designate any objective property of the material concerning its material specificity. What one can feel by touching a material (and what one may then call warmth or cold) is, after all, not its temperature but its thermal conductivity. However, what one calls a material's coldness or warmth in atmospheric sensing is something completely different and this, its synaesthetic characteristic, can be produced by various objective properties. Thus, cold can be produced by smooth, glassy surfaces, but also by the colour blue. Warmth, by contrast, can be produced by the colour red and also by characteristics pertaining to wood, such as a mat surface. True, particular materials are prototypical of some of these characteristics, or the latter are named after the first, as in *icy* or *wooden*. But that does not mean that ice always has to appear icy, or wood wooden. Just think of a frozen pond under a lantern's light, or of a Rococo armchair's legs. Again, a material's character is named after the atmosphere that emanates from it, and the same character can derive from qualities belonging to quite different sensory fields. Thus, the term *synaesthetic* character.

A distinction must be made between the synaesthetic and the social character of materials. At stake here is what Goethe called *sinnlich-sittliche Wirkung der*

---

[5]Whereas *corporeal* here refers to the body as experienced from the outside, through sight and touch and particularly objectified in the observation by others in medicine and natural sciences, *bodily* refers to the body as the nature we ourselves are (Böhme, 2010a), or as given to our own sensory perception, within (but not necessarily limited to) our material body.

Farben (the sensuous-ethical effect of colours) in his *Theory of Colours* (1840). In the context of current language use, however, the German term *sittlich* is likely to lead to misunderstandings. Goethe employed the expression *sittlich* not in a moral sense but in the sense of the Greek expression *ethos*, meaning *form of life*. Materials possess social character insofar as they radiate an atmosphere that belongs to a particular form of life. Splendour, in the sense of grandeur, can be such a character, and so are wealth and solidity. Other social characters are, for instance, rustic, elegant, and noble. These, too, represent only the most general characterizations. What is important is that these characters are subject to cultural change and even fashion. This applies both to social characters as such – thus, *cool* as an atmosphere of a form of life, for example, has emerged only recently – and to the question of which objective material qualities constitute a social character in each case. Goethe already noted this concerning colours: depending on cultural context, for example, either black or white can be a colour of mourning. And in Goethe's time, grey would have certainly not contributed to the character of elegance, but it does so today in many areas of design.

Thus, the aesthetic qualities of materials cannot be linked immediately to their objective properties, nor to those established through sensuous-practical dealings. Rather, these qualities consist in their *character*, that is, in the specific mode in which they are atmospherically experienced or, respectively, contribute to an atmosphere. This character is experienced not through direct physical contact, or even just through sense perception, as the uptake of sensory data by the classical five senses – rather, it is experienced through bodily sensing. A material's aesthetic quality is the most characteristic way in which it is *sensed*.

In speaking like this about aesthetic material qualities in general terms, a great spectrum of possible characters opens up. Thus, the question arises as to which among them counts as beautiful. The example of the golden ladle shows that even entirely diverse characters can contribute to the formation of the complex character *beautiful*. Surely, in the case of gold, the social character of wealth adds to its character, but there are also its splendour and gentle warmth. As for fig wood, what matters is its character of naturalness, its scent and warmth. In any case, one can probably say that materials are considered beautiful if they increase the feeling of vitality. Which material can do this in each case will certainly depend on the chosen form of life or, conversely, on a material's belonging with the atmosphere of a form of life.

Particle board

To return to the golden ladle: the material aesthetics that unfolds for us in the conversation between Socrates and Hippias remains, however reflected, in one respect naive. Socrates and Hippias discuss the question of material aesthetics as a question concerning what things should consist of. The golden ladle is rejected, *inter alia*, because it would be heavy and massive and might therefore smash the earthenware vessel in which the soup is cooked. But how about a ladle that looks golden but does not consist of gold? In fact, delusion and imitation are rare in the Greek classical age. The Greeks painted their sculptures and buildings for the sake of chromaticity, not to dissemble materials other than those actually used. The latter occurs extensively later, though, in Rome, where brick columns were frequently veneered with marble, and especially in Egypt. One could even say that ancient Egypt is the origin of surface finishing, and one can recognize the origins of alchemy in the range of glazes, enamelling, dyeing techniques, imitation precious metals and stones on which Egyptian art drew when dealing with material. The two oldest alchemy papyri, kept today in Leyden and Stockholm, are full of pertinent recipes – in which one can also observe that *gold making* (later such an ideologically charged term) originally meant, quite soberly and naively, producing the appearance of gold (Stillman, 1960: 80f).

By now, modern design of materials has far exceeded the goals of original Egyptian alchemy. *Gold making*, by anodizing clocks and jewellery with titanium nitrite, for example, is so successful that the question of whether something is really made from gold touches not on the aesthetics of the matter but merely on its economy.

In particle board, paradigmatic of modern design, the characteristic of contemporary materials design becomes evident, namely the separation of interior and surface design. Particle board: on the inside messy, brown, without character; on the outside imposing as beech, oak, but also as marble or metal, and in that case shining variously as decorative Formica. A similar parting of materiality and surface, of being and appearance, is found in plastics. In the case of plastic, though, which has positively been referred to as the epitome of anaesthetic material, the aesthetic presentation is usually defined by form or colour and not – or at least rarely – by the fact that, via its surface, it presents itself with the character of a material that it is not.

The interior design of particle board is determined by a twofold rationality, namely, of function and of economy. Characteristically, both mesh in the rationality of production. The interior design of particle board is determined by the preferred manufacturing qualities of this material in the process of production; a high adaptation to its designated use or function, for instance in furniture or cladding; and, finally, by the economic imperative of guaranteed quality. Over all this, however, dominates the principal demand for homogeneity. Some quotes taken from Michael Paulitsch's standard work on *Modern Wood-Based Materials* illustrate the latter:

> It is imperative to source, over long periods, raw material of a similar kind, made as homogenous as possible through classification. The tensile strength of the wood grain [...] is about five times as high as that of flawless wood. The log's inconsistencies can reduce the strength of a regular

wooden body to approx. 25 %. [...] For mass products, we are left only with the methods of homogenisation through crushing and recombination. [...] Globally, composite wooden boards have enabled many people for the first time to purchase furniture with wood character. This is inseparably connected with the development of a versatile surface finishing technology, be it through veneer, paint coating, or laminating. (1989: 25, 50, 141)

The latter quote, in particular, clearly shows the concurrence of aesthetic and economic aspects that leads to the separation of the design of interior and surface. Aesthetically, the surface design is of primary relevance. It complies with an economy that is quite different from the economy of production. While the latter is all about low material prices, the possibility of standardized production techniques, and the prospect of predictable and thereby guaranteed material qualities, the former hinges on saleability, customer wishes and the aesthetic production of forms of life.

Internal design and invisible aesthetics

Even though material aesthetics is a matter of surface design, this does not mean that surfaces do not also have their own specific function, that of use value. The separation of internal and surface design is also a consequence of the different functions a material's surface and interior have. This parting of ways between the external and internal functionality of things, sometimes to the point of a dichotomy, is a consequence of modern technology. For one no longer uses modern equipment as one would have used a ladle – rather, one touches it externally, if at all. This has important consequences for surface design; thus, abrasion and scratch resistance move into the foreground. But this functional surface design, too, is basically internal design and concerns not the material's appearance but its construction or composition.

Apart from the production of alloys, there was no internal design in antiquity. According to the classical model of form and matter, humans contributed form to the being of things during their production. Matter, by contrast, was considered to be given by nature. Today, the construction of materials is a highly developed science and technology, which should actually be called internal material design. It is tasked with constructing materials for precisely specified functions and applications. The set of possible materials, as a consequence, expands towards infinity. Here are but a few examples:

In high performance switches, that is, switches that close very high voltage power circuits, these high voltages cause arcs. Therefore, cadmium oxide is embedded in the switch material, which consists of highly conductive silver.

Characteristically, cadmium oxide evaporates at high temperatures, which means that it quickly extinguishes an arc when it occurs.

The material for the pistons in an Otto motor essentially has to have three properties. It has to be light, stable and resistant to abrasion on the cylinder wall. Therefore, aluminium is selected as the base material, into which silicon is embedded in two forms: very small silicon particles ensure the solidity of the whole, and larger, lamella-shaped particles prevent abrasion. Such highly sophisticated structural design takes place out of sight, as it were. It is irrelevant for material aesthetics. However, microphotography presents us with fascinating and sometimes even very beautiful sights. The latter reference could be regarded as an aside but this aspect of material aesthetics is not without significance, for these images matter to materials scientists and engineers, that is, to the makers of the internal design. They strengthen the makers' motivation and self-understanding, and they also help with the identification of a material. Thus, images of the *beautiful* internal aesthetics adorn the title pages of professional journals for material science which otherwise, as to be expected, contain measured data, formulae and graphs. Such images can occasionally also be found in advertisements for new materials.

Another reason makes the reference to the invisible (or at least observable only with the aid of technology) material aesthetics more than a mere excursion: the technically mediated aesthetic experiences that can be had here are by no means isolated cases. Rather, in technological civilization, human perception is increasingly technically mediated and the most relevant aesthetic experiences – one could almost say aesthetic socialization – take place within technically mediated perception. Views through the microscope, televised images of outer space, colour and light experiences while diving or through televised underwater photography, clouds and atmospheric impressions during flight – these are fundamental experiences that shape viewing habits, not to mention taste. It is even fair to assume that beauty is typically sought after in such experiences, in a turning away from the *mêlée of objects* in the modern world. Characteristics of the contemporary sense of beauty are not regularity and symmetry but precisely indeterminacy, event, and atmosphere. In this way, the artificially visualized internal design of materials might indeed be related to the external design, after all. For this, the frequently asserted relationship between microphotography and modern painting may provide a clue.

Contribution to the critique of aesthetic economy

The results of this analysis so far could be summarized in the following paradoxical thesis: the aesthetics of material is not the same as material aesthetics. The extravagant presentations of materiality, which constitute a basic feature of our reality, are not about a coming-into-appearance of the matter of things. In this respect, the correspondence asserted at the beginning, namely between material aesthetics in modern art and the presentation of materiality in industrial design, is an illusion. In reality, these developments work in opposite directions. Artists present stones, sand, bird feathers and wood as art works precisely because, in the world of commodities, the experience of these materials as concrete matter is diminishing. Here, we have to speak of an anaestheticization of material and a dematerialization of aesthetics. The oppositions that break open here demand a socio-critical interpretation. Not only does economy, as the paradigm of particle board has already demonstrated, determine aesthetics in the prevailing aesthetic economy, but, conversely, aesthetics also determines the economy. The aesthetics of material that is characteristic of our present must be understood within an aesthetic economy.

Aesthetic economy denotes a particular phase of developed capitalism which can be characterized in two ways:

1. Aesthetic work, or the work of staging, represents a large part of the work of society as a whole. Aesthetic work generally refers to the production of appearance and atmospheres, that is, all those activities that are not about production, or the maintenance of processes, but aim to give things and people a particular appearance and to present them in a favourable light. Designers are of course among the aesthetic workers but then also cosmeticians, stage designers, interior architects, advertising and fashion professionals, and many others. In statistics, aesthetic work is not yet aggregated into a separate category, as is the case for service operations or data processing. However, aesthetic work is likely to amount to a large and ever-increasing part of the total work of society.

2. The values produced in this phase of developed capitalism are increasingly aesthetic values. In fact, the category *aesthetic value* really only emerges during this phase, even though it has of course always existed *as a side effect*. Karl Marx' binary distinction between the use value and the exchange value of commodities proves inadequate today. The use value of a commodity is composed of all the qualities that make it useful, or by which it can be used. To increase a commodity's exchange value, further qualities are added that are likely to make it particularly marketable. Among those are presentation and packaging. To be sure, use value and exchange value can indeed enter into an opposition, and the exchange value can, as Haug has shown in his well-known book *Critique of Commodity Aesthetics* (1986) dominate

over the use value. Now, a commodity's aesthetic value is, in a manner of speaking, the exchange value turned use value, but it is also what exceeds both exchange value and use value. In any event, the pure exchange value of a commodity also has a use value, of course, for example when it serves as a status symbol. On the other hand, there are more and more commodities that serve exclusively the staging, or let us say the beautification of the world and intensification of life. This shows that the aesthetic or stage value is indeed an autonomous type of value. The aesthetic economy, then, is marked by the transition to independence of this value type and by the relative increase of commodities that have only aesthetic value.

This relative increase in the production of aesthetic value can be explained by an analysis of the structure of consumer needs. In the case of human needs, a particular distinction must be made between needs, strictly speaking, and desires. Needs in the strict sense can be satisfied, that is, saturation can occur; examples are hunger and thirst and also the need to clothe oneself. Other needs, which I shall call desires, are not slaked but intensified by their gratification. Of this kind are the desires for wealth, recognition, and generally everything that does not serve reproduction and the bare maintenance of life but rather its intensification. Aesthetic values, particularly, belong in this last category. Since capitalism as an economic system can only stabilize through growth, its basis cannot be needs in the narrow sense but must be desire. In developed capitalism, exactly, where needs are in principle already satisfied, the arousal of desire and its intensification are of increasing importance. In this way, developed capitalism has turned into aesthetic economy.

Certainly, this outline casts a critical light on the economy of developed industrial nations. In view of the fact that, globally, people's elementary needs remain unsatisfied, a large part of these economies' production can only be regarded as luxury production. Nonetheless, not only life but also the intensification of life is a fundamental feature of human existence. To show oneself, to step into appearance, to stage oneself and one's world: beauty is a legitimate human concern.

Material splendour, the parting of ways of surface design and internal design, the dematerialization of aesthetics, and the anaestheticization of material are expressions of the aesthetic economy as an advanced phase of capitalism. It is about the staging of commodities and the self-staging of people. It is about the staging of politics and the self-staging of companies. It is about the staging of whole cities (Durth, 1988), even of the great capitalist festival itself.

4

Atmospheres in Architecture

Weather and feelings

The term *atmosphere* originated in meteorology, where it designates the totality of earth's aerial envelope. However, in most European languages, this expression has for centuries also referred to the emotional tone of a space or spatial constellation. In this sense, atmosphere can be called with Elisabeth Ströker an 'attuned space', or with Hermann Schmitz a 'quasi-objective feeling'. I would call atmosphere the *sphere of felt bodily presence* (Böhme, 2013).[1] As a starting point, this term can refer to the weather but also to the felt space one finds oneself in (*in dem man sich befindet*). To clarify, let me give you some examples for both:

> What is the weather like where you are?
> It is a cheerful morning.
> There is a threatening thunderstorm.
> It is a gloomy day.
> There is an autumn chill in the air.
> What is the mood at your end?
> We live in tense expectation.
> There is an aggressive atmosphere.
> The atmosphere is very homely.
> Discussions are taking place in a cool atmosphere.

These examples should show clearly that weather and feelings are closely related: both are atmospheres. Of course, in this case, weather is regarded as a subjective fact, as a bodily, sensibly felt weather condition, and feeling as

---

[1] See 'Learning to live with atmospheres: a new aesthetic humanist education', p. 111ff, below.

something quasi-objective, an emotionally tinged space. This affinity has its limits, though, and I will address them in due course. Before I do so, let me quote the author who has worked out the relationship between weather and feelings most clearly, under the wider heading of *bodily felt space*.

Hermann Schmitz writes in his book, *Der Gefühlsraum* (Felt Space):

> Amongst the examples [of felt space, G.B.], I list in the first instance climatic space, that is, an undefined broad expanse of weather or climate which we spontaneously feel when, without consideration of our body and sense data in the ordinary sense, we are aware that today, for instance, it is muggy, damp, balmy or fresh and cool, or spring-like or exciting in a blustery and stormy way, or that something else is in the air. Phenomenologically, what we feel in those moments is actually not a condition of our body but an enveloping, formless, seamlessly diffused atmosphere. In its expansiveness, our own body no doubt stands out as something that is specifically affected by this atmosphere – slackening, for instance, in muggy weather or tightening in fresh, clean air. Likewise, feelings are, as we have already observed, atmospheres that haunt people by bodily affecting them; they are, however, not simply body states but the undefined, expansively diffused powers encompassing them. (Schmitz, 1969: 361)

Architecture and felt space

Atmosphere is therefore a fundamental fact of human perception, that is, of the way in which people sense at once where they are, through their disposition. Seen in this way, atmospheres shape a person's being-in-the-world as a whole: the relationships to environments, to other people, to things, and to works of art. That is why atmospheres are extraordinarily significant for the theory and practice of architecture. In explicitly addressing the relationship of atmosphere and architecture here, we first need to deconstruct a common preconception, namely that architecture is a visual art. Of course, one can see works of architecture – but it is not clear whether seeing is the key and most important way of accessing them. Of course, photos are important in the mediation of architecture – but if it is also correct that architecture consists essentially in the production of atmospheres, then the most genuine way of accessing has to be through bodily presence. This concept, therefore, requires explicit definition. For in the era of telecommunications, questions concerning bodily presence have their own significance. For architecture, though, the examination of bodily presence is tied to a differentiation of types of spaces: narrowly thinking architecture exclusively in terms of geometric space gives way to recognizing that architectural creation takes place in bodily felt space as well.

Atmospheres as the subject matter of architecture

This places architecture into relation with the experiencing subject and his or her disposition. It is difficult to render account of this relationship and particularly difficult, at least according to classical aesthetics, to speak about architecture because buildings should be both functional and, *qua* artworks, purposive without a purpose.[2] Out of this contradiction or, better, out of the dialectic unfolding from it, Hegel later developed a bold schema for architectural history. It supposedly develops in three steps from antiquity to his own time, beginning with a symbolic phase and proceeding via a classicism to romanticism. In each of these phases, architectonic form is oriented towards human purposes in different degrees (Hegel, 1975: 631). Insofar as the architect has to create in each case a work of art that simultaneously mediates artistic and utilitarian concerns (quite unlike artists in other genres), this approach is correct. However, it also entails a temptation to try to understand the artistic character of architecture through comparisons with examples from other art forms like sculpture, painting, literature, or music. Thus, a building is said to have a sculptural effect; an architect approaches his or her design like this or that painter; a space has poetic expression; or a construction is structured like a fugue by Johann Sebastian Bach. Such comments are intended as compliments, of course, but one has to wonder whether they are not purely an embarrassment or even whether they degrade architecture. Is there really nothing that is proper to architecture? While the relationships and interdependences between the arts are certainly important and worth noting, this way of talking about architecture damages its reception by shrouding architecture's genuine entitlement in a mist of metaphors borrowed from the other arts. It is also dangerous for architects themselves, misleading them to approach their work with a self-understanding and understanding of art that was borrowed from other arts. And with that, we come full circle and the discourse becomes consistent: one architect designs his or her buildings like sculptures, another experiments with painting, the third aspires to buildings that are like texts, the fourth wants them to be like music. Why not? Why should such relationships not be fruitful heuristic devices for architects and illuminating metaphors for viewers? They are. And yet, they can also be prevarications, avoidance of the real concerns of architecture. But what are these? When, to short circuit the argument, we include in our considerations terms like *form* and *matter*, *expression*, *meaning*, and *harmony*, as comparisons with

---

[2]This phrase derives from Kant's *Critique of Judgement* (2007: § 15). 'Purposiveness without a purpose', as a concept, allows Kant to think of the internal organization of living beings as a principle of order in nature and to define the appreciation of the beautiful as disinterested pleasure in art.

the other arts would indeed suggest, then sculpture seems to be closest to architecture. Do they not both work in the realm of the visual, giving form to matter? Already, the temptation here for architects is to work towards visibility and to understand their design as shaping masses. In this respect, we need to ask whether it is really seeing that leads to a genuine perception of architecture, or whether it is much rather feeling? And do architects give form to matter or much rather to space?

The perception of architecture

Hegel, who categorizes the arts according to the senses, includes architecture without much thought among the visual arts. Perhaps he was influenced by a philosophical privileging of sight, inherited from the Greeks. Today, there are quite different reasons to include architecture in the visual arts. Above all, the self-representation of the architectural profession or, better, the presentation of architectural works has led to this opinion. Long before building begins, for example, the presentation of architectonic projects via drawings, models and, for some time now, computer simulations and animations is essential for competitions and clients. Later, when the building is finished and the project completed, the photographic representation of the work is equally or in some respects even more important than the work itself. The architect's presence in professional journals, catalogues, feature articles, brochures and the like, and by association his or her reputation, depends on the successful photographic representation of the works. How many people could travel the world in order to form their own impressions of the effects of the works of great architects *in situ*? It would be surprising, then, if the thought of future photographs did not enter the design process as well. This leads to a third factor in architectural work: architecture must not only be useful and perform a function, it should also be a work of art and, finally, it must be paid for, and that means it has to fit in with the market. Accordingly, advertising and branding require architecture to be staged and, therefore, there is always an element of self-staging in contemporary architecture.

And yet, if it is true that architecture is essentially about spatial design, then it does not belong to the visual arts. One cannot see a space. It is tempting to prove this claim by referring to the inadequacies of perspectival representation. But that is based on a hasty presumption that what one actually sees are images, that is, something two-dimensional. The trivial conclusion would be that spatial phenomena, despite all possible tricks, cannot be rendered adequately in two dimensions. The whole fallacy results from our habit of taking the camera as the model of ocular vision – with one eye! Of course, we actually see with two eyes, and what they show

FIGURE 4.1 At the foot of the Eiffel tower, Paris / © 2014 Gernot Bohme.

us has so far not been replicated by any technology without recourse to the eyes. One does indeed see space, through the spatiality generated by seeing with both eyes. But what do we actually see, and what does binocular seeing achieve? We tend to understand this performance technically again, that is, according to the model of a binocular rangefinder. And it is true that the distance between objects can be determined by reference to a fixed base, aiming from both ends of the instrument. This is similar to how we estimate distance in seeing. Another effect of seeing with two eyes is important, though, incidentally one that radically contradicts perspectival seeing. Quite correctly, the art historian Ernst Gombrich has identified the concealment of one object by another as a crucial aspect of perspectival representation. To paint in perspective means to paint in such a way that nothing appears that would be concealed to an eye fixed rigidly on one point (Gombrich, 1969, particularly p. 178f). Precisely this principle does not apply in binocular seeing: it is possible to look around obstacles, as it were, and the resulting blur makes things appear to float in space. Further, eye movement produces a constant change of perspective in which things are in a sense experimentally shifted around. As paradoxical as it seems, the impression of things being in space results precisely from the indeterminacy of their location. One obviously has to differentiate between the physicality of things and their existence in space or, to put it another way, their ability to provide space through their form or arrangement. Perspectival drawing can, indeed, represent the physicality of things, but not their spatiality nor space itself. We gain an impression of the latter in binocular seeing, moving our eyes around – this impression, however, remains peculiarly schematic as long as it is isolated from other experiences. This becomes quite clear when looking at 3D projections.

Once another visual potential is used, namely the alternating fixation on different distances, a three-dimensional image becomes more animated. In this way, one can virtually (i.e., through sight) roam into the depth of space – the only way of experiencing space as something that one is within. The scene changes, and space is genuinely experienced by being in it – through bodily presence. And the simplest and most convincing way to ascertain one's bodily presence in a space is through movement. Therefore, the elements in seeing that best give us an impression of spatiality all entail movement, that is, varying perspective and changing fixation. Seeing itself, however, is not a sense for being-in-something but, rather, one that establishes differences and creates distance. By contrast, there is a specific sense of being-in, called disposition (*Befindlichkeit*). In our disposition, we sense where we are. Sensing our own presence is simultaneously to sense the space in which we are present. Where we are (where we find ourselves) can still be interpreted topologically, as a positioning in space. And indeed, in sensing our bodily presence, both the distances to things (or, better put, their oppressive closeness or their receding expanse) and the geometry of space come into play. However, here, too, the process is better understood in the sense of movement impressions (*Bewegungsanmutungen*, see p. 49), like *aspiring* or *weighing down*. But sensing the Where is actually at the same time more integrative and specific, as it refers to the character of the space in which one is. We sense what kind of a space surrounds us. We sense its atmosphere. This has consequences for the perception of architecture: if it is true that architecture creates spaces, then to evaluate them one must go inside these spaces. One has to be bodily present. Of course, one will then also consider the buildings and their structures, judging their scale and content, but to do so one need not be present. To have the definitive experience, one's disposition has to be tuned by one's presence in the space in question, that is, by its atmosphere. This finally shows the sentence attributed to Polykleitos or Vitruvius: 'Man is the measure of architecture' – in a different sense from that intended, of course.

Architecture and space

Geometry is about the laws of lines, plane surfaces, and three-dimensional bodies in space. Geometry can help us understand how to handle space in architecture. In architecture, there are two possibilities of spatial composition: the closed architectural body which isolates space within itself, and the open body which embraces an area of space that is connected with the endless continuum. The extension of space can be made visible through bodies such as slabs or poles placed freely or in rows in the spatial expanse of a room. (Zumthor, 1998: 21)

It seems here as though architect Peter Zumthor had forgotten his own observation, according to which the most important aspect of architecture is how people feel in and around buildings. He delegates responsibility for space to geometry and claims that spatial design in architecture consists in making space visible. Making visible, according to the aforementioned quote, occurs in the delimitation of space through objects and the placement of things. Architecture does design things, of course, and it cannot do without geometry – though geometry is actually far more relevant for the structural or civil engineer. However, something else happens in the creation of material reality in architecture and the placement of things, something that is much more relevant to the power of buildings 'to appeal to our emotions and minds in various ways' (1998: 18). Buildings accentuate and focus the sense of space, they entail movement suggestions, they convey experiences of narrowness or expansiveness, and they articulate space itself as an expanse.

There are examples, not all of them taken from architecture, that nevertheless illustrate what is in principle possible for architects: the placement of a castle on a hill, Jonathan Borofsky's *Man Walking to the Sky* (Kassel, Germany), the curved forms of Japanese and Chinese roofs, and the installation of a distant source of light or sound in space. Following these examples, one can see how they presuppose a spatial concept or, better, a spatial experience that does not require things. While spaces marked by location and distance are essentially determined by things, the space of bodily presence is initially nothing more than a perceptible indeterminate expanse, out of which diverse spaces can emerge through articulation. Orientations, movement impressions and markings are such forms of articulation. They create spatial concentrations, directions, and constellations. Since these articulations do not presuppose concrete space, but effectively inscribe themselves into the void, they remain reliant on the experiencing subject, that is, human beings in their bodily presence. The space of bodily sensing – a sensing that reaches out into the indeterminate expanse – takes shape through such articulations.

Once the decision is made that this is the space fundamental to architecture, that is, fundamental both as *topos* and as *spatium* (since architecture does not create buildings and constructions as such, but for people), it also becomes easy to accept non-classic, that is, non-objective means of constituting space in architecture. These are primarily light and sound. Light as such can create spaces – think of stepping into the cone of light from a street lamp. Sounds, noise and music can also create independent but non-objective spaces, as experienced most impressively when listening with headsets. Architects, of course, have always made use of these means, yet it seems that their time has come into its own only now, or a short while ago. That is partly because the technical production of light and sound affords independence from the vagaries of time of year or day, or from the festive seasons. Thus, while it is true that Abbot Suger already deployed light architectonically, he still depended for its effects on the weather and the seasons. Today, lighting and acoustics can become integral parts of architecture. When referring to light and sound as moments of spatial design, one immediately thinks of their deployment as quasi-objects. Thus, Axel Schultes creates capitals and walls made of light. However, to treat light and sound as objects would be to underestimate their spatial significance. They actually create spaces of their own kind, or endow spaces with a character of their own. The light that fills a space can make it serene, buoyant or gloomy, festive or homely. The music that pervades a space can make it oppressive, energizing, compact or fragmented. One experiences the character of such spaces through the disposition they impart. And with that, we have come back to atmosphere.

FIGURE 4.2 View from Skuspelhuset (Lundgaard & Tranberg), Copenhagen / © 2009 Gernot Bohme.

The atmosphere of a city

To talk about the atmosphere of a city is nothing unusual. The expression turns up in everyday talks and literature, in cities' promotional material, and in the travel supplements of newspapers. Two things are relevant for the everyday use of this expression: first, atmosphere is usually talked about from the perspective of the stranger. Second, it is an attempt to say something that is characteristic of a city.

When atmosphere is discussed as something experienced by strangers to the city, this does not at all mean the city from a touristic perspective. Rather, atmosphere means, on the one hand, precisely what is ordinary and natural for the residents and, on the other, what the natives constantly help produce through their daily lives, but which strikes visitors only as characteristic. The atmosphere of a city, then, is not the same as its image. The image of a city is what it consciously projects about itself to the outside, or else the totality of preconceptions held about it externally.

On the other hand, coming to the second aspect, the atmosphere of a city refers to something characteristic, that is, something that is proper to a city, something individual about it and therefore difficult to convey in general terms. This is not to say that one cannot talk about the atmosphere of a city, and we shall see in due course that this is, in fact, entirely possible. Rather, it means that atmosphere is something that has to be sensed in order to understand what such talk is really about. The atmosphere of a city is quite simply the manner in which life takes place in it.

Elaborating the day-to-day talk of atmosphere into a concept of aesthetic theory primarily offers advantages for aesthetic theory itself (see Böhme, 2013), in this case concerning urban aesthetics. The introduction of this concept liberates aesthetic theory from the restriction of being visual or semiotic, which meant that everything that cannot be conceived of as structure was shifted into the realm of interpretation. In this vein, Christian Norbert-Schulz speaks of *Meaning in Western Architecture* (1975), or Charles Jencks considers the *Language of Post-Modern Architecture* (1987). This, however, is only to follow the trend of semiotics, failing to recognize that the era of representation has long since passed (Redner, 1994). To put it another way, the multicultural world of our big cities contains more and more commonly understood pictograms but no longer symbolisms understood by the general public. And that means that what appeals to us in a city cannot be interpreted as a language but enters our disposition in the form of impressions.

With that, I come to the second advantage of an urban aesthetics that draws on the concept of atmosphere: such an aesthetic is not just about how a city might be judged from the point of view of aesthetics or art history but about how one feels in it. This is a decisive step towards the inclusion of what is rather awkwardly called the subjective factor. On the one hand, an atmosphere is always sensed only in one's own disposition. On the other hand, it is precisely sensed as something external, something emanating from other people, things, or the environment. In this sense, it is something subjective that can be shared with others and about which one can communicate. What matters in the study of atmospheres is how one feels in environments with particular qualities, that is, how one senses these qualities in one's own disposition. About such dispositions one can communicate by indicating the character of an atmosphere: relaxed or oppressive, busy, serene or festive. Language provides countless expressions to characterize atmospheres, which fall into several main groups. I will only mention two here.[3] First, language describes synaesthetic characteristics, which are sensed primarily through the modification of one's bodily disposition. Second, there are social characteristics that are partially shaped by social conventions. Examples of the latter are *elegant*, *petit bourgeois* or *impoverished*. From an historical perspective, the analysis of urban environments using atmospheric characteristics could be seen as an expansion of something Hirschfeld introduced in 1779 into the description of park scenes (2001). His aim was to define urban environments by how residents or visitors felt about their lives – he even considered the causes of potential pathologies.

FIGURE 4.3 Kärntner Straße, Vienna / © 1990 Gernot Bohme.

---

[3]Among the other groups are moods, physiognomics, and movement impressions (*Bewegungsanmutungen*, see p. 49).

The third advantage of the concept of atmosphere lies on the side of the object. Exposure to atmospheres allows them to be studied from the side of the subject, but they can indeed also be studied from the side of the object, that is, through the entities by which they are produced. The stage set serves as the paradigm for this approach. A general goal of scenography is to produce atmospheres, using light, music, and sound, or through spatial constellations and the deployment of characteristic objects. This paradigm falls short of the mark for urban planning, though, since atmosphere is not produced for external observers here. Rather, it is produced for the actors themselves, as it were – that is, for the participants in urban life, who co-produce urban atmospheres in their own activities. In fact, the paradigm of the stage set actually entails dangers for architecture. Decades ago, Werner Durth already noted the dangers of approaching town planning as a *mise-en-scène* (1988: 141). These dangers consist of something akin to the aestheticization of politics criticized in his time by Walter Benjamin: to grant the masses 'not their right, but instead a chance to express themselves' (1969: 241). Nevertheless, the paradigm of the stage set does offer the advantage of providing a rich spectrum of categories and instruments with which to define atmospheres on the side of their production. The question concerning the entities producing atmosphere considerably enlarges planners' [critical] perspectives and possibilities and thereby, hopefully, their responsibility.

Conclusion

Finally, I want to come back to the relationship between atmospheres and weather, since this relationship is particularly obvious in the case of cities. After all, the atmosphere of a city is always also determined by regional climate and the seasonal patterns characteristic of an area. In old European cities, architecture and urban planning still responded, to an extent, to the regional weather conditions. The colour schemes of houses, for example, refer in some regions to the specific local light conditions, just as the design of roofs and gables is functionally adjusted to local atmospheric conditions. It is due to these factors that one can speak of *the* Italian city or *the* Dutch town. While architecture and urban planning reflect, on the one hand, wind and weather patterns of a region, the weather conditions are, on the other, the natural producers of a city's atmosphere in the sense of local dispositions and forms of life. To be sure, it is not only the historical period of modernity that separates us from the old European city today, it is also climate change. In that respect, new forms of correspondence between the two types of atmosphere in a city – atmospheric conditions and characteristic dispositions – are waiting to be established in architecture and town planning.

FIGURE 4.4 Flat Iron (Daniel Burnham), 175 5th Ave, New York / © 2008 Gernot Bohme.

5

The Presence of Living Bodies in Space

Developments in architecture and art history

The theme of *bodily presence in space* is important not only in architecture today, it is topical in a more general way. In fact, that bodily presence is again becoming an interesting topic for architecture today is owed to this more general relevance arising from our current stage of technological civilization.

That bodily presence is given such weight today might seem paradoxical to some analysts. Do we not live in an age of telecommunications? Do our lives not increasingly take place in virtual realms? What could our body mean to us, then?[1] Increasingly, people's social existence is defined by their technical interconnections. Their presence consists less in their personal, physical manifestation than in their connections. Homepage, internet address and mobile phone are prerequisites for the participation in social games. People's contributions to what happens in society as a whole – to work, consumption or communication – is increasingly handled via the network's terminals or nodes. For many professional activities, it is irrelevant where the person who practises them is located at any given time – as long as he or she can be contacted somehow. Is that really the case, is this the future of technical civilization: a social existence without a body or, at least, an existence for which bodily presence is redundant?

Many facts contradict this scenario. For instance, travel has not decreased with the expansion of telecommunication but increased. This not only applies to

---

[1] See, for instance, Donna Haraway (1991).

tourism, which has definitely not been replaced by Internet surfing or domestic video consumption – that is the stuff of eco-phantasies. Reality looks different: consumers do not make do with the image but want to have-been-there. This extensive tourism could be regarded as a compensation for an otherwise disembodied working environment, but this interpretation is contradicted by the fact that it also happens at the heart of social development, namely the management of large companies. The prediction that teleconferences – technically entirely feasible, after all – would replace travel has turned out to be wrong. People drive, they fly, they want to congregate: *face to face*.

Apart from extensive travel, the rediscovery of the human body occurred in parallel with twentieth-century development of modern technology. From philosophy to the mass practices in countless yoga, tai chi, and similar groups, a new human self-understanding concerning the body is beginning to be articulated. This, too, is a paradoxical phenomenon. Do transplants and gene technology not realize *l'homme machine* (see La Mettrie, 2011)? Has the automation of production not rendered the human body superfluous as a labour force?

Only when applying a one-dimensional concept of technological civilization does this situation appear paradoxical. In reality, this development is deeply ambivalent and can be read like a flip-flop image in two ways. Humans have had their bodies returned to them precisely by technological developments: released from being a labour force, the body potentially becomes the container of personal fulfilment. In fact, the threat to human nature by the technological reproduction of human bodies highlighted bodiliness as a central concern of human dignity. Thus, it was the destruction of external nature that has first brought into discussion the fact that humans are themselves nature.

To sum up: while the basic conditions of our civilization may be technical – within this frame and partially in contrast with it, people insist on their bodily existence and in that way define their dignity, which they demand to be respected, and their needs, for which they expect satisfaction.

Against this backdrop, the renewed actuality of human bodiliness in architecture is not surprising. Architecture operates on both sides, in any event; it is shaped as much by the progress of modern technology as by the development of human needs. Only temporarily and under particular temporal constellations can architects focus on the side of the object, believing that the goal of their construction is properly buildings. Classical modernity was such a period, and particularly the tradition inaugurated by the Bauhaus. Rationality, construction technology and functionality determined building in what appeared to be, from socialist, national-socialist and capitalist perspectives alike, a mass society. The creation of spaces for bodily presence was not regarded as an essential aspect nor human dispositions as an important topic. Nevertheless, that the human body is currently taken seriously again represents a renaissance in architecture, resuming a development going back to the end of the nineteenth century when it was initiated by art historians. Thus, Wölfflin had worked out that the spatial character of architecture is not just a matter of opinion but that it is, rather, experienced in and on one's body and, in a sense internally matched. This led to the discovery of movement impressions (*Bewegungsanmutungen*) as essential elements of architectural form. However, Wölfflin not only conceived of existing architecture in its bodily sensory effects but interpreted it, conversely, also as an expression of bodily disposition.[2] Thus, he saw the great periods of European architectural history as manifestations of changing bodily self-understandings. August Schmarsow subsequently tried to provide Wölfflin's intuitions with a psychological base (Schmarsow, 2001).[3] Thus, the characterization of architecture was set free from its previous stasis, and architectural works were assessed through the movement of experience. This view was first adopted by *Jugendstil* (art nouveau) architects. The turn is articulated in August Endell's book *Die Schönheit der großen Stadt* (The Beauty of the Metropolis) when he writes: 'When thinking of architecture, people always think of construction members, facades, columns or ornaments first – and, yet, all that is secondary. Form is not the most effective but rather its reverse: space, the emptiness spreading rhythmically between the walls that delimit it, its liveliness nevertheless more important than the walls' (Endell & David, 1995: 199f). In Endell's words, the turn from building to body, from object to subject, is characteristically conceptualized as a paradigm shift from the design of architectural objects to that of space. For architects, this formulation was more meaningful and practical than Wölfflin's rather phenomenological version or Schmarsow's psychological one. However radical the change of view was, though, and Endell was right to call it a turn, the relationship was still like that of positive and negative in photography. It stayed within the same dimension and the same metier. Nevertheless, the reversal was a kind of liberation. If the building is no longer the main concern of architecture but the space it creates, inside and out, the perspective is opened up towards infinity, or to ambiguity, as it were.

Spatial structures in bodily experience, architectural forms as movements, architecture as the design of emptiness – with these concepts, Wölfflin, Schmarsow and Endell inaugurated a potential that has in no way been

---

[2] Wölfflin speaks of the '*Empfindung seines Körpers*', the 'sentiment of his body', in the German text (1914: 217). For the English edition, this phrase was rather unfortunately translated as the 'new outlook upon the human body' (1952: 231).
[3] Original publication Leipzig: Hirsch 1897.

exhausted yet. To the contrary, as mentioned, it was soon covered over again by modern functionalism. But still, we can identify at least three strands along which these impulses were taken up and further developed.

First, there is the detachment of architecture from the norms of horizontality and verticality. This fundamental structure, which permeates all classical architecture theories, takes support and load as the basic pattern of architectural form. This basic form seemed so natural that it was believed to be moored in the human intuitive faculty. Meanwhile, modern architectural developments, as well as psychological experiments, have proven this to be thoroughly wrong. Seeing the world in horizontals and verticals is more likely to be connected with traditional building materials and forms, for example, brick, wall, and load-bearing beam. The new building materials used in railway stations and artificial greenhouse paradises, above all steel and glass, first break with this schema. Interestingly, at about the same time a break with the Euclidean world occurs, if one can put it that way, for instance, in van Gogh's paintings.[4] This development has continued into the present, where it first comes to full flower in the use of materials like steel, concrete, acrylic glass and other plastic materials. They make feasible the jettisoning of straight line, level surface and right angle and thus demonstrate that architecture, rather than realizing a given spatial structure, first and foremost constructs for human experience.

The second main strand is also related to materials, but it now demonstrates a deliberately altered relationship between architecture and space. Mies van der Rohe's and Frank Lloyd Wright's buildings,[5] above all, have opened enclosed space towards space outside. This risky step into the *outside* first puts the issue of space on the agenda: in the classical construction of buildings, the spatial sequence always originated as a matter of course, without there being a need for a particular design. The dissolution of the distinction between interior and exterior, however, not only exposes the occupant to the *open* but, in a sense, also demands that the architect reach out into nothing with his structures. As a consequence, buildings would have elements that had almost no function for their construction or use. One has to admit that this explicit reaching out into space demonstrates in retrospect that architects even of earlier periods have more or less intuitively done the same. Of course, in their case it was hardly a reaching-out into nothing, since it still took place as a practice of urban interior design, for instance, of open spaces in the inner city.

---

[4] Abandoning the horizontal – vertical schema is not yet the same as a departure from the Euclidean world, of course. However, it becomes clear that the Euclidean approach, as it manifests particularly in the laws of perspective, is nothing *naturally* given but rather something forged by rules of action, particularly craft rules.

[5] The surrounding space becomes a natural part of a building's interior (see Lloyd Wright, 1972).

The third strand, which takes up the eruptive potential of 1900 in Germany, was probably inaugurated in the encounter with traditional Japanese architecture. Bruno Taudt stands out for discovering, among other things, the importance of the imperial palace of Katsura, Kyoto.[6] Traditional Japanese architecture, with its sliding and translucent walls and its playing down of support and load structures (so that roofs seem to float, columns and beams look like frames), has an entirely different relationship with space than classical European architecture. Space here, it could be said, is already no longer experienced from the side of the thing, and architecture is regarded as design in space. The conscious vacation of centres, the non-centric arrangements of vistas, are also part of this approach. One could say that, by now, such elements have entered modern architecture in general.

Thus, the potential at the start of the twentieth century was taken up along these three strands, even though, it seems to me, it has in no way been exhausted. To the contrary, one could almost talk of a kind of professional damage control regarding the explosion that occurred between Wölfflin and Endell. Architects took up only what they could, as it were, without abandoning their profession. This restriction of potential is already evident in Endell. For when I said earlier that Endell understood the paradigm shift in architecture almost like a positive-negative reversal in a photo, this interpretation allowed the architect to stay *with what he knew*. The same space that had previously been occupied by the volumes of buildings was now understood as an open space delimited by buildings and structured by their outreaching lines. The question of space itself was still not raised. The issue was still the space of geometry, in which the architect inscribes excluding or enclosing structures. With that, the question of the space of bodily presence – to all intents and purposes already posed by Wölfflin – was still not at all taken up. The architect's job remained, despite all turns, the work with large, walk-in sculptures.[7]

---

[6]This was in the 1930s. Twenty years before Taut, Frank Lloyd Wright had been in Japan, building the Imperial Hotel in Tokyo and absorbing and processing Japanese architectural ideas.

[7]Sigfried Giedion who, as Wölfflin's student, was interested in matters of perception, realized in the 1960s that modernist architecture's sculptural intentions were out of step with the ability of many architects to handle the relationships of volumes. In the Foreword to the 1967 edition of *Space, Time and Architecture*, he notes that while, in Le Corbusier's hands, each building 'emanates and fills its own spatial atmosphere and simultaneously [...] bears an intimate relationship with the whole' (Giedion, 1967: xlvii–xlviii), 'a building like Ronchamp could be a disaster in the hands of a mediocre architect' (xlix). Mainstream practitioners ever since have tended to produce walking sculptures, rather than atmospherically charged spaces emanating their own atmosphere and resonating with bodily presence. By contrast, Giedion quotes Georg Bucher's 1851 description of the Crystal Palace later in the same book: its blue expanse confused the viewer's sense of distance and, in a 'dazzling band of light', 'all materiality [was] blended into the atmosphere' (Giedion, 1967: 254).

What is the space of bodily presence?

Within European culture, there are essentially two spatial concepts, which can both be affiliated with the names of great philosophers and were also shaped by mathematics. The concept of space as *topos*, place, goes back to Aristotle; that of *spatium*, distance, to Descartes. Mathematically, topology is the science of a manifold with positional and environmental relationships, and geometry is the science of a manifold with metric ones. According to Aristotle, space qua *topos* is defined as the inner surface of the surrounding bodies. In this sense, space is essentially delimited, it is something *within* which one is located, a place. The manifold of places constitutes regions that mutually surround each other. Space in the sense of *spatium* is the gap between bodies. It is distance that can be traversed or volume that is filled. Both terms, *topos* and *spatium*, refer essentially to bodies, and that relates them to each other. Bodies delimit space, or space is the extension of bodies, that is, their dimensions. Space, then, is where bodies find a position and through which bodies move. This conception of space, which I will call summarily geometrical, is natural for architecture, in some sense, given that it has to do with the creation of bodies, namely the erection of buildings. Does this conception of space, however, grasp the discovery of space in architecture as it was conceived from Wölfflin to Endell? Is the space conceived as *topos* or *spatium* a space or sphere of human presence? Or, to put it the other way round: is the space of bodily presence the space of geometry?

A human being is, doubtless, also a body among bodies. Humans are subject to the laws of physics, so that two bodies cannot occupy the same place; or that they move through space according to the laws of mechanics. Alive, humans must certainly also deal with themselves as bodies, they have to avoid collisions with other bodies when they move and perform changes of position that consume energy and are subject to the laws of inertia and friction. Humans are bodies among bodies only when regarded as objects – and be it if they regard themselves as objects. In that case, mind you, space is also structured for them as *topos* or *spatium* by other bodies. Then, the structures of space are structures of geometry for them, too.

What happens, though, when I assert my human subjectivity, when I query how I experience the space *in which I find myself here*, or what I experience as space? It turns out that his space is not at all, or definitely not only, structured by bodily relationships.

To start with, I will provide a few examples of spaces in which the experience of being in them is articulated without reference to bodies. At the same time, I note the relevance of that experience for architecture.

FIGURE 5.1 Street lantern, Görlitz / © 1995 Gernot Bohme.

First, there are light or colour spaces. Everyone is familiar with the experience of being in the light beam of a street lantern or a work lamp. Here, we still speak of a lantern or lamp because we know that this beam has a source, but this knowledge is irrelevant for the experience of the beam as space. What is important, on the other hand, is the contrast with the surrounding darkness and therefore, conversely, the experience of being in the light. This experience is at the same time tuned by, for example, security and homeliness, or conversely by exposure. In any case, the relationship to the surrounding darkness plays an important role. The design of spaces through light, then, is obviously an essential element, which needs to be integrated into contemporary architecture, or has already been taken up insofar as the perspective of human presence is taken seriously. I might add that the classical dogma, that colours are always colours of bodies, does not apply in the design of spaces through light. James Turrell has realized bodiless, hovering colour spaces in his art works.

This phenomenon is related to another worth mentioning, so-called aerial perspective, which is well known in classical landscape painting. While the painted landscape itself could be seen as a bodily structured space, it nevertheless includes something that is bodiless, namely the atmosphere, or air space. Accordingly, we could say that the classical experience of landscape already implied an element that transcended the conception of space as *topos* or *spatium*. The experience of landscape thus includes space as the *open* and indeterminate, as pure *expanse*. Classical spatial theory has tried to appropriate and thereby restrict this openness in the aerial perspective. The classical example in the context of *topology* is the interpretation of sky blue as an enveloping body, namely the sphere of fixed stars surrounding us. The experience, or at least our experience, is different – it is the experience of indeterminate vastness. This change vis-à-vis the conception of antiquity is characteristically demonstrated in that famous picture in which a man penetrates the spheres surrounding the earth and looks out into an uncertain outside. Today, we could say that this experience of space (which is, as we have seen, contained in the aerial perspective of classical landscape painting, for example) has its ground in bodily sensing. This means, of course, that the discovery of space formulated by Endell, as the negative of body shape and physical boundary, was still insufficiently determined. This type of space, space *qua* expansion, can be experienced quite independently of bodies, perhaps even best when bodies are absent or not perceptible. The spaces of night or mist can be such. Certainly, architects can use constellations of objects to render spatial expanse perceptible. It is nevertheless important for them to know that what is experienced in such spaces is itself independent of objects; and it is important to think of other, non-corporeal means to facilitate this experience of vastness. And that leads me to my third example of body-independent spatial experience.

There is an experience with which everyone who has ever been involved with New Music in any way is familiar today – and in the term *New Music*, I absolutely include both classical and popular music. Developments in music over the last decades have helped overcome the prejudice that music is a temporal art. Spatial installations, events like techno parties, and also new types like *ambient* music have turned music into a spatial art.[8] In this context, the development of reproduction and production technologies was an important factor. Tunes, sounds, noise – as we now know – have their own spatial forms: they move in space, unfurl a space, configure together in space. Such experiences were perhaps already available traditionally, in concerts taking place in gothic or romantic churches, for example. Modern technology now demonstrates that this experience of acoustic spaces can take place entirely independently of bodies or physically shaped acoustic chambers: listening to this kind of music using headphones, one finds oneself in and moves through acoustic spaces. The acoustic discovery of the space of actual experience took place entirely parallel to this development in music. Under the umbrella of the global Soundscape project, research into landscapes and cityscapes as acoustic spaces has been carried out. Acoustic spaces, particularly, were shown to be potentially characteristic of the atmosphere of a city, or fundamental for the sense of home in rural environments. In our present phase, the development of Soundscape flips over from a descriptive to a productive approach. The first projects considering the design of sounds and noise in city and landscape planning are underway.

Disposition

These examples may have already plausibly demonstrated that the notion of bodily presence opens up new perspectives and design possibilities for architecture. Nevertheless, it is important to establish a supporting theoretical background building on the term *bodily presence* itself. What does bodily presence mean, and what does it mean for architecture that its concern is the design of spaces in which humans will be bodily present?

The question of bodily presence cannot be discussed here fully. In particular, one cannot expect that the question of bodily presence, as an aspect bearing on the work of architects, will at the same time generate an answer to the question why, in an age of telecommunications, people still prefer face to face communication (or, better, communication in bodily presence). In that respect, I can only sketch an idea here that generates a particular perspective

---

[8]See Böhme, *Musik und Atmosphäre* (Music and Atmosphere, in 1998a) and p. 131ff, below.

on the question concerning bodily presence in space. Telecommunications always relate to specific channels, which means that the partners can only ever communicate according to individually differentiated parameters. This is also the case when partners can see each other's image on a monitor. As a result, the communicating partners merely *appear* for each other, like actors on stage. After all, actors are present to the audience only in their roles and not as *humans.* In bodily communication concerning business or scientific matters, of course, the participants encounter each other as representatives, or in a role, as well. At the same time, however, they are also present as humans. The decisive aspect in bodily communication appears to be that this difference is always *in play* in communication. That means that an issue or a firm is in a sense incorporated by its representative, who can never simply be identified with a position or a thesis, and thereby categorically *checked off* – that is, he or she always represents an indeterminate possibility and has to be taken seriously as a person.

We shall see that the significance of bodily presence for architecture similarly hinges on keeping a difference in play, namely the difference between the objective (*Körper*) and the felt body (*Leib*). One could say that, until today, architecture has not yet taken up the very theme of the felt body that was part of the turn that was beginning to be felt around 1900. We shall see, however, that the conception of human beings as bodies (*Körper*) must by no means be abandoned. Rather, the play of difference between objective and felt body is fundamental to the question of bodily presence.

The central term for the description of the phenomenon of bodily presence is *disposition* (*Befindlichkeit*). In German, we are extraordinarily lucky that the term *sich befinden* (to be positioned, to find oneself, to feel) entails an ambiguity that corresponds very well with the phenomenon of *bodily presence in space.* On the one hand, *sich befinden* means *to be in a space* and, on the other, *to feel in such and such a way*, to be disposed in a certain way. Both meanings are connected and form a whole of sorts: in my disposition (*Befinden*), I sense what kind of a space I am in.[9]

A space, of course, is more than what I sense of it, namely its atmosphere. A space also has its objective constitution, and much of what belongs to it does not enter into my disposition. And, of course, my disposition is not only determined by my sensing where I am; rather, I always already bring moods with me, and stirrings arising from my body also determine my disposition. And yet, there is this centre, this connection between space and disposition, and it is always active and palpable. Disposition, insofar as I sense where I am, generates a kind of basic mood, which tinges all other moods that also come upon me or arise in me internally. We would not normally be conscious of this

---

[9] Regarding the relationships between these terms, see Introduction, p. 8, above.

FIGURE 5.2 Bruder Klaus Field Chapel (Peter Zumthor), Mechernich-Wachendorf / © 2007 Ross Jenner.

basic mood as such, but it has nevertheless an extraordinary significance – even when downplayed, repressed, and therefore unconscious – insofar as it has a psychosomatic effect via an organism's general tone. That is why we need to take atmospheric spatial effects seriously – not only for special occasions, as in tourism or for festivities, but also for our everyday work, traffic and living environments.

So, what is space as the space of bodily presence? The key term has already been mentioned: *atmosphere*. I prefer the term *atmosphere* to *attuned space*,[10] since the latter suggests that a space has to be assumed first, which can then take on a mood, as a kind of tinge. Factually, as the three examples above have already shown, the space of bodily presence is an atmosphere into which one enters, or in which one finds oneself (*sich befindet*). The reason arises from the nature of the experience, which is bodily sensing. And, by contrast with objective, physical space, it is in this sensing that the space we call bodily felt space is unfurled. We sense expansiveness or tightness, we sense uplift or depression, we sense closeness and distance, and we sense movement suggestions. These are some basic moods of bodily

[10] I have adopted the term *atmosphere* from Hermann Schmitz (1964), the term *attuned space* derives from Elisabeth Ströker (1987).

felt space as it is given in sensing. They could be expanded into a bodily alphabet, which might be a starting point for *spelling out* the bodily experience of space (see also Schmitz, 1964). Comprehensiveness, however, is less important here than access to categories of spatial experience prior to any bodily experience. Further, it is important that these categories be, from the beginning, characteristics of disposition or attunement, that is, possess mood qualities. Felt space is the modulation or articulation of bodily sensing itself. To be sure, this modulation or articulation is caused by factors that need to be identified and treated objectively. I call them the *generators* of atmosphere. Architecture, insofar as it is concerned with the disposition of people who are bodily present in the spaces created by it, will need to take an interest in those generators. They can indeed be of an objective kind, and that is precisely what Wölfflin raised as an issue with his idea of movement suggestions, which emanate from architectural forms. But there are, as the examples show, also non-objective or non-physical generators of atmospheres, like light and sound in particular. They, too, and this merits emphasis, modulate bodily felt space by creating tightness or expansiveness, orientation, and enclosing or excluding atmospheres.

Atmospheres are, as it were, the object pole of bodily presence in space: they are the medium in which one finds oneself (*in dem man sich befindet*). The other pole is subjective disposition (*Befinden*), which opens up to an even broader spectrum of characteristics by which atmospheres can be described. So far, I have described atmospheres as bodily felt spaces of presence predominantly through spatial categories that are also characteristic of a disposition, for example, *depressing*, *uplifting*, *expansive*, or *restrictive*. Expressing a disposition, one might say accordingly, I feel depressed, I feel uplifted, I feel expansive, or I feel restricted. Proceeding from there, one arrives at a type of disposition that need not necessarily be understood in a spatial sense. Or else, its spatial character is not immediately apparent, for example, *serious*, *serene* or *melancholic*. Of course, I have chosen these expressions because they were already used by Hirschfeld in his *Theory of Garden Art* (2001), in which he described park scenes for English gardens which landscape architects were commissioned to design. Such terms designating dispositions may therefore very well characterize spaces of bodily presence, that is, atmospheres, as well. And that, of course, does not only apply to park scenes, in which, according to Hirschfeld, one can seek out particular moods or find a suitable sounding board for one's own mood but also to architectural spaces in a wider sense. An interior, a square, a region can appear serene, majestic, frosty, cosy, festive. One can see that a broad spectrum of characteristics of atmospheres, and thereby of spaces of bodily presence, is opened up by the rich repertoire of descriptions of our dispositions. This spectrum may seem confusing and, at first, offer only few avenues for architects to find the generators that lend a space its various mood qualities. A practice perspective, and particularly that of stage design where spaces with a particular mood quality (usually called a *climate*) are created all the time, might help to create an overview. I suggest three groups of characteristics (or characters, as Hirschfeld calls them) in the first instance: first, movement impressions in a broader sense. In terms of generators, these are above all the geometric structures and corporeal constellations that can be created in architecture. In terms of disposition, they are essentially not only experienced as movement suggestions but also as volume or load, and particularly as a tightness or expansiveness of the space of bodily presence.

The second group are synaesthesia. The term *synaesthesia* is usually taken to mean sensory qualities that belong to multiple sensory fields at once; thus, one can speak of a sharp sound, a cold blue, a warm light, and so on. This intermodal character of some sensory experiences is grounded in their reliance on bodily sensing, which means that they can be assigned to the respective sensory fields in an ambivalent way only. This becomes particularly evident when one asks about the generators, that is, about which arrangements can produce an experience of such synaesthesia (Böhme, 1991). Once that question is asked, it becomes clear that a room can be experienced as cool, for example, because it is either completely tiled, or painted blue, or else has a comparatively low temperature. What is interesting for architects about synaesthesia is precisely the fact that one can produce the same spatial mood by different means. That is to say, it raises the question for their practice, not of which qualities they should give the objective space they design, but what kind of dispositions they want to produce in that space as a sphere of bodily presence.

Finally, I come to a possibly surprising group, which I call *social characters* or *characteristics*. In a way, I have already mentioned one such character, namely cosiness, insofar as cosiness indeed contains synaesthetic elements but at the same time conventional ones. That means that the character of cosiness may very well be culturally specific; or, put another way, what is called cosiness may vary from culture to culture. References to the atmosphere of the 1920s or a foyer; to a petit-bourgeois atmosphere or to the atmosphere of power, however, make the social character of atmospheres even clearer. Architects are well accustomed to dealing with such characters. Of course, they tended to be regarded as important in interior architecture more than in urban planning and construction. Nevertheless, who would deny that architects have always sought to endow their buildings with sacred or grand atmospheres? While these social characters imply, indeed, suggestions of movement and synaesthetic characteristics for example, they also include purely conventional elements, that is, characters that are associated with meanings. The fact that porphyry as a material creates an atmosphere of grandeur, or the nineteenth-century idea that granite exudes a patriotic atmosphere (Raff, 2008), depends on culturally specific conventions. Evidently, there are also elements of a semiotic character among the generators of atmosphere, from materials to objects to insignia more specifically.

Actuality and reality

Concluding analysis at this point could create the impression that the task of architecture is essentially one of staging, given that people will be bodily present in the spaces it creates. In that case, it would be impossible to distinguish architecture from stage design systematically. From that perspective, it would no longer be architecture that is at stake but the staging of spaces of bodily presence, which would convey particular dispositions to their users and visitors. In fact, this moment of staging has recently grown rather prominent in architecture – too prominent as some critics would say. Architectural theorist and historian Werner Durth, for example, remarked critically on the *staging* of cities already in the 1970s (Durth, 1988). However, simply to equate the task of architecture with staging, in an effort to give subjective perspective and human bodily existence their dues, would amount to throwing the baby out with the bathwater. Architecture will continue to deal primarily with bodies, and it will have to consider humans as bodies too.

Once again, what does bodily existence in space mean? What do people want when they attach importance to being in a particular place, bodily and personally, with other people?

The relationship between environmental qualities and dispositions, which is mediated by atmosphere as the central moment of bodily presence, I have already articulated in detail. This was to draw attention to the actuality of architectures, meaning their effect on a bodily present person. But the third example, above all, listening to music, showed that the associated spatial experiences can certainly occur in virtual space; that means that the respective dispositions can be generated by simulations. This should serve as a warning. Concentrating on architecture as staging, on the one hand, and on the dispositions of visitors and users, on the other, could lead to a world of pure surfaces, accessories, simulation and, ultimately, the virtual. However, to say that bodily presence in certain places, particularly in front of art works and with other people, is important to people only because they want to experience the associated dispositions is, in fact, only half the story. The craving for bodily presence is directed not only towards actuality but also towards reality, the thingness of places, objects and people. One indication of this is the almost obsessive tourist practice of touching, tapping and scratching the buildings and things they visit. Really to be there, then, also means to experience the resistance of things and, perhaps even more important, to experience one's own corporeality in this resistance. Buildings and spaces are in reality not free and easily available; rather, one has to access them, one has to walk around them, and that takes time and effort. The experience of one's own corporeality embedded in these acts is, like disposition, central to bodily presence. This shows that the need to feel one's bodily presence is at once the need to feel one's own liveliness, to feel vitality. Architecture, consequently, has to continue to provide the opportunity for the users of its works to experience bodily resistance through them. Technical facilities must precisely not be used to render the visit of modern buildings something like effortless surfing.

In summary, traditional architecture has conceived of space from the perspective of geometry and considered the people in it as bodies. In contrast, what matters today is to strengthen the position of the experiencing subject and to foreground what it means to be bodily present in spaces. This aspect will take architecture to a new level of design potential. Neither side, however, should be made into an absolute. Rather, the truth resides in the interplay between the two, between felt and objective body, between disposition and activity, and between actuality and reality.

6

Atmospheres of Human Communication

The utterly familiar

Atmosphere has proven to be a useful concept within aesthetics in various ways. Interestingly, individual analyses initially involved examples in which atmosphere is encountered *externally*, as it were: the atmosphere of church spaces, the atmosphere of dusk, the atmosphere generated on stage, or the atmosphere of a city (Böhme, 1998a). Again and again, however, these analyses made use of the fact that we know atmospheres close up, *amongst us* as it were, that is, in the social sphere. Thus, we talk of the tense atmosphere in a meeting, the gloomy atmosphere of an assembly, the merry atmosphere of a birthday party. In politics, too, atmospheres are frequently mentioned, as when, for instance, the meeting of two statesmen is said to have improved the atmosphere, or a discussion reportedly took place in a friendly atmosphere. Investigations in which atmospheric phenomena appear to emanate primarily from the environment, then, seem to be underpinned by the fact that we are so familiar with atmospheres in the social realm. All the more important, it seems, to figure out what is involved in the social experience of atmospheres.

I did not explore social, interpersonal atmospheres at the outset for a particular reason: all the atmospheres in the examples provided still have a quasi-objective aspect; one can end up in them, or one can elude them. Although it is true to say that such *external* atmospheres, too, are co-determined by the subject, it is only correct insofar as the subject represents something like a sounding board for them. That is different in the

FIGURE 6.1 Audience at a public screening during the Football World Cup, Tübingen / © 2006 Gernot Böhme.

case of interpersonal, social atmospheres: the subject or, better put, the participating subjects constantly co-produce an interpersonal atmosphere. Objectification, consequently, is difficult. Further, the participating subjects themselves would find it difficult to provide a description since their embeddedness in the atmosphere makes the situation appear overly complex. This impression is likely to result from the fact that participants in an interpersonal atmosphere cannot really see themselves as fixed elements, because this atmosphere constantly co-determines them in their being. There is no question that there are excellent literary descriptions of interpersonal situations, and they can be meaningfully analysed in this context. If, however, it is generally true that atmospheres can only be experienced through exposure, then literary examples of atmospheres can at most be play things; what we really need to find out is what interpersonal atmospheres mean to people when they are affected by them, that is, when things get serious.

Provided the difficulties of this exploration have become sufficiently clear now, it is also clear why I shall not try my hand at the description of interpersonal atmospheres. Instead, I ask how atmospheres can be changed by behaviours – already assuming the various atmospheres into which people are entangled.

FIGURE 6.2 Jacopo Pontormo, The Visitation (1528–29), Florence / © The Yorck Project, Wikimedia.

Interpersonal communication is always embedded in a particular atmosphere; put another way, there is a specific mode of communication that amounts to the production of a common atmosphere. In saying this, I have already taken up opposition against dominant communication theories. I will briefly characterize those theories now in order to clarify the particularity of communicative atmospheres.

Jürgen Habermas' theory of communicative action (2014) is likely to be the most important theory of communication at the moment. Habermas builds on Austin and Searle's speech act theories, which regard communication as a linguistic interaction, that is, as mutual speech acts. In this perspective, the currently widespread view of communication as an exchange of information is *preserved* (*aufgehoben*) and embedded in a wider context. Linguistic utterances, insofar as they name facts in some way, indeed always also have an informational aspect. However, it is the act of linguistic utterance that determines whether such facts are being claimed, desired, threatened, ordered, and so on. Linguistic utterances are therefore understood as acts within communicative events, and they are consequently called illocutionary acts. The particular type of speech act is, while it can also be articulated in the utterances themselves, usually determined by the context. For example, when I say, *it is raining outside*, this can be pure information, as when someone previously said: *have a look outside – what's the weather like?* However, the utterance can also express regret, or it can constitute an amplified request, as in: *put your boots on!* When the illocutionary character of speech acts is made explicit, they take on the form of *I say that it is raining outside; I order you to put on your boots; I regret that the weather is so bad*, and so forth.

The theory of communicative action is undoubtedly relevant for the question of communicative atmospheres. Nevertheless, it seems that it actually excludes the phenomenon of interpersonal atmosphere. For the theory creates the impression that subjects are what they are, independent of the way they express themselves, and that they remain unchanged in their being by others' forms of utterance.

Taken by itself, communicative action conveys the impression of a parlour game – and, indeed, it is underpinned by Wittgenstein's theory of language games. Dieter Mersch, therefore, correctly argues in his critique of these theories that they both emphasize and assume the speaker's perspective (Mersch, 2007). In contrast, he argues the importance of taking seriously that participants are always already *entangled* in a conversation, and that speaking presupposes hearing as much as it is an answering. Consequently, he returns to Austin in order to strengthen the notion of perlocution. Speech acts are illocutionary insofar as speaking itself involves action, but they are perlocutionary insofar as they have an effect. These two aspects cannot be neatly separated, yet Austin's original examples nevertheless demonstrate the difference. The example he provides of an illocutionary act is:

In saying I would shoot him I was threatening him.

His example for a perlocutionary act is:

By saying I would shoot him I alarmed him. (Austin, 1962: 121)

In the latter example (the perlocutionary act), we actually get closer to the theme of communicative atmospheres: it shows how an utterance can modify the mood of a partner in communication. On closer consideration, though, even the first example of an illocutionary act proves to be atmospherically effective: it changes the constellation between the speakers. Thus, the utterance of a threat generates a tense atmosphere between them. We can see that the performance of speech acts is in no way simply a move in a language game but always has, we might say, a performative effect, that is, an effect on the conversational atmosphere. An utterance can relax or tighten the conversational atmosphere, making it serious, threatening, and tense. The allocation of different roles, as an effect of the respective linguistic utterances, simultaneously changes the participating speakers. They are turned into underlings or expected to participate in a feeling, like a disappointment; or they may be pushed into the role of having to justify or know something. Language psychologists have therefore correctly emphasized the difference between the informational and the relational aspect of linguistic utterances. This difference cuts, as it were, across the earlier one, for its informational aspect not only includes the propositional content, that is, the so-called factual situation, but also the illocutionary character. A command, too, is in a certain way information, after all, insofar as I tell someone that I am giving an order. It is through the relational aspect of an utterance, on the other hand, that a new constellation between speaker and listener is established.

Obviously, then, one can usefully draw on the theory of communicative action for questions of communicative atmospheres, but only when (in part against it) the perlocutionary and relational aspects of linguistic utterances are strengthened. On the other hand, one has to say that, for speech acts to be able to take place, and for illocutionary acts to be adequately understood, communicative situations always have to be presupposed already. This is easily demonstrated in the above example. For an utterance like *it is raining* to be understood as an urgent reminder to put on one's boots, the situation would presuppose certain earlier interactions and thereby imply a hierarchical difference between speaker and listener and so on. On the other hand, it is difficult to conceive of a situation in which the utterance *it is raining* would be understood as an assertion. In the aforementioned example, I introduced it as a pure piece of information in response to a question. Situations in which *it is raining* is understood as an assertion must be rare, even if *I assert that it is raining* is added, and would presumably imply that none of the participants in the conversation is able simply to look out of the window. One could imagine a situation, for example, in a closed space, in which the participants hear a pattering sound. The assertion would then presuppose a conversational situation characterized by insufficient information and, consequently, by uncertainty. Even if one says, then, that speech acts create communicative atmospheres and social constellations between participants, they can still be effective only if they are spoken into already existing communicative atmospheres and constellations. This leads to the principal question, might communicative atmospheres not be something prelinguistic?

With that, we turn to another theory of communication, which is, in a sense, the antithesis of Habermas' orientation towards language games, namely Hermann Schmitz' theory of bodily communication. It starts from the observation that an antagonism between tension and expansion characterizes the inherent sensing of the body. This sensing does not stop at the visible body's surface, but it tends to reach out towards the whole world. Thus, objects or people can enter into this sensing and modify it. In this *bodily communication*, as Schmitz calls it (or, 'communication by means of the felt body', Schmitz, 2002: 492), the Other leaves, when intervening into the inherent economy of one's body, in some way an imprint, a fascination.[1] Depending on the type of fascination, Schmitz speaks of excorporation (*Ausleibung*) and encorporation (*Einleibung*). Encorporation is the displacement of the pole of tension from inside one's body towards the outside, for example, by an object that carries one along (his examples are taken from tennis and soccer) or a person by whose gaze one is captivated. Excorporation is the diffuse slippage resulting from the fascination by something outside, for example, when getting lost in a sight.[2] These comments, of course, only provide a formal framework for a theory of bodily communication. Nevertheless, the latter certainly succeeds in capturing the bodily sensing of presence – of other human beings or of objects. It can register something like movement impressions (*Bewegungsanmutungen*, see p. 49), perhaps also the synaesthetic characters of the environment, and, further, whatever we know about body language, eye contact and the like. Having said this, regarding our topic, communicative atmospheres, a

---

[1]Since phenomenology does not question causes, this fascination is not pursued further. Accordingly, Schmitz does not discuss the possibility that something one encounters may not mean anything. Only situations in which a fascination takes place are studied under the heading of *Leibliche Kommunikation* (*communication by means of the felt body*).

[2]See Schmitz (1978: 242 and 1990, section 3.2, *Leibliche Kommunikation*, 135–140).

similar critique is called for as Mersch's, regarding the speaker's perspective in Habermas' theory. Quite naturally, one imagines bodily communication from the perspective of the participating subjects (embodied subjects, to be sure) and their interaction. By contrast, communicative atmospheres are to be found between subjects, notwithstanding that these subjects constantly coproduce these atmospheres.

Radiance

With that, it is time to turn to Hubert Tellenbach, an author who originally introduced atmospheres as an interpersonal reality. In *Geschmack und Atmosphäre* (Taste and Atmosphere 1968), he first made atmospheres the subject of a scientific investigation. As a psychiatrist, his prime concern was to develop an instrument for the identification of psychological dysfunctions. His investigation is notable for forging a connection between the sensing of atmosphere and the sense of taste. Strictly phenomenologically speaking, it must be noted that he dealt with the sense of smell – but for sense physiologists, these senses are the same. Atmosphere is for Tellenbach consequently smell, in the first instance, which emanates from a person – literally and metaphorically. He considers this smell as basic to communication, in the sense that people like one another (in German, *einander riechen können*, to like one another's smell) or not. Atmosphere, then, is for Tellenbach primarily a person's radiance, or his or her personal aura: 'A person has and transmits atmosphere in more or less intensive ways as a characteristic radiance that marks his [or her] personality' (1968: 48). The same objection to an excessive concentration on the subject, which was already raised against Habermas and Schmitz, could be raised here. But ultimately, it does not apply to Tellenbach: he does not stop at the concept of radiance. Interestingly, this is partly due to his productive engagement with the influence of his Japanese colleague, Kimura Bin (1995), who tried, in parallel with Tellenbach, to render Japanese experiences of *Ki* productive for psychiatry. *Ki* does not necessarily emanate from people; it can denote something that is in the air, an intensity of betweenness, in which individual persons can participate or be seized by. Tellenbach himself accessed the issue via developmental psychology: as an adolescent, one finds in one's own family an already existing atmosphere; one goes with its flow, as it were. 'The child initially accepts the existing family atmosphere, and needs to accept it, because no *differentiation between person and environment* has as yet taken place' (1968: 52).[3] Tellenbach observes an analogy here, between family

---

[3]The phrase in italics derives from L. A. Spitz (1950: 19).

atmosphere and nest odour for animals. Similarly, he develops the idea that communicative atmospheres represent the basis of interpersonal trust and a protective function of individual development.

Tellenbach's psycho-developmental perspective made it possible to recognize the relative autonomy of interpersonal atmospheres vis-à-vis the participating subjects, as well as their precedence in relation to individual contributions. It would be a mistake, however, to restrict the relative autonomy and precedence of interpersonal atmospheres to childhood or even early childhood periods. To the contrary, relative autonomy and precedence also apply to adult communication. This recognition helps prevent the reduction of interpersonal atmospheres to something like individuals' personal charisma. There is no denying, of course, that individuals do have a more or less characteristic personality, but they actually contribute to a common atmosphere in this way, even if they dominate it. Further, they contribute to this common atmosphere not only through their personality but also through their behaviour, their speech, their gestures, their presentation, their simple bodily presence, their voice, and so on.

Actualization and disturbance of interpersonal atmospheres

That interpersonal atmospheres are the basic condition for communication suggests one begin their investigation from the perspective of negative aspects, that is, looking at disturbances rather than attempting to grasp their constitution proper. And yet, there is a lot to say about atmospheres as something presupposed, namely from the perspective of behavioural patterns by which participants attempt to actualize presupposed atmospheres. According to Tellenbach, atmospheres secure basic trust and establish a base note for the solidarity of the partners in communication. The individual communication partners, for example the members of a family, do indeed feel that they rely on interpersonal atmosphere. They experience, for example, that it is difficult to feel cheerful all by oneself. People need a resonance for their own mood, and so their own cheerfulness will always lead them to attempt to brighten the general mood. The reverse effect, namely their infection by moods, is rather impressive. For example, there is a common observation that children who do not drink alcohol themselves nevertheless give a merry impression in the company of revellers. Conversely, a whole family atmosphere seems gloomy when one of its members is sad or depressed – even individuals who attempt to withdraw still suffer from the depressed atmosphere in the house.

In the case of interpersonal group atmospheres, one must distinguish between the atmosphere that is actualized at any one time and a keynote, which represents a kind of basic consensus and the mutual trust of the participants. It appears that the bulk of interpersonal verbal communication serves the actualization of atmospheres between people. This is what gossip, small talk and chitchat are good for. This is also where explanations using language game theories fall short: primarily at stake here are neither information exchange nor verbal interaction, rather, above all the act of talking itself. And this has, as it were, a procedural function – that is, its main purpose is the actualization of an underlying interpersonal atmosphere.

This is still clearer when the atmosphere is actually positively invoked. Such conjuring manoeuvres take place, for example, between people who have not seen each other for a long time or are threatened by mutual estrangement. They might call up memories in order to activate shared feelings; deploy keywords to conjure up a shared atmosphere; or use external resources like music, images, or places to revive mutual vibrations between the people involved.

These efforts at actualizing interpersonal atmospheres show already how delicate and ephemeral this resource is, whose loss one has to fear. Consequently, one can learn the most about interpersonal atmospheres in situations where they are under threat or even being destroyed – that is, through negative examples.

The most serious disturbance is probably the collapse of interpersonal atmospheres. It can be so catastrophic that it features in the aetiology of emerging schizophrenia (Huppertz, 2000). But one can also observe this collapse in rather mundane events, like the materialization of a suspicion. This suspicion can, depending on its nature, arise in all human groupings. Perhaps the best known is the suspicion of jealousy which destroys the relationship between lovers. It seems entirely possible that Tellenbach arrived at his identification of atmospheres, as the basic function of ensuring trust, via this type of destruction of atmospheres. Another possibility of atmospheric decay is shock. This is usually passing, and the shock need not affect the fundamental tone of an interpersonal atmosphere, but it is likely to impact its actualized form. A shock can destroy both the merry atmosphere at a party and the serious atmosphere of a state ceremony. Interestingly, reactions to the collapse of an atmosphere can manifest in diametrically opposed emotional expressions, that is, in one case in hysterical sobbing and in another in hysterical laughter.

Another form of ruination of atmospheres is the corruption of meaning. This is the widely known experience of alienation, in which the world becomes utterly meaningless, people become strangers, and potentially even take on the character of things. I have merely described this process so far, which is very serious and verges on the psychopathological, without as yet hinting at possible causes for the destruction of atmospheres. It is probably impossible to name general causes, but the fact that the collapse of meaning is also called a disenchantment provides a clue. Indeed, the sharing of an atmosphere is something like a collective enchantment. It is possible to break away from this enchantment, more or less consciously, or to destroy it as a commonality. We recognize this effect in the exclamation of the small child in Andersen's story *The Emperor's New Clothes*, which released all those involved from their shared illusion. Another example is the Stoic, Marcus Aurelius, whose deliberate destruction of shared meanings in his self-reflections was performed to still his own and others' fears. When everything is meaningless, there is nothing left to lose.

These examples of decaying atmospheres show that interpersonal atmospheres are capable of casting a spell on all those involved, possibly keeping them trapped in an illusion, but in any case securing an unmediated connection with others and the world. Their decay throws the individual back on him- or herself, and it throws into question the relationship with other people as well as with the world.

Less dramatic negative effects on atmospheres can be described as disturbances. These leave the matter itself intact but highlight its proper nature through irritations and actual endangerment. The *faux pas* is a characteristic example here: it is a form of expression, or an expression, or a type of behaviour that is out of line in a particular company and, when it happens, challenges these lines momentarily, makes the perpetrator stand out and somehow irritates everyone, so that spontaneous communication comes to a halt for the time being. A *faux pas* is not simply the violation of a rule – which it is also, of course; but rule violations can simply be detected and, if necessary, punished. The *faux pas*, on the other hand, is a perlocutionary act in an Austinian sense, that is, its occurrence has a direct effect on the interpersonal atmosphere.

A similarly disturbing phenomenon is the so-called wrong note, which could be considered, in a sense, as a mild form of *faux pas*. However, the wrong note is precisely not a step or an act, but only an error of judgement about the modality (*Wie*), the pitch, or the style of wording. When Kant says, about the tone in which a verbal expression is presented, that this tone 'indicates, more or less, a mode in which the speaker is affected, and in turn evokes it in the hearer also' (Kant & Walker, 2007: 157), he has struck on an important aspect of verbal communication: the tone in which an utterance is presented modifies the interpersonal atmosphere. Normally, one has to tune into this atmosphere to communicate successfully. To let a *wrong note* slip into one's utterance effectively means disturbing the interpersonal atmosphere. In that case, one has to expect resistance, no matter what one says in terms of contents and language, because it is the shared atmosphere that makes communication partners willing to take up the other's utterances.

The appearance of a stranger has to be considered another disturbance of interpersonal atmospheres, because she or he is not tuned into a common atmosphere or the community is not attuned to him. This case is interesting insofar as it opens up ethical perspectives concerning the theme of shared atmospheres. For, as is obvious in this example, an interpersonal atmosphere cannot always serve as the base of communication, and its preservation cannot be the ultimate goal of every action, either. It must also be possible rationally to distance oneself from a shared atmosphere and to act on the basis of reason – perhaps even in order to restore an interpersonal atmosphere following the disturbance, so that everyone may share in it. This leads me to the last example of disturbances, which I would like to call the *tearing open* of the atmosphere. When the atmosphere is torn open, it is not destroyed but becomes in a sense visible as such and transparent. Modes of behaviour that result in such a *tearing open* are, for instance, teasing and irony. They presuppose an interpersonal atmosphere but in a sense also break away from it; they generate distance and threaten to destroy the atmosphere. In some cases, this may well happen, and one therefore has to be careful about those practices, particularly in one's relationships with children. However, these behaviours show, precisely, a potential in dealing with interpersonal atmospheres, so that individuals are not simply dependent on them but can, in principle, positively contribute to them. In the final section, therefore, I want to touch briefly on some possibilities of generating interpersonal atmospheres. They suggest, if one can put it this way, that more is possible than modifying the always already presupposed atmosphere, in one way or another.

Contributions

The discussion so far has demonstrated how important interpersonal atmospheres are for the possibility of communication. They connect communication partners before they address each other. An interpersonal atmosphere provides assurance that one moves, somehow, already on shared grounds. We need interpersonal atmosphere also as a sounding board for our own moods. By modifying the interpersonal atmosphere through our mood, we share this mood with others. On the other hand, an interpersonal atmosphere is also the source of our own feeling: we are affected by and enveloped in it, and we drift with it in our own feelings, so to say.

Given the importance of interpersonal atmospheres, it is remarkable how little explicit attention and interest they have received. It is worth noting that a concern with interpersonal atmospheres can be observed, of all places, in politics. If confidence-building measures are taken to improve an atmosphere in politics, one wonders why similar practices are not adopted in everyday communication. An awareness of everyday communication, and of skills required in this area, helps us to keep this communication as focused and factual as possible. In technical civilizations, these are valuable virtues, indeed. At the same time, however, we observe a decline of everyday culture and ritual. That is, for the sake of goal orientation and objectivity in communication, we neglect to nurture the performative aspects of communication and let the forms that could create space for it to occur go to waste.[4] That something like interpersonal atmosphere is important becomes obvious to us only when something goes wrong, that is, through what I have called *collapse*, *disturbance* and *tearing open*. To place these modifications at the forefront of the analysis here was, after all, not just a methodical strategy. Yet, one way of nurturing interpersonal atmosphere as such emerged as chatting, gossip or small talk. Granted, this is a trivial way of nurturing interpersonal atmospheres, of which people may not even be conscious as they participate in it. Considering, though, that the cultivation of life consisted, for an author as dry and logical as Immanuel Kant, in the inclusion of others in one's own feelings (see Böhme, 2005b) should give us pause. Even further, there may be something like a responsibility for interpersonal atmospheres, insofar as they make up the shared space of a common mood.

Therefore, in closing I want to ask tentatively in what way an individual can contribute to an interpersonal atmosphere. I choose the term *contribution* deliberately because here, too, atmosphere has to be presupposed, as something independent of an individual. In a certain sense, of course, we are actually quite well trained in the production of atmospheres today, that is, through the manipulation of external conditions such as furniture and spatial layout, music, and lighting. However, interpersonal atmosphere is substantially sustained by the behaviour of individuals, in the same way in which they, conversely, sustain their own behaviour through it. What matters here, above all, is the How of this behaviour, and less its intentions or content. As they say, it's not what you say, but how you say it.[5] That is, what matters is voice, intonation, speech melody, or pitch. What matters is the attitude one takes to one's partners, the movement suggestions one exudes, closeness or distance expressed through posture and spatial vicinity; and besides, the play of glances, or vivaciousness. All that happens, of course, even by itself. One is not normally aware that these actions and behaviours can be conscious

---

[4]I have criticized this decline of everyday culture in greater detail in *Briefe an meine Töchter* (Letters to My Daughters, 1995b).

[5]In the German original: '*Der Ton macht die Musik*', the tone makes the music, or what matters in music is the tone.

contributions to a common atmosphere. What can be done to let a creative atmosphere emerge; how can one contribute to a healthy atmosphere in a family; what is it that makes an atmosphere calming, hospitable, and beneficial for children? These questions are difficult to answer, but one thing can be said generally: a willingness is required to turn one's attention to this interpersonal phenomenon as such, and a form of communication that is itself *restrained*, that is, in which people hold back their expressive and active intentions and confine themselves to contributing to something that *has to develop*.

7

Learning to Live with Atmospheres

A New Aesthetic Humanist Education

Objectives of aesthetic education

A curious oscillation between resigned modesty and exalted claims is typical of *art* as a teaching subject in schools. Just as physics lessons cannot turn students into little physicists, or mathematics turn them into mathematicians, the task for art education in schools cannot be to turn students into artists or even art critics. All the same, a substantial part of art teachers' efforts consists precisely in conveying elementary knowledge in this direction and to develop corresponding skills. Students are supposed to learn about art techniques, to train their perceptive abilities and to know how to express themselves. In addition, they are expected to acquire knowledge about visual arts genres: it is anticipated that they will construct categories, analyse works of art and discuss them competently. All this does not amount to much and holds manifold disappointments for both teachers and students. It would better, then, to be modest about aesthetic education.

Regardless, the expectations of this discipline are extremely high and amis to establish fundamental principles to contribute to self-development, to develop individuality and the capacity for emancipation, to nurture innovative thinking, inventiveness and problem solving, to provide cultural orientation, and, finally, to contribute to career guidance. These aims are taken from the Hamburg *Rahmenplan bildende Kunst* (Framework for Visual Arts) for lower secondary classes – similar expressions can easily be found in other frameworks. The peculiar collection of objectives shows that expectations of art as a school subject significantly transcend subject specific aspects: *Bildung* (education) is expected – not in the sense of knowledge acquisition but in the sense of character formation. This expectation may be justified, but its expression reads like a smorgasbord of assorted goals, since neither beginnings nor ends are guided by education. Neither are we told what the subject of art, in its efforts to form human beings, has to engage with (that is, the world in which we live and the way in which humans, including children, are determined by it), nor is there a question about the meaning of being human, that is, what the goals mentioned above are to achieve.

I will try to explore these two questions by turning, as one might expect, to Schiller's letters in *On the Aesthetic Education of Man*.

Schiller's *On the Aesthetic Education of Man* in a series of letters

To understand Schiller's letters today, one must remember when they were written: in 1795, that is, under the impression of events during and immediately after the French Revolution. This is a text by the Republican Schiller, who shared the goals of the revolution but was dismayed when faced with the bloody violence by which it proceeded. If one of the general concerns of the Enlightenment was the transition from the given to the man-made (or, from nature to technology),[1] this was equally characteristic of the *project of modernity*. In particular, the transition from the state of Nature to the state of Reason was considered necessary by Schiller (Third Letter, 2004). His thesis is that the direct transition from the state of Nature to the state of Reason leads into barbarism, because humans are not properly prepared and their liberation from one compulsion, that of Nature, causes them to fall under another, the constraint of principles.[2] Consequently, Schiller concludes that the transition to the state of Reason (or a moral state, as he occasionally puts it) requires humanistic education. For the contrast between Nature and Reason is also found in humans themselves, and it is there, *inside*, that it must be mediated and healed.

---

[1] See Böhme (2001b), Chapters I.2–I.6.
[2] The archetype of this catastrophe for Schiller is probably the figure of Robespierre.

FIGURE 7.1 Sea view, Kamakura / © 2004 Gernot Böhme.

FIGURE 7.2 View of the Botten, Greifswald / 2005 Gernot Böhme.

The disintegration of sensuousness and reason is, according to Schiller, a product of social organization, particularly of the division of labour. In his view, the desire for efficiency causes individuals to be educated entirely one-sidedly, and thereby also utterly incompletely as human beings (Sixth Letter, 2004). He sees the same separation of abilities, or their asymmetrical development, reflected in the class divisions in society. The 'lower and more numerous classes' (Schiller, 2004: 35), as he puts it in the Fifth Letter, turn towards sensuousness, whereas the 'civilized classes' (he obviously thinks of the bourgeois and feudal classes here) are alienated from it and try to organize their lives rationally. From his Eurocentric perspective, he reflects this difference once more as the difference between savages and civilized states (Fourth Letter).

The solution, he thinks, lies in aesthetic education, which is given the task of reconciling the conflicting human capacities via a third, which he will call play impulse. With this proposal, he follows certain lines Kant sketched out in the *Critique of Judgement*. It is worth remembering those here, because they help make Schiller's propositions easier to understand and more plausible. Following Kant, an object is called beautiful if its presence gives rise in the imagination to a free play between sensuousness and reason.[3] The enjoyment of beauty consists in the freedom of this play – hence the important role play assumes for Schiller. Simultaneously, Kant assigns beauty – incidentally in accordance with Edmund Burke – a role in the formation of society. Our ability to arrange our environment with taste (i.e., to furnish it with beautiful things) allows us to let other people share in our sentiments. Hence, Schiller's idea of socialization through beauty, which culminates in the concept of an aesthetic State. Finally, Kant justifies moral appearance, that is, the endeavour to give oneself the appearance of being good through civilized behaviour. His hope is that that a person will become moral in the long run, that is, goes beyond appearance. Anyway, in the education of humans to become human, which, according to Kant, leads from civilization to cultivation to moralization, moral appearance represents the middle phase. In Schiller, one could be led to believe that cultivation is the real goal or, at least, the *conditio sine qua non* for true humanity.

Decisive for Schiller is the connection between play, beauty, and freedom. The aesthetic education of man to become human consists in stimulating the play impulse. It is given the task of mediating the tendencies allocated to sensuality and reason respectively – that is, sense and form impulse, as he calls them. Schiller deduces that the play impulse is about beauty, because the sense impulse is about material, the form impulse about form, and both together and in combination are *living form*, which, for Schiller, is beauty. When following the play impulse, one is thus concerned with beauty, and in this way achieves freedom both from the demands of Nature and the laws of Reason. Schiller does not hesitate to illustrate this by way of the contrast between play and seriousness. Life loses its seriousness in play: 'In a word,

---

[3]Regarding this interpretation of Kant, see my book *Kants Kritik der Urteilskraft in neuer Sicht* (1999b).

as it [the mind] comes into association with ideas, everything actual loses its seriousness, because it grows *small*; and as it meets with perception, necessity puts aside its seriousness, because it grows *light*' (Fifteenth Letter, 2004: 78).

So, how does aesthetic education take place? One might think that Schiller foregrounds performance, that is, theatre. However, this is not at all the case; rather, he obviously expects the mediation of material and form to be already completed in the work of art, so that the aesthetic education of man can take place in the contemplation of art. Through the latter, he believes, humans end up in a middle disposition, which he calls aesthetic (Twentieth Letter, 2004: 78). For, while humans are receptive and let themselves be determined when in a sensuous condition, they want self-determination when in a condition of reason or rationality. The play between both, which Kant had already identified as the play of the imagination, is the floating aesthetic condition.

> The mind, then, passes from sensation to thought through a middle disposition in which sensuousness and reason are active at the same time, but just because of this they are mutually destroy their determining power … This middle disposition, in which our nature is constrained neither physically nor morally and yet is active in both ways, pre-eminently deserves to be called a free disposition …. (Twentieth Letter, 2004: 98–99)

Schiller does not seem to deploy the expression *disposition* here in the sense of *mood* but rather in the sense in which one speaks of the tuning of an instrument. For aesthetic education is not supposed to lead to a fleeting sentiment but to a new state of mind.

This raises the question concerning the goal of aesthetic education. The reference to Kant and the reflection on the French Revolution might suggest that the aesthetic condition is only a passing phase, and that play is merely an exceptional situation. After all, the overall goal is the state of reason, and the particular goal the moral human being – and there is no way of getting rid of the serious side of life.[4] This, however, is not at all clear in Schiller's text; he concludes his letters with the idea of the aesthetic state, and he identified true humanity as play already in the Fifteenth Letter:

> For, to declare it once and for all, Man plays only when he is in the full sense of the word a man, and he is only wholly Man when he is playing. (Fifteenth Letter, 2004: 80)

---

[4]Kierkegaard's sharp opposition between aesthetic and ethical life, in which he contrasts the playful with the serious, may well be a reaction to Schiller's letters.

Aesthetic humanist education under the conditions of technical civilization and aesthetic economy

When asking how one could reconstruct Schiller's idea of humanistic aesthetic education under our current conditions, the very first thing one has to learn from him is: education is not about writing on a *tabula rasa* nor about the delicate care for a self-developing little plant. Rather, education always takes place on the basis of a predisposition by, and in competition with other, educational instances. Like Schiller, who took account of an already alienated human being and a divided society, we must take into account that the project of aesthetic education in schools involves young people who are conditioned by a powerful life and consumer world. Pedagogy must therefore ask itself the question which corrective, if not therapeutic role in the development of young people it might take on. To that end, the life world and present society have to be explored as educational entities. It seems expedient to do this under the headings of *technical civilization* and *aesthetic economy*.

Over the last decades, our life world and society – the world of work and transportation, communication, perception, and art – have been subjected to a rapid process of technification. The most recent phase of this process involves the technification of the human body. With regard to *aesthetics*, what does life under the conditions of technical civilization mean? Human communication and perception in technical civilization are extensively and, regarding means and possibilities, even dominantly impacted by technical media. A very large part of social activity, from communication to, more recently, shopping and banking, are processed telematically. Even where unarmed (i.e., occurring without equipment) perception is dominated by norms and models of technically mediated sensing. Seeing is oriented by camera and video, not the other way round. The need to adapt to, and to act adequately in, a technified world of work and transportation has led to an habituated objectivity, a radical separation of functional behaviour and emotions. Emotional needs are sated less in reality, and more likely within worlds of images, that is, in film, television, and so on.

The second organizational form that dominates our life may be called *aesthetic economy* (see Böhme, 2003).[5] It characterizes that phase of economic development in which we find ourselves at present in Western industrialized nations. The economy is still capitalistic and can therefore function only as long as there is growth. The necessity for continuous

---

[5]See also pp. 33 and 66.

economic growth, however, contrasts with the fact that basic needs have long been sated within the realm of this economy. It, therefore, necessarily banks on needs, or better, desires that are not slaked through gratification as thirst is quenched through drinking but rather intensified. These are the desires for decorations, staging, or consumption as such. Commodity production, therefore, can no longer rely on the use value of goods but has to create stage values – and that is characteristic of an aesthetic economy. In sum, our economy is no longer based on scarcity but on extravagance. Puritan ethics, according to Max Weber the foundation of early capitalist development, becomes obsolete in its late phase. The maxim is no longer saving but spending, no longer stock but turnover. This style, this way of thinking shapes both the reproductive and the productive sphere, the private as much as the public. Our society has therefore correctly been called a consumer and event society.

What do technical civilization and aesthetic economy mean to the people who live in them, and how are the people shaped by those social structures? Asking this question, and looking back to Schiller, one has to say the phenomena of separation and alienation are no longer class specific phenomena; likewise, the one-dimensionalities of human development are no longer assigned to specific groups of people. Rather, they concern everyone, and the rift runs right through each individual. With Kant, Schiller spoke of the separation of sensuousness and reason. He diagnosed a life of lust and receptiveness, a life of inclination and materialism on one side, with one type of person, or one class. On the other side, with the other type of person, the other class, he found a dominance of rationality, a rigidity of principles and the development of will and autonomy. What would be the equivalent today? As I already said: the rift runs right through each person today, depending on the situation, competencies and abilities are called on differently and they are trained one-dimensionally and in isolation by the definitive forces of the respective spheres. On the side of reason according to Kant and Schiller, there is today the personality shaped by work and transportation. He or she is objective, punctual, functional, and mobile, intensely fungible, but precisely not autonomous. In today's consumer society, the sensuous side according to Kant and Schiller should find its correspondence in a human type who relishes life beyond the reality principle. However, we know already from Marcuse (2011) that the reality principle as performance principle dominates even the realm of free time and consumption. For some time now, we meet people who are not socialized by enjoyment but rather tuned for turnover and consumption; who are at bottom incapable of passion; live at a distance from their bodies; represent themselves as *cool* and unreceptive in their social relationships; and become increasingly relationship-poor, if not unable to commit.

It would be wrong to think that our young people still grow into these structures. As participants in public transport, as consumers of music and fashion, as nodes of telecommunication networks and floating, permanently changing social relationships, they were socialized into the entire system of technical civilization and aesthetic economy a long time ago. What can aesthetic education mean in such circumstances, and what is the task of the arts subject in schools?

Atmosphere as the object and medium of aesthetic education

Under contemporary conditions, I propose that atmospheres could take on the role Schiller once assigned in his aesthetic education to play. But what are atmospheres? To use an expression by Elisabeth Ströker, atmospheres are attuned spaces, or, following Hermann Schmitz, quasi-objective moods. I would define atmospheres as the spheres of felt bodily presence. Much better than such definitions, though, everyday language can lead us to an understanding of *atmosphere*. We speak of a *serene valley* or of the *tense atmosphere in a discussion*, we speak of an *autumnal atmosphere* or the *atmosphere of the Twenties*. These are turns of phrase by which one can easily communicate about a mood that is in the air, or about the emotional climate that prevails in the room. Here, I do not wish to repeat in detail the theory of atmosphere as a central element of *Aesthetics as a General Theory of Perception* (Böhme, 2001a),[6] rather, only sketch some basic traits in outline.

An atmosphere must be palpable, which presupposes bodily presence – one must be in a landscape or a space, or one has to expose oneself to the aura of a work of art. One can feel the atmosphere in one's disposition towards a particular mood. One is *tuned* by an atmosphere.

Each atmosphere has its own distinctive character. Indeed, we habitually talk about atmospheres by describing their character, and everyday language provides a surprisingly rich repertoire for this purpose. To start with, some of these characters are moods, so that people call an atmosphere serene or serious. Then, movement suggestions: atmospheres are felt as uplifting or oppressive. Next, synaesthesia: these are atmospheres that are identified by qualities that, as it were, cross sensory fields. Accordingly, one speaks of a cold or a rough atmosphere. Further, there are atmospheres of communicative character: they prevail during conversations or meetings between people. An atmosphere can be tense, for example; a conversation can be conducted in a rough tone; or the atmosphere can be engaging or aggressive. Finally,

---

[6] *Ästhetik als allgemeine Wahrnehmungslehre* (Aesthetics as a general theory of perception) is the subtitle of my book *Aisthetik* (2001a).

there are social atmospheres, which are determined particularly by their conventional aspects. Thus, one can talk of a petty-bourgeois atmosphere or of the atmosphere of the 1920s.

Another important aspect of the theory of atmospheres is the fact that atmospheres can be produced. They are, then, not just something one feels but something that can be generated deliberately by specific, indeed material constellations. The paradigm here is the art of scenography, where stage designers habitually produce a *climate* by arranging things, spatial constellations, light and sound in specific ways. As a result, a space of a particular basic mood arises on stage, within which the drama can then unfold.

We must now ask regarding aesthetic education in schools, is there something like *atmospheric competence*? To pursue this question, we first have to remember that atmospheres are exceedingly commonplace. They are what we live our lives in; we are determined by atmospheres and we determine them. We sense the atmosphere of a conversation we are part of. We feel the atmospheres of the rooms we enter, which are created by their architecture (i.e., physical mass and volume) and also by lighting conditions, acoustics, colours, and so on. Architecture and interior design, however, are not alone in providing atmospheres for spaces. There are also specific atmospheres we experience that are partially consciously produced: the sales atmosphere in boutique clothing and department stores, or the leisure atmosphere on promenades and in hotels. We are also familiar with atmospheres in the theatre and, generally, in art. Atmospheres prevail particularly in music, be it in concerts or as acoustic furnishings of everyday spaces that envelop us in atmospheres. In everyday life, we experience these atmospheres in passing, mostly unconsciously, and yet they have a great effect. An atmosphere provides us with a basic mood and affects us precisely because we do not specifically pay attention. It determines our disposition – even to the extent of potentially causing psychosomatic upsets.

Considering the ubiquity of atmospheres and the fact that we do not notice them explicitly, even as they affect and influence us, the first call of an aesthetic education must be to learn to perceive atmospheres. This has immediate, far-reaching consequences. First, it teaches us the meaning of bodily presence. By contrast with a telematic society, particularly, bodily presence stands out and gains greater appreciation. This is relevant particularly for the visual arts subject, where reproduction and representation are too easily the norm.[7] Second, the body itself is rediscovered as a medium of emotional participation: dispositions are felt physically, and they are always dispositions in a spatial setting. Finally, we must learn or practise an attitude of patience: to perceive

---

[7]Regarding the reclamation of aura as a principal characteristic of modern art in the late twentieth century, see Dieter Mersch (2002).

atmospheres takes time and openness, and we must allow ourselves to be involved and touched by them.

Just as we have to learn to perceive atmospheres and to be consciously involved in them, we also need to learn the opposite, productive side of atmospheres: we have to learn to make them. In this context, as said, the paradigm of scenography can provide an orientation. We must further realize, however, that the aestheticization of our world occurs, in large part, according to this paradigm: the design of cities, parks and landscapes; the *mise-en-scène* of the commodity world in department stores; the production of atmospheres in bars and hotels. We can learn a lot from the practitioners in this field, particularly that they do not operate by sign-posting or by suggesting meanings but, rather, by attempting to endow things, constellations, spaces or art works with an *aura*. By practising the production of atmospheres in the design of spaces or communicative scenes, young people learn to understand the function of *generators*, acquiring a dynamic relationship with the atmospheres they live in. Above all, however, they will be in a position to critique the production of atmospheres and the resulting manipulation as well.

There are, thus, atmospheric competencies consisting of the ability to perceive atmospheres, on the one hand, and the ability to make them, on the other. The backdrop to the explicit development of these competencies is, however, the fact that we always already live in atmospheres. We principally know our way around them and discover in our work with them that we even have a rich vocabulary to name them.

This, however, does not yet get us to our destination. The practice of atmospheric competencies could indeed be framed within the modest claims of visual art teaching, namely as an introduction to basic artistic techniques and to culture as art world. Is there more at stake with atmospheres? Does work on atmospheres stake a claim comparable to Schiller's aesthetic education of humans to be humans? I would say so. To start with, there is a formal relationship: like play, an atmosphere is something medial, or mediating; it is an in-between, between subject and object, between determination and reception, between action and passion. And, just as play was meant to help Schiller's contemporaries to achieve integrity between sensuousness and rationality, so can atmospheres help us overcome the split between consumption and functional objectivity. Except that people today are even worse off than the depraved individual Schiller had in mind in the eighteenth century. While Schiller still trusted his contemporaries possessed sensuous passion, on the one hand, and moral rigidity, on the other, there is reason to fear that our contemporaries lack the characteristics of the respective opposite of pleasure and autonomy. What is at stake, then, is not just the mediation of lopsided capacities but the fulfilment of depraved forms of life. The worlds of work and consumption fall apart and do not yield what they stand for: pleasure and autonomy. So, let us once again return to the two faces of atmospheres: perceiving and producing.

To perceive atmospheres means to open oneself emotionally. This can offset the externalization of the environment and counteract the lack of contact, the coolness of modern individuals. Getting involved in atmospheres is tantamount to wanting to participate and to expose oneself to impressions – a prerequisite for the experience of pleasure in life and the discovery of one's body as a medium of being. Considering the immense pressure exerted by telecommunication, and how young people regard themselves as terminals in telematic networks as a matter of course, this rediscovery of bodily presence is of great importance. They can again feel that they are carriers and recipients of emotions and, rather than avatars in virtual space, bodies of flesh and blood, in traditional parlance.

Producing atmosphere, one steps out of slavish consumerism. The permanent staging of our everyday world, with its aesthetic emanations and acoustic furnishings, ensnares people in an entirely passive attitude of consumption, and particularly so in the area of aesthetics. Exercises in which atmospheres are shaped hone critical potential at the same time as possibilities of atmospheric creation are introduced, and they thereby strengthen the ability to resist economic and political manipulation. Finally, young people learn that they factually always co-produce atmospheres, particularly communicative atmospheres. Therefore, they will learn to take responsibility for what they contribute atmospherically to a discussion, a peer group, or a class session and, with that, retrieve part of their autonomy – precisely in an area in which everything appears to simply evolve by itself.

To conclude, it is worth noting that the appeal to Schiller's letters, particularly, might suggest that the plea for an aesthetic education as the education of humans to become humans is a plea for a conservative project, or even a critique of contemporary culture. However, a conscious engagement with atmospheres does not reject the contemporary world. Quite the contrary, it is open to basic features of contemporary life, precisely, and engages with them critically. *Atmosphere* as the basic concept of a new aesthetics has been suggested by the leaning of contemporary art towards the performative, the tendency of new music towards spatial art, and the aestheticization and staging of everyday life. To learn to engage with atmospheres enables each individual to participate critically and to contribute to this world in which we live today.

8

The Grand Concert
of the World

Introduction

A theory of music worth retrieving, in the light of developments in modern music since Schönberg, lies in our archives of cultural history. It is part of the teachings of philosopher and mystic Jakob Böhme (1575–1624) and contained in his text *De Signatura Rerum* (1651). Here, Böhme conceptualizes things (or, more precisely, all of Being) along the model of a musical instrument. The body is regarded as a sounding board, and its form and materiality as tuning or character (*Stimmung*, called *signatura* by Böhme), which is accountable for the characteristic expression a thing can have. The essence, *essentia*, resting inside the thing needs excitation to appear. For that, Böhme holds God responsible in the greater scheme of things. In individual cases, however, this excitement can come from another thing, or from a human being who blows to make a thing sound.

Crucially, in Böhme's theory of understanding, we understand an utterance when it strikes our *inner bell*. That means that understanding is a co-vibration, a resonance. Thus, what we call interaction is for Böhme a phenomenon of resonance. Things affect each other not via pressure and thrust, as they would for Descartes later, but through communication. The coherence of the world appears to Böhme as a grand concert. Might music, as we call it, be a part of this grand concert, or might it even be our way of participating in this concert?

Modern art and the aesthetics of atmospheres

Since the onset of aesthetic modernism, that is, roughly since Baudelaire's times, a constant race has taken place between artistic development and aesthetic theory. It was not only in visual arts that avant-garde developments transcended, again and again, what art was supposed to be – the same applies to music. *Musique concrete* and sound installations, in particular, forced a revision of the theory of music. Beyond that, they quite generally changed fundamental aesthetic concepts. To mention some key words in advance, these changes concern the diversification of sound material, a new conception of music as a spatial art, the priority of hearing,[1] and the return of the voice.

Aesthetics was conceived by Alexander Gottlieb Baumgarten in the middle of the eighteenth century, initially as a theory of sensible cognition. Too quickly, however, it turned into a theory of taste concerned only with works of art. In Kant, aesthetics still seemed essentially an aesthetics of nature;[2] in Hegel, though, the latter was already no more than a vestibule for aesthetics proper, that is, for the theory of the work of art. Henceforth, aesthetics was primarily to serve aesthetic judgement and thereby art criticism, completely abandoning the field of sensible experience and affective concern. As a consequence, aesthetics has shown itself incapable of grasping developments in modern art after Schönberg und Duchamp. This becomes quite clear in Adorno's aesthetics, which hovers on the threshold, as it were: Adorno was unable to recognize or else acknowledge the artistic character of jazz.

Since then, a new aesthetics has developed, which has the concept of atmosphere as its core. An aesthetic of atmospheres offers the extraordinary advantage of taking up a wide range of everyday experiences. It allows us to communicate easily about phenomena like a *serene valley*, an *oppressive thundery atmosphere*, or the *tense atmosphere of a meeting*. The notion that atmospheres are moods that are in the air designates a phenomenon everyone is familiar with. Furthermore, we have at our disposal an almost inexhaustible fund of expressions to speak about or to characterize atmospheres. One talks of a *serious atmosphere*, a *threatening atmosphere*, a *sublime atmosphere*; but one also speaks of an *atmosphere of violence* or of *sacredness*; one even speaks of the *atmosphere of a boudoir*, of a *petty-bourgeois atmosphere*, or of the *atmosphere of the 1920s*.

---

[1]The English distinction between hearing and listening has no direct equivalent in German. While, aside from *hören* (hear), there exist *zuhören* (listen) and *lauschen* or *horchen* (listen intently), the semantic reach of *hören* overlaps, in practice, partially with that of listening.
[2]This impression disappears on closer inspection, though, and it becomes apparent that examples from the field of design are particularly relevant. See Böhme (1993b; 1999b).

Building on these everyday experiences and phrases, the term *atmosphere* has meanwhile been developed into a scientific concept. What is particular about it, but what is also theoretically difficult, is that it designates a typical phenomenon of the in-between. Atmospheres are something between subject and object: one might call them quasi-objective feelings that are indeterminately diffused in space. However, insofar as they are nothing without a perceiving subject, they also have to be called subjective. Their value lies, precisely, in this in-between state, bringing together what was traditionally separated into the aesthetics of production and the aesthetics of reception. One can indeed produce atmospheres, and there are elaborate art forms specifically devoted to this task that involve quite objective, technical means – not as causal factors, though, but as generators of atmospheres. Paradigmatic for this approach to atmospheres is the art of scenography. On the other hand, atmospheres are experienced in a mode of affective concern; one has to expose oneself to them in bodily presence, feeling them in one's own disposition, to be able to identify their character. This is a classical aspect of the aesthetics of reception.

Both contrastive and ingressive experiences are appropriate to study atmospheres: the specificity of atmospheres is best experienced when their characters are offset, that is, before they have already, as part of all that surrounds one evenly, sunken into inconspicuousness. Thus, for example, they are experienced in contrast when one finds oneself in atmospheres diametrically opposed to one's own mood, or upon entering when changing from one atmosphere to another. Atmospheres are then experienced as *impressions* (Böhme, 1998a), namely, as a tendency to induce a certain mood.

The aesthetic of production, on the other hand, is interested in the generators of atmospheres. These are objects, their qualities, arrangements, light, sound, and so on. However, what is decisively at stake in thing-ontology in particular are not the qualities pertaining to a thing, which define it and differentiate it from other things, but rather the qualities it radiates outward into space. More precisely, it is about reading qualities as *ecstasies*,[3] as ways in which a thing steps out of itself and modifies the sphere of its presence. The study of ecstasies is particularly relevant for design and scenography, where the objective qualities and functions of things matter less than their scenic value.

The aesthetics of atmospheres, which began as part of ecological aesthetics (Böhme, 1999a), came to rehabilitate Alexander Gottlieb Baumgarten's original approach of aesthetics as *aisthesis*, that is, a general theory of perception (Böhme, 2001a). It has meanwhile demonstrated its revelatory potential in a

---

[3]Regarding this term, see *The Ecstasies of Things*, p. 37ff, above.

series of case studies, for instance of city atmosphere, light as atmosphere, the atmospheric of dusk, the atmosphere in church spaces, music as atmosphere, and, finally, atmospheres of interpersonal communication.[4]

The aesthetic conquest of acoustic space

Since ancient Greek times, music as a theory of art has consisted of the knowledge of tones, which were determined by intervals, or their harmonic distance from a basic tone. This understanding of music seems unbelievably narrow to us today. By comparison, the twentieth century introduced a vast expansion of musical material unfolding in many dimensions and amounting almost to a conquest of acoustic space. From tonality via chromatics, the path led to a step-by-step expansion of acoustic material admissible in music, eventually including even pure sound and noise. At first, tonal nuances in the chromatic intervals played a role, together with the emergence and inner life of a tone (blowing, stroking, or plucking); later, the interest shifted to the instruments' individuality and their voices, and the importance of sound increased. Then, an ironic take on instruments, involving beating and scratching of sound boxes and ever new percussion instruments, admitted a wealth of sounds, no longer just tones, into music. Eventually, recordings of everyday sounds, street scenes, sounds from nature, and the acoustic world of the factory found their way into music making. Today, sampling techniques render all kinds of acoustic material available for compositions.

Apart from this diversification of musical material, there is evidence of a principal change or, better, an expansion of the character of music. Until well into the twentieth century, dogma held music to be a temporal art, which finds its very essence in the temporal coherence of musical processes spanning beyond the present moment. From the basic requirement of cadence and return to the tonic to melody and theme to the structure of movements and to the unity of a symphony: coherently bound succession was considered typical for music. Even in Schönberg's twelve-tone music, the adoption of fugue technique placed the musical proper into successive unity. This understanding of music was not superseded but certainly put into perspective insofar as music was then discovered as a spatial art and, in new music, more or less explicitly developed as such. The fact that music fills spaces and that space, via resonance and reverberation, represents an essential element of its effect, has always been known. Newly discovered were the spatial shapes, that is,

---

[4]See 'The atmosphere of a city', p. 77ff; 'Light and space', p. 143ff; 'Church atmospheres', p. 167ff; 'The grand concert of the world', p. 123f; and 'Atmospheres of human communication', p. 97f.

form figures and ensembles in space, of the individual tone, the ensemble of tones, and also the succession of tones (or, better, the succession of sounds). These had never before been an issue for music. Quite likely, contemporary electronic techniques of reproduction and production in music first made this area workable and thereby also drew attention to it. To make a tone buzz through a space like an insect, or perhaps rise above a dully tuned volume of sound to atomize like a firework – these possibilities first arose with contemporary technology. They drew attention to something that, in a certain sense, had always already belonged to music. The Greek terms for high and low (oxys, ὀξύς, and barys, βαρύς, meaning pointed and heavy or broadly set) already hinted in that direction. In new music, however, practitioners began to shape the spatial form of music quite consciously, partly using classical instruments, partly electronic installations. Consequently, they advanced the recognition of space as an essential dimension in the creation of music generally. Under certain conditions, this can become the key dimension of a musical work of art, of which something like a beginning or an end, or a principle of shape operating across time, can then no longer be reasonably expected.

The tendency of music towards spatial art, particularly, has brought it into the realm of an aesthetics of atmospheres. For the spaces that are relevant here cannot simply be identified with geometrical space but with topological space at best. Musical space, of course, has its own directions, and there are shape-like phenomena and something like a mutual externality – all of which, however, should be seen not as separate but as changing, merging, appearing and disappearing forms. Further, this space is affectively experienced; something broadly set, for example, as heavy and oppressive, something rising as soothing and joyful, something shattering as funny, and so forth. Taken together, these aspects show that musical space equates, strictly speaking, to an expanded bodily space; that is, it amounts to an outward sensing into space, formed and articulated by music.

The discovery that music is the foundational atmospheric art has solved an old, always annoying yet irrefutable problem for music theory, namely the question of what the emotional effect of music actually consists. By contrast with the helpless theories of association, or theories deploying phantasy as an intermediate element, the aesthetics of atmospheres can provide the simple answer that music as such is the modification of bodily felt space. Music shapes the listener's disposition in space, it intervenes directly into one's bodily economy. Practitioners have made use of this phenomenon long before the theoretical insight arrived: already in silent movies, music bestowed both spatial and emotional depth to the image. Subsequent film music followed this practice. In German, one even speaks of an Atmo in the context of audio drama or radio feature; it is backgrounded to an action through music, or acoustic events more generally, in order to endow the narration with atmosphere. In a similar way, atmospheres are generated in bars through particular sounds, and the wait in airports, subway shafts, a dentist's clinic, department stores or hotel lobbies, is made pleasant, or cheerful and active, by music.

What applies to atmospheres generally is also an everyday reality for acoustic atmospheres: the character of a space is responsible for the way one feels in that space. Meanwhile, it has been discovered that the sound of a region significantly mediates one's sense of home; likewise, the characteristic feeling of a life style, or an entire urban or rural atmosphere, is determined essentially by the respective acoustic space. It follows that the notion of a landscape can no longer be restricted to the visible today, and also that town planning, for example, must cease its preoccupation with noise prevention or protection and start concerning itself with the character of acoustic atmospheres of squares, pedestrian zones, and whole cities.

Music and soundscape, or the music of the soundscape

If twentieth-century music expanded acoustic space by diversifying tonal material, including technical sounds, everyday samples and even noise, and if music eventually developed from a temporal to a spatial art that deliberately creates affective spaces, this conquest of space was facilitated by an entirely independent development. By this I mean R. Murray Schafer's worldwide project Soundscape, founded in the 1970s (2010). Soundscape was concerned with the research and documentation of the world of natural sounds, the acoustic life of a city, or the characters of technology and work. The resulting material was then used for compositions. Acousticians and sound engineers collaborated with musicians, if they were not composers themselves. Seen from the side of music, this was a development towards the diversification of musical material; from the side of Soundscape, it was a discovery of the world's own musicality. While it was certainly always acknowledged that birds or whales, for example, have their own music, this project was about more. It was about the discovery of acoustic characters or, better, the acoustic form of living environments – be they natural, like the sea, the forest and other landscapes, or lifeworlds in cities and villages. It became evident that condensation and composition were required even for the documentation of such acoustic worlds, to mediate them to those who are not from these regions. What could have been more logical than to make this condensing and composing an explicit form of creativity and, in that way, partially meet with music and partially to join forces with it. John Cage's composition, *Roaratorio* is an example of the latter.

FIGURE 8.1 Seaside, Kamakura / © 2004 Gernot Böhme.

The work of Sam Auinger and his various collaborators falls into this area, too. Like nobody else's, his productions let us participate in the Grand Concert of the world. This is not entirely simple, of course, and contemporary people, whose everyday listening is rather a form of not-listening, might need to pass through music like Auinger's to discover and appreciate this Grand Concert. Auinger proceeds differently from Cage; for example, he does not produce tone or sound files to use them subsequently for composition by sampling. Rather, the transformation of a given sound occurs in music on site, *in actu*. Sounds are tuned with the help of a resonating body, usually a resonance tube, that is, they are perceived by the way in which they make a resonating body vibrate, that is, mediated by the natural frequencies of this body. This is a fascinating process, which repeats materially, as it were, something that can be taken as the beginning of music per se, namely, the fact that attunement (i.e., the *signatura* of the resonating bodies) turns sounds into tones. It is well worthwhile considering, using the experiences provided by Auinger and others, whether our hearing of the grand concert of the world may perhaps consist of such a tuning of sounds that close in on us, a tuning performed by our own ears. Is it not also the case that our vision turns the chaos of optical frequencies in the world into a relatively ordered spectrum of colours?

Of course, tuning does not level all sounds into a series of keynotes and overtones. Some, rather, depending on their amplitude, retain their independent existence. In that way, Auinger and others achieve what the collaborators in the Soundscape project call the difference between tonality and characteristic event. Tonality is the basic mood of a landscape, a city or a port, and the rare and distinguished bundle of sounds making up the physiognomy of a landscape are characteristic events, as it were. Such events may be, as in Auinger's music, the sounding of pipes, for example, or the sound of the brakes on a train. Important is, again and again, the appearance of the human voice, not in its linguistic articulation, but as an idiom, as the characteristic sound of a language. Auinger does not shy away from using the sound of a classical instrument from time to time either.

Arising from this are pieces, as we might call them, of the grand concert of the world Jakob Böhme talks about; not, of course, as God might hear it, but tuned, calibrated for our ears and thereby turned into music. And yet, we are likely to hear the music differently, too, in the way Auinger and others enable visitors of their installations as listening participants: at the Grand Central Station in New York, in the *Haus der Kulturen* in Berlin, or, more generally, at an airport, a motorway, a pedestrian zone. Once engaged with it, *understanding* what one hears there as music, that is, receiving it resonating according to Jakob Böhme, one performs, indeed, yet another reclassification of music: music is the play of acoustic events in a space unfurled by tonality.

Both developments, music in the twentieth century and the Soundscape project, as well as their connections, cannot be considered outside the context of technological development. Just as the unfolding of music as a spatial art is almost unthinkable without electronic technologies of reproduction and production, so is the research into acoustic landscapes without electronic recording and reproduction technologies. Twentieth-century developments in acoustic technology, however, also had another, quite independent effect; namely, the ubiquity of music. Music, which in the European tradition over the last centuries was associated with festivities and special occasions, has become a cheap general consumer good. It is constantly available through radio and television channels and our acoustic environments are usually already occupied by music, or at least infiltrated by it, due to the acoustic furnishing of public spaces. Wherever that is not the case, contemporary humans carry their own acoustic world with them, first on Walkmans, today on MP3-players.[5]

What does this development imply? While the last aspect above would certainly suggest an acoustic pollution of our environment,[6] the acoustic awareness of the average person has, on the other hand, undergone a significant expansion. This not only means that the musical needs of a broad sector of the population have been significantly augmented, and with them

---

[5]See the classic text by Shuhei Hosokawa (1984).
[6]A critical response is offered by Hildegard Westerkamp (1988).

acoustic expectations, but also that listening as such has become a dimension of many people's lives and an area of satisfaction. Of course, the noise of contemporary environments and the occupation of public space by music have also led to a general practice of not-listening. Nevertheless, listening has unfolded from an instrumental activity – I hear something – to a way of participating in the life of the world. The aforementioned developments have blurred the boundaries of music. While, at the beginning of European music history, the drawing of such boundaries was central to its definition, the subsequent constant expansion of its field has tended to render all boundaries vague. Thierry de Duve's comment – in reference to visual arts – also applies to music: after Duchamp, the basic question of aesthetics, *What is beautiful?* has changed to *What is art?* (1996).

Acoustic atmospheres

The reference to acoustic atmospheres may have provided a tentative answer to this question. Tentative, because it is an answer that defines the character of musical experience for our time. It is to be expected that different answers will apply in other times after us, even soon after us. What is certain, though, is that the great period of Platonism has come to an end in music. Plato criticized people who tried to find out with their ears what harmonic intervals are (Plato, Ferrari, & Griffith, 2000: 239 [5321a]). And Adorno was still able to say that the appropriate way of hearing a symphony is to read the musical score. How far have we moved since then! It is now questionable whether contemporary music can even still be adequately notated. It seems as though sensibility has been rehabilitated in music and that we have to uphold, *contra* the whole of the Platonic period, that music can only be grasped by hearing. Perhaps one even has to say that hearing as such is the proper theme of music. It has been said about modern art generally that it is reflexive, and that its topic is art itself, its social position, its anthropological significance, its pure appearance. In visual art, this becoming-reflexive had a clear and demonstrable meaning. Many modern works of art were no longer about the representation of something but about the experience of seeing itself. This may have started already with Turner or the Impressionists, but it becomes utterly clear with artists like Joseph Albers, Barnett Newman, or Mark Rothko. In music, this development may not have become so obvious because music is, in a certain sense, far more natural. By contrast with the image, it has always been clear that music is *non-representational*, that it does not represent anything. Of course, there was painterly music or programme music. However, these attempts undeniably went astray and tended to put music into the service of something else. Already Kant said once that music is the language of feelings. One could interpret this dictum, of course, to mean, according to the usual semiotic understanding of language, that music designates feelings, that is represents them. However, this is not what Kant meant, for he distinguished in spoken language precisely the tone, in which something is said, from the content mediated by signs, that is, it is the tone which allows one to participate directly in the speaker's feelings (Kant & Walker, 2007: § 53, p. 157). Music was for him the coming-to-independence of this form of communicating feelings. Today, we have cause to generalize this thought: the crucial factor in music would then be the thematic development of acoustic atmospheres as such. This would provide an entirely different definition for music from what we found in the Platonic tradition, where music was defined essentially by the restrictions placed on the tonal material or, better said, by the restriction of the acoustic space that defines musical tones. Today, we can say that we are looking at music whenever an acoustic event concerns the acoustic atmosphere as such, that is, when it is about hearing as such, not about the hearing of something. This may need more explanation. But in advance, one can already say that music, according to this definition, no longer needs to be exclusively made by humans.

What does it mean to say that it is hearing itself that matters and not hearing something? In posing this question, one first discovers how much hearing normally refers to objects. *I hear a car driving past*, *I hear the bell tolling twelve*, *I hear someone talk*, *I hear a mosquito*, *I hear the horn of a*

FIGURE 8.2 Philadelphia Harbour / © 2004 Gernot Böhme.

ship. This way of hearing is useful and plausible; it serves us in identifying objects and their location in space. However, in a certain way, hearing itself is overheard in this type of hearing. Granted, one can say *I hear the barking of a dog* instead of *I hear a dog bark*. But this refers, in fact, to a different kind of hearing. As a mode of the dog's presence in space, the barking is certainly part of the dog. However, characteristic of voices, tones, and sounds is that they can be separated from their origins, or detach themselves, and fill space and wander through it almost like things. To perceive acoustic phenomena in this way, that is, to perceive them as such rather than as expressions of something, requires a change in attitudes. Living in the twenty-first century, we have often trained ourselves in changing attitudes precisely by using acoustic devices, particularly by listening with headphones. Many of us find it embarrassing that we were only able to discover in this way that acoustic spaces are something in themselves, independent of things and non-identical with real space. While acoustic space is, of course, also experienced in real space, this experience takes place in bodily felt space, in the space of my own presence that is unfurled by the expanse of bodily sensing. In a hearing that does not skip over tone, voice and sound to reach the objects that may cause them, listeners can sense voice, tone and sound as modifications of the space of their own presence. When listening like this, one is dangerously open, letting oneself enter the vastness outside, and is thus liable to be hit by acoustic events. One can be carried away by sweet melodies, knocked over by thunderclaps, threatened by droning noises, or wounded by a piercing tone. Hearing is being-outside-oneself and, for this very reason, potentially the joyful experience of sensing one's being in the world, at all.

One has to go through these experiences, they cannot be mediated verbally. Nevertheless, there is a useful analogy: Descartes, a philosopher who basically thought mechanistically in principle, was once asked whether someone who uses a stick to probe a stone actually senses that stone. His answer was, like that of twentieth-century Gestalt psychology, a stone is sensed where it is. This has been called *embodypathy* (Staemmler, 2007) – not entirely wrongly. Strictly speaking, however, what is involved here is the expansion of bodily felt space. Even more so than about probing with a stick, one can certainly say about hearing that one is *outside* while hearing. And this being-outside of ours not only meets voices there, and tones and sounds, but it is itself shaped, moved, modelled, nicked, cut, lifted, squeezed, widened and constricted by those voices, tones and sounds.

In the best model of hearing we have so far, people internally participate in what they hear. This resonance model of hearing drew its plausibility from the well-known experience where people sing along internally, as it were, with a melody they hear. But this model suffers from an inadequate topology of inside and outside, and it quickly meets its limits in the face of the complexity and foreignness of all that is heard. After all, it is highly unlikely that someone could internally sing along with the sounds produced by a nacelle, with its whirring, shrilling, whistling and droning. These sounds are also not even heard inside but rather, precisely, outside. It is the bodily felt space itself that starts to resonate, and in which these voices, tones and sounds happen. This experience admittedly occurs only rarely or, better said, only rarely in pure form; for in a certain sense it primes each and every listening experience. Except, the self does not normally lose itself to listening but maintains itself by displacing the voices, tones and sounds towards their origins, thereby skipping over the experience of in-between.

Conclusion

At last, we should once more return to the beginning. Twentieth-century developments in music have turned music itself into a component part of the environment. Functionalized as an aspect of interior architecture (one speaks of acoustic furnishing), it has been reduced to something atmospheric, as it were. On the other hand, both avant-garde music and the Soundscape Project have, from two different flanks, even promoted acoustic atmosphere as the essence of music. Thus, the voices of things and the concert of the world have attracted increasing attention, and listening has gained in importance for life. Taken together, these facts imply that, in the area of acoustics, ecological aesthetics is not only a complement to natural science ecology but, rather, that it has its own task of producing knowledge about and of preserving and shaping acoustic space. The question concerning the nature of a humane environment is recast as one concerning the characters of acoustic atmospheres. Here, too, it is important to go beyond a purely scientific approach, which can do little more than measure noise in decibels and to ask which acoustic characters the spaces we live in should have.

9

The Voice in Spaces
of Bodily Presence

Spatial sounds

The expression *spatial sounds* seems tautological. Does not all sound exist in space? While this is actually true, phenomenologically speaking, this truth sometimes needs to be defended against people who claim to hear something *in their heads*. Indeed, one hears spatially even what one hears with headphones – though obviously, in that case, not in a concrete, surrounding space with walls and furniture but in an acoustic space unfurled by the sounds themselves.

Nevertheless, the notion of spatial sounds become meaningful in confrontation with a claim by music historian, Carl Dahlhaus, who, following Herder, holds that music is essentially a temporal art (1982: 10).[1] This thesis has a lot to recommend it, since nobody will regard a single tone or an incoherent sequence as music. A sequence of tones is considered music only when it has a form, that is, when it is organized into a whole by a theme. Kant already, in his *Critique of Pure Reason*, designated this kind of thematic unity a particular type and, more than a century later in Bergson's *Time and Free Will*, it became the central phenomenon in the experience of time. This unity is not based on identity but on a synthesis in which the manifold elements organize themselves or blend into a whole. Both philosophers mention melody as a prototype in this respect, but this kind of unity is potentially much more comprehensive, including even the unity of a symphony.

---

[1]Herder, in turn, had adopted Lessing's programme of defining the arts by their characteristic limitations in his *Laocoon* (1766). Both Herder and Lessing stood in an Aristotelian tradition.

Contrasting with this approach to music as a temporal art, a significant shift in the understanding of music, if not a revolution, took place within the twentieth-century avant-garde. In its wake, it is now poignant to speak about spatial sounds. It was most likely Marcel Duchamp who, in a 1913 note, first spoke of an *acoustic sculpture*. This idea, which was recently performed by the *Recherche* ensemble in Darmstadt on the occasion of a Duchamp exhibition, builds on the notion that music can also be – or perhaps always is – a spatial form (*Raumgestalt*). Musicians and composers have probably always been more or less aware that sounds exist in space, form space and themselves have spatial form; there are Baroque compositions, for example, which were performed by several choirs distributed across a church. However, it was only during the twentieth century that a new genre arose from this approach to music, namely the genre of sound-art or spatial installations (La Motte-Haber, 2004). This genre is explicitly concerned with the spatial movement of tones and the spatial form of sounds, or *vice versa*; at stake is the acoustic formation of spaces. This development in music was certainly first made possible by the significant twentieth-century advances in electroacoustics. They not only made the thematization of the spatial aspects of music possible but also enabled new listening experiences and, on this background, recast the question concerning hearing itself. If the line of thinking suggested by Herder and Dahlhaus conceived of hearing essentially as a form of temporal existence, the exploration of acoustic space has given rise to a new understanding of hearing: as bodily presence in space.

The rehabilitation of the voice

In the tradition of the *artes liberales* tradition, since antiquity, music belonged to the *quadrivium*, that is, to the mathematical sciences, along with arithmetic, geometry and astronomy. It was only in the seventeenth century that music moved away from the *quadrivium* to be included in the *trivium*, along with grammar, poetry and rhetoric. This meant, in fact, that the emotional character of music took on greater importance vis-à-vis its rational aspect. In practice, the human voice, individual or choral, was increasingly considered to be essential for music whereas instruments were primarily an accompaniment. The music historian Dahlhaus, mentioned earlier, establishes a new development from about 1800, though, which he calls the *emancipation of instrumental music* (Dahlhaus, 1982: 24ff). Beethoven's symphonies, Dahlhaus suggests, mark the development of a type of music that could do without any vocal elements at all, representing the essential nature of music precisely *instrumentally*. It is important to note, though, that vocal music was understood as song, and that therefore the import of words was considered essential for the meaning of a piece of music (this is quite plausible when thinking of Bach's oratorios).

Advocates of vocal music held that only words can give music meaning and elevate it from pure enjoyment to a cultural experience. Conversely, partisans of instrumental music argued that music which needed words to convey meaning had not yet come into its own and that the true nature of music therefore would come forth with its emancipation from the human voice. Hegel spoke of *independent music* in his aesthetic lectures (1975: 951ff).

> But the proper sphere of this independence cannot be vocal music, an accompaniment always tied to a text, but instrumental music. For the voice, as I have already stated, is the sounding belonging to the entire subjective life which is not without ideas and words also and now in its own voice and song finds the adequate organ when it wishes to express and apprehend the inner world of its ideas, permeated as they are by an inner concentration of feeling. But the reason for an accompanying text disappears for instruments, so that here what may begin to dominate is music restricting itself to its own, its very own, sphere. (1975: 953)

Dahlhaus highlights that Hegel's view that music proper was instrumental music never gained full acceptance; nevertheless, he believes he can identify a *hegemony of instrumental music* (Dahlhaus, 1982: 29). This makes sense when considering two further aspects: on the one hand, the notion of instrumental music as music proper included the requirement for music to have meaning, in order to qualify as culture, thus conceiving of music itself as a language. Accordingly, Hegel argued that music must 'draw entirely out of itself [...] the development of a principal thought, the episodic intercalation and ramification of others' and 'limit itself to purely musical means, because the meaning of the whole is not expressed in words' (Hegel, 1975: 952). On the other hand, the musical use of the human voice was itself conceived along the lines of an instrument. Accordingly, the training of singers was focused on the *purity* of tone. That was, incidentally, already the case in opera, the *Queen of the Night* aria in Mozart's *Magic Flute* being a classic example.

This leads us to a second musical revolution during the twentieth century, namely the emancipation of the voice in music. This is a twofold emancipation: on the one hand, twentieth-century avant-garde music emancipates the voice from language, so that its musical significance no longer depends on the suggestion of *representations* (*Vorstellungen*, in Hegel's terms). On the other, the voice no longer obeys the dictate of instrumental music, such that singers style themselves as instruments among instruments. An excellent example for both aspects are Michiko Hirayama renderings of Giacinto Scelsi's *Canti del Capricorno* (2007), performed around 1980. To understand this better, we must refer to an author from whom we normally do not expect any profound insights concerning music – Immanuel Kant.

The analogy between music and language I criticized above is deployed by Kant, as well. However, as he does not believe that music is constituted by signs that have meanings, Kant uses the term *language* as no more than an analogy – music is a *language of sensations* (Kant & Walker, 2007: 157). His considerations draw on the role of the voice in speech, and he distinguishes between the expressions of language and the *tone* in which they are uttered:

> Its [the art of tone's] charm, which admits of such universal communication, appears to rest on the following facts. Every expression in language has an associated tone suited to its sense. This tone indicates, more or less, a mode in which the speaker is affected, and in turn evokes it in the hearer also.... (2007: 157)

Thus, Kant regards music as an artistic articulation of our everyday experiences with speech, namely that the tone or the sound in which something is said carries the emotional part of the utterance and, in his words, 'evokes it in the hearer'. Language and speech comprehension, therefore, are discussed here in a totally different sense from that of language as a system of signs or expressions. Understanding here does not mean imagining the referent but rather co-performing the speaker's affect by listening.

In this view of music or the role of the voice in speech, Kant draws on a theory of language that was probably first given expression by Jacob Böhme in his text *De Signatura Rerum* (1651). Here, Böhme develops the concept of a thing according to the model of a musical instrument: like an instrument, each thing has its genuine character (signature) and, when it is struck, its characteristic tone (p. 77). Hence, the interaction between things, that is, also the coherence of nature as a whole, is conceived as communication. However, communication is not symbolically mediated, as most linguistic theory today would suggest. Rather, the utterance of a person or a thing is understood through the listener's internal co-performance (*innerer Mitvollzug*), such that its tone or voice causes vibrations, or strikes an inner bell. Understanding is a phenomenon of resonance.

With this, we have an extremely radical concept of voice and, if we regard music with Kant as an artistically elaborated system of voices, also of music. It is radical because the theory takes seriously the effect of voices and music (which we experience in affective concernment, *affektiver Betroffenheit*), both in their power and depth of penetration. By contrast with communication involving linguistic signs, where understanding is always a matter of interpretation and therefore implies a gap between the perception of the sign and its comprehension, understanding through resonance is much more exposed to tone than any form of symbolic mediation in communication could be. Besides, affective concernment is never purely an intellectual matter – it is sensed, rather, in bodily stirrings. Music as a language, in this sense, resembles much more the language of angels or perhaps that of whales and dolphins.[2]

The voice as an articulation of bodily presence

Following Jakob Böhme, we can now say with greater clarity what the voice of something or someone actually is, namely, the articulation of bodily presence. A thing or a person can indeed exist inconspicuously so that it, or he or she, goes unnoticed. Normally, though, the presence of something or someone in space is noticeable – most commonly, the outer appearance or a face. In brightness, the appearance of things and people makes them noticeable in a characteristic way. However, Jakob Böhme adds to this much more poignant modes in which the presence of someone or something is felt. He mentions smell and reverberation, which are both modes whereby a being penetrates its entire surrounding space (classically termed *sphaera activitatis*), and in which the smell or voice endow the atmosphere of this space with a character. What is felt is not only the presence of some general thing but the presence of this particular one. In this context, it is worth remembering that individual knowing and recognition are vitally mediated by smell and voice, both in the animal and the human world. It is remarkable how animals like penguins can locate their young, among thousands of their fellow species, by their voices. But this is also true for human beings: everyone knows how one can recognize a partner on the phone without any verbal communication. Likewise, the individuality of personal odour is, after all, even deployed in criminal investigations. Voices, however, are not therefore limited to individual or personal use; to the contrary, a theatrical use of the voice is obviously possible, as well. It is worth noting here that the character experienced in somebody's voice is therefore not necessarily identical with this person's character but is really only *character in appearance*, that is, precisely someone's articulated presence. In this respect, Bernhard Waldenfels is wrong to say that 'one has to be *somebody* in order to have a voice' (Waldenfels, 2006: 191).

Each voice has a character, and a singer or actor can lend a different character to his or her voice through its intonation. This makes a person noticeable in her presence (even more so than through appearance or through what is said verbally). In terms of affective concernment, someone is perceived as friendly, serene, threatening, earnest, and aggressive. Drawing on a very nice expression by Roland Barthes, this phenomenon has been called the 'Grain of the Voice' (1977). It is obvious from whence Barthes' intuition stems: the

---

[2]Regarding the language of angels, see Hartmut and Gernot Böhme (2010), Chapter IV.4; regarding the language of dolphins and whales, see Joan McIntyre (ed.) (1982).

singing of Louis 'Satchmo' Armstrong, in which words are almost no longer relevant but instead, as it were in that case, the *sound* or, as Roland Barthes puts it, the *grain* of the voice as such. Except, Roland Barthes misinterpreted his own discovery when he said, 'The "grain" of the voice is not – or is not merely – its timbre; the *significance* it opens cannot be defined better, indeed, than by the very friction between the music and something else, which [is a particular] language…' (p. 185).

Music like the *Canti del Capricorno*, in particular, shows that the grain of the voice does not depend on some relationship with spoken language or even, as Roland Barthes suggests in the text above, with writing. For that would mean that things, and even animals, have no voice. On the other hand, Barthes is right in saying that '[t]he "grain" is the body in the voice as it sings' (p. 188). That is it, and Jakob Böhme already said the same when he modelled the body of something or someone on a musical instrument. A person in his or her bodily existence and a something in its thingness are palpable in the expressions of someone or something, because a vocal expression is characteristically moulded by the body from which it emanates.

This insight also explains why the rehabilitation of the voice in twentieth-century avant-garde music led to an entirely novel use of musical instruments. Granted that the importance of sound in music had been steadily growing since the triumph of jazz, and the specific character of each musical instrument – the horn, the saxophone, and so on – is palpable in its sound. New music has pushed this further by pursuing the material character of musical instruments beyond tones – by blowing, striking, scratching, and so on.

In this way, musical instruments were acknowledged, not merely as instruments generating tones as clearly as possible, but now also in the specific character they have as bodies.

Conclusion

In our everyday modes of hearing focused on meaning and information, we generally do not hear the voice. And yet, the voice of the person we communicate with generates the communicative atmosphere in which communication takes place; it makes us favour or reject someone, and it imbues what is said with an affective tone. Twentieth-century developments in music have liberated the voice from this subsidiary and ancillary function, so that we can not only theoretically appreciate its extraordinary import for our being in the world today but have also learnt practically to hear voices as such. A voice is the atmospheric presence of something or someone and one of the dimensions along which something or someone steps out of it-, him- or herself and essentially tinges the surrounding atmosphere with emotion. Unlike verbal forms of expression, a voice is highly individual so that the atmosphere it determines can in each case be distinguished and described as proper to its owner.

If the voice is the atmospheric presence of something or someone, the question arises as to which way this presence is perceived. This cannot simply be by 'constative' hearing after all, although that also happens, for instance when one recognizes someone by her voice on the phone. As an atmospheric presence, however, the voice is felt in affective sharing (*Teilnahme*). That is, the voice affects one's own mood negatively or positively. But how does that happen? Jakob Böhme would say, through resonance. The emotional tone a voice imparts to a space tinges, in a manner of speaking, one's own mood – one resonates with what one hears. Does that mean that the voice is perceived by inwardly singing along? Indeed, there is that, too, but hearing by inwardly singing along is very limited and ultimately fails with polyphony or strangeness. The whole theory of hearing as inwardly singing along suffers from the same weaknesses pertaining to all theories based on perception-as-representation. If the perception of a house consisted of inwardly imagining a house, then surely this inner image of a house has to be perceived itself, in turn. So, no, just as we see things where they are in visual perception, in space outside, so with hearing, too: we hear the voice in space. That it affects us is due to the fact that the voices we hear modify our own bodily presence in space. To find oneself in a space means to reach out into this space through bodily sensing, feeling narrow or expansive, oppressed or elevated, and many other things. Our disposition, as a sensing of where we are, is in each case modified by the qualities of the space in which we are. This fact is of great importance for the emotional impact of architecture. Architectural forms, lighting conditions, colour schemes, materials, and other qualities, or the atmosphere that architectural structures radiate or contain, determine one's disposition in spaces or built environments through bodily sensing. Voices, which are stronger generators of atmospheres than most other phenomena, are part of that. Just as voices constitute, on the senders' part (if that is a good way of putting it), their bodily presence in space, they constitute on the receivers' part the modifications of their disposition – that is, of the way in which they themselves feel their presence in space. The extraordinary effect voices have on our emotional condition at any given time is due to the direct modifications they effect in our felt presence in space. They can make it feel narrow or expanded, can be uplifting and releasing, or oppressing and threatening. Just as we call tones high or low, heavy *(barys)* or acute and sharp *(oxys)*,[3] so our sensations follow the impressions of such tones, inviting or forcing us to be present in space in this or that way through our bodily sensing.

---

[3] See p. 127, above.

10

Light and Space

FIGURE 10.1 View across the river Elbe, Magdeburg / © 2006 Gernot Böhme.

City lights, artificial light, new media – night turns into day, the city into an ocean of light. [...] In the evenings, mediated by artificial light, even an ugly metropolis like Tokyo transforms into a glittering, vibrating, fluorescent, oscillating sea of luminosity, an ecstasy of colour and movement, full of nerviness, mad haste and speed, and stimulating intensity. (Schnell, 1993: 67)

This sentence is taken from the essay 'City Lights', in which Ralf Schnell sets out to articulate his enthusiasm for night time Tokyo in terms of media theory. Even if one is as fascinated as Schnell – with respect to dynamism and lighting spectacles, Shibuya is likely to outperform Times Square today – one still has to wonder whether he is able to articulate his aesthetic insights appropriately. Is Tokyo ugly as such, only transforming into a princess at night? Is the nocturnal light magic no more than a dress thrown over a dreary architecture? Or would one not, rather, have to say: This night life is life in Shibuya, and those bright strings of signs, those light points and spotlights, those swaying monitors are an essential part of architecture. Spaces are created not just by walls but also by light; vanishing points and perspectives are defined not only by stone ledges and cantilevering beams but also by light; façades are not only shaped by series of windows and stucco reliefs but also by light. Architects have always known that it is possible to build with light, and they sought to work and create effects with light. The Egyptian priests oriented their temples so that the sun entered through the open doors at dawn and caught the god's statue; the Pantheon opened upwards towards the light; and Abbot Suger wanted to celebrate the epiphany of eternity in his church Saint Denis by flooding the building with light. In contrast with this classical way of considering light, a fundamental change began to take place when light could be technically controlled around the middle of the nineteenth century. Traditionally, considering light had been part of considering a building's integration with its environment, including its cosmic orientation and amounted to the interaction of architecture and light. With the development of lighting technology, however, light gradually became an integral means of architecture, a kind of building material or design element. Without a doubt, the development of steel and glass constructions significantly increased the integration of natural light into architecture. However, the real revolution in the relationship of light and architecture occurred with artificial light. Even though its nineteenth-century development – from the Argand lamp to gas and incandescent mantle, right through to arc and incandescent lamps – was extremely arduous and incomplete, and even though lighting design involving reflectors, glass containers and screens was only beginning to emerge, buildings like the Parisian arcades, the architecture of display windows in department stores and, finally, modern theatres would be unthinkable without artificial light (Schivelbusch, 1988).

Only during the twentieth century, however, light was made truly accessible by a sheer infinite multiplication of technical light production and design: apart from burning and glowing also ionizing; apart from mirrors, prisms, lenses also polarizers, lasers, photomultipliers, optic fibres, and much more besides. Modern technologies of light production and modulation place such an abundance of light types and effects at our disposal that it seems urgently necessary to find an orientation. As long as the techniques were restricted as during the

FIGURE 10.2 Staircase Kunsthaus (Peter Zumthor), Bregenz / © 2007 Ross Jenner.

nineteenth century, people had to be content to ask what could be done with the techniques available to them. Today, we can turn the question on its head and, taking expectations in architecture, stage design or entertainment as the starting point, ask by which technologies they can be realized. This reversal, however, presupposes an ability to articulate our experiences with light and find an orientation among them. It requires, in short, a phenomenology of light. We can safely assume in the development of such a phenomenology of light that almost all experiences that it could name are ancient. Nevertheless, the differentiating engagement with light made possible by technology may well have first set such phenomenology on its path. Even Goethe's theory of colours, however much it polemicizes against Newtonian optics, owes its origin to the prismatic, that is, technical production of the spectrum.

The phenomenology of light

But what is a phenomenology of light?[1] In answering this question, I recall Goethe's beautiful definition of colour: 'colour is a law of nature in relation to the sense of sight' (1840: xl). Perhaps this phenomenology is indeed precisely about studying this law of nature in relation to the sense of sight. Very quickly, though, it will become apparent that one cannot at all limit this study to colours and that all phenomena of light – luminescence, brilliance, flickering, shadow, and much else – must be included. I want to highlight the particular aspects of this study of nature in relation to the sense of sight by an example.

Arthur Zajonc's achievement was the attempt to bring together in a book all our experiences and ideas of light, from physics to mythology. He actually starts the book, titled *Catching the Light: The Entwined History of Light and Mind* (1993), with a strange, entirely non-phenomenological claim, namely that we cannot see light. To prove this, he constructed a box into which he projected light; he enclosed this light inside the box by some contraption, such that it could not be reflected anywhere. That Zajonc does not say anything concrete about the technology of this enclosure is a little worrying, but the effect produced by this modern magician is all the more impressive: attempting to look through a hole in the side of the book, one could not see anything at all. Everything was dark. Of course, you might say, how could one see anything? If light cannot exit, nothing can be seen.

What is un-phenomenological about Zajonc's approach is that he already knows in advance, completely independently from seeing, that light is an electromagnetic radiation within a certain frequency spectrum. Physically, there are good reasons to say that this radiation is in the box and that we cannot see it. Phenomenologically speaking, however, there is no light, at all – given that light is the law of nature in relation to the sense of sight. It would be absurd to claim that light itself cannot be seen when talking about light as a phenomenon. Clearly, Zajonc cannot deny his professional background in physics, however much he cares about phenomenology. Granted, though, the claim that light cannot be seen also has a meaning, even if weaker, that comes closer to the phenomenon. It is well known that light slanting into a dark church interior is

---

[1] See also my essay 'Seeing Light' in Bachmann (2006: 115–135).

seen as such particularly via the dust particles it hits. It is a gross abstraction to claim that there would be nothing but pure blackness between the church window and the floor hit by the light ray if the church interior were completely *clear*. In any case, it is wrong to deduce that light in itself cannot be seen, except when it hits bodies, because we can also see it, after all, when we look directly into a light source – without thereby seeing anything yet. Evidently, even this weaker claim about not being able to see light as such contains an assumption, or rather aprejudice, which turns it into a mere tautology. For the claim, which assumes that seeing equates to seeing *something*, or, more precisely, something concrete, is an empty one since light is, indeed, nothing concrete.

This brings us to a fundamental phenomenological fact regarding light: as a phenomenon, light is primarily and properly brightness.[2] We shall see that there is also an abundance of other types of light phenomena, but brightness is fundamental. The first thing I notice, when I open my eyes on a day on which I slept too long, is: it is already bright daylight. This noticing of brightness is primary and fundamental. It precedes every particular perception, for example of colours, shapes or things. All of those things I do perceive, but in *brightness*. And this noticing of brightness is the fundamental experience of light.

Before turning to singular phenomena in the realm of light, I would like to clarify light's basic character as brightness a little further. Philosophers tend to call this character *transcendental*. *Transcendental* in this context means as much as the *condition of possibility for* ... When we engage in the phenomenology of visual appearances, we notice that, among those visual appearances, light as brightness plays a special role. For everything we see, we see only insofar as it is bright. Brightness is thus a condition of possibility for seeing as such. It is transcendental to seeing.

This special position of brightness in the realm of the visual contains great potential that can be used artistically. For one can say that, in brightness, appearance itself appears, or, the other way round: that brightness co-appears in each visual appearance. Conversely, this means that the art of light always simultaneously makes seeing a consideration. Already Plato suggested in his famous Analogy of the Sun that light as brightness is the condition of possibility for seeing as such. He writes:

'If there is sight in the eyes, and its possessor is trying to make use of it, you surely realise that even in the presence of colour sight will see nothing, and the colours will remain unseen, unless one further thing joins them, a third sort of thing which exists for precisely this purpose.

'What thing do you mean?'

'The thing you call light.' (Plato et al., 2000: 214)

---

[2]See *Licht als Atmosphäre* (Light as Atmosphere, in Böhme, 1998a).

FIGURE 10.3 Kolumba Museum (Peter Zumthor), Cologne / © 2008 Tina Engels-Schwarzpaul.

Clearly, Plato means light *qua* brightness here. Brightness is itself a phenomenon, but a phenomenon with transcendental significance. Strictly speaking, brightness first makes sight a real faculty, and makes it possible that visible things can indeed be seen.

In what follows, this fundamental insight will have to be delimited, yet, still be adhered to: light is not the only condition of visibility: darkness is another. There is, however, an asymmetry between light and darkness, in that light is the condition for seeing at all; darkness is, in the interaction with light, the condition for seeing something, that is, that there are conditions providing delimitation, articulation, and certainty.

Cleared space

The first effect of light as brightness is to unfurl a space. In a sense, space is even created by light. To grasp this, though, one has to be clear about which sense of space is being deployed here. It is obviously not mathematical or physical space, which could be measured in the dark if necessary. Rather, it is about experiential space – and even then only about the space of a particular experience. We know, for instance, purely acoustic spaces from the spatial experience arising from listening with earphones. Naturally, such spaces have nothing to do with light. Rather, the space created by light is a space of distances and intervals, intervals from me. This space is best described as a cleared space (*gelichteter Raum*), whose characteristic quality is *lightening* (*Hellmachen*). Spatial experience also takes place in the dark, but the space can then be close and pressing in, or one can conversely get lost in the indeterminate expansion of darkness. The characteristic sudden change occurring through lightening is the realization that one is placed in intervals and that, at the same time, space surrounds one as a leeway for free movement. Therefore, the term *cleared space* suggests itself here for this type of space, in reference to *clearing* (*Lichtung*). For a clearing, a piece of land cleared in the forest, is determined by distances, too: by limitations, on the one hand, and by the possibility of free movement, on the other. It is characteristic of space created by light that the possibility of moving within it not only includes that of *de facto* but also of potential movement, that is, of mere eye movement: one can let one's eyes wander within the cleared space. This experience cannot be had in photos, which shows that it is indeed a significant spatial experience. The reason for this is that the focus in a photo is fixed at the moment of exposure. By contrast, I can wander into the depth of the cleared space in which I find myself, that is, I can not only let my eyes wander from one object to another but also fix my attention in space at varying depths. This possibility of wandering with our eyes in the depth of space may indeed be decisive for our very feeling of being in a space.

The primary emotional experience of cleared space is one of safety and freedom. Of course, one can also encounter threats in cleared space but, really, the basic experience is that everything is at a distance, and that this distance means both safety and freedom of movement for the individual. This aspect of safety in cleared space receives the character of security whenever the cleared space itself is delimited, that is, stands out against the indeterminate space of darkness. Seen from the cleared space, on the other hand, darkness becomes a realm of uncertain threats.

Day is cleared space without boundaries. We can see here that day also has a spatial character. Day, as such, is unlimited, yet initially it has to expand in the morning and later withdraw and disappear in the evening.

One could ask whether the experience of cleared space requires the simultaneous experience of a light source. Since we have connected the phenomenon of cleared space to the simple experience of brightness, and in particular the possibility of wandering through space with one's eyes, we probably have to say that the perception of a light source is not necessary for this experience. That is a very important statement since light is all too easily confused with the emanation from a light source in a physicalistic manner. Even the Greeks (or, more specifically, Aristotle, who did not think in a physicalistic way) always thought of light with reference to a source. Aristotle defines light as *parousia* (παρουσία), that is, the presence of the sun or occasionally of fire. However, given our experiences with indirect light or *light-like objects*, we can and must make a distinction. I call things like luminous ceilings, or even the coloured glass windows of Gothic churches (which are, as stated again and again, experienced like luminous walls), light-like objects. It may be debatable here whether it also makes sense to speak of an experience of brightness without a light source. Decisive, however, is that we can perceive brightness as such, and that the experience of cleared space therefore does not depend on the perception of a light source. There is just one effect that could give us pause here, namely the quasi-shadowless illumination of a room as it is produced, for example, by computer diodes, in which the room loses depth, or is flattened out, as it were. In some circumstances, the space can acquire almost surrealist aspects, since it is difficult just by looking to assess the relative distance between things and thereby indirectly the depth of space. That would mean, however, that precisely what I have called freedom in cleared space, as the possibility of wandering with one's eyes in the depth of space, might be related to the rendering of contours by shadows. In that case, then, a simultaneous indirect experience of the light source, namely through the shadows cast, would be important for the full experience of cleared space.

The space of light

Light creates space – that was the first statement – and I called the space unfurled by brightness the cleared space. The cleared space is a space in which I am present, and I experience my presence in space in a particular way through brightness. It is, however, also possible to see a space created by light from the outside, as it were, like an object. This phenomenon became properly evident only with new lighting technologies and has been demonstrated in often unsettling ways in light art. I am thinking here above all of James Turrell's work, installations of various forms in which spaces of light, like cuboids or pyramids, are seen to be floating in darkness. Characteristically, these installations require a preparatory phase in which visitors pass through a light trap before they enter into a dark space. In the Frankfurt Museum für Moderne Kunst (Museum for Modern Art), one begins to perceive after a while an image floating in front of the wall, for example, or, better perhaps, a cuboid – because the shape seems to have a certain depth – made of uniformly coloured light. Getting closer, the space within the wall opens up onto an indeterminately deep, nebulously illuminated *exterior*. The experience of these spaces made of light has dreamlike aspects, probably precisely because they are so completely independent from the experience of objects. This is perhaps also what makes them confusing, perhaps even frightening for some. The three-dimensional impression of these shapes depends, incidentally, also on a relative closeness of the viewer. Seen from a greater distance, they would perhaps simply appear as a light source. This phenomenon, demonstrated in its pure form in art, might also play a role in other experiences of light, albeit in less pure, that is, mixed form and overlaid with other phenomena. Thus, the experience of illuminated spaces, say, on stage or in an office looked at from the dark street, oscillates between that of spaces and sources of light. The magic of this experience may be related to that of projecting oneself, as it were, into these light spaces, and perceiving them as potentially cleared spaces, thus being transposed from the exterior in which one is located into an imaginary interior. This is also what illuminated shop windows apparently rely on, at least whenever a significant differential between the light levels of display and street is preserved. Benjamin's remark in the Arcades work, namely that commodities are presented as on a stage, may have been made with that in mind.

The genre of spaces of light also includes holographic figures produced with light, which float freely in space due to interference effects. While this effect has, strangely, so far not yet been widely used in advertising, it has been deployed in the area of entertainment. In Disney World, for example, ghosts made out of light are on display sitting around a table. These phenomena show perhaps most clearly that light is a transcendental appearance, that is, an appearance that makes something else appear but also makes an appearance itself. We can say now that this self-manifestation of light can, at the same time, also simulate a something – a cuboid or a pyramid in Turrell's case, or the robbers in Walt Disney's. Therefore, these phenomena are only appearances – just as one speaks of ghosts – that is, appearances without something appearing.

As a rule, *mere appearances* still have to manifest themselves on something real, that is, at least on a projective plane or a monitor. However, there has been no doubt that the shapes one can see in a range of situations, from the *laterna magica* right through to the virtual worlds on our screens, properly consist of light, indeed, that they are *photo-graphs*, as they have also been called: drawings with light (*Lichtbilder*). The easier it is to forget about the piece of reality on which they manifest themselves, the more fascinating they become.

Lights in space

The starry sky is the prototype of the phenomenon of lights in space. Here, too, one could somehow say that light unfurls space; yet, we have to think of a different light and a different space than in the case of brightness. Stars are lights precisely in dark space, but they take away the pressing aspects of dark space or the indeterminacy in which once can get lost. They do not, as brightness does, constitute space as a space of distance. Stars do not permit an assessment of distances but they do provide space with a form, because they structure it by establishing directions. This, too, makes the sense of space reliable to a certain extent, and we know, after all, that navigation is possible only with this kind of reliability. The space that is structured by stars, however, remains itself dark. This means also that lights in space are not really perceived as light sources, even though they, incidentally, provide the clearest evidence that light can be seen. In order to be perceived as light sources, they would have to shine on something. They are, of course, factually light sources, and they do lighten up the night a little on the whole. This lightening is indiscernible and not perceived as originating from the stars – this is quite different in the moon's case. The phenomenon of lights in space should actually be defined by this characteristic: they are perceived as points of light, not as sources of light, even if that is what they factually are. Also, this type of light is not always found unadulterated in nature. Even blurry sight or mist suffice to create a halo around stars. Fireflies are another good example of lights in space – in their case, movement adds to the effect, particularly of irregularly hovering movement. This makes explicit that lights in space are experienced as something autonomous, with a life of their own; actually something that can already be sensed when looking at stars. This may well be an effect of *bodily communication*, or perhaps of identification – in any case of a tendency to project oneself into the locale of light in space and even, from there, look back down onto our world.

Lights in space have meanwhile been discovered for interior architecture, probably because they afford a basic illumination in a space, without distracting light sources. They are also used for decoration, illumination and advertising. In terms of atmosphere, the association with the starry sky always plays into this deployment of artificial light. There is, however, another classical phenomenon of the type lights in space that also comes into play, namely the fireworks display.

Adorno called fireworks a basic type of ephemeral art (Adorno et al., 2002: 81). It is the celebration of impermanence. By contrast with the stars and the fireflies, there are an additional flaring up and dying down, as well as the colour and splendour of the sheaves of light, of course.

Glass fibre technology has meanwhile made the phenomenon lights in space available almost without restrictions. It promises an abundance of light phenomena that are bound to expand the spectrum from starry sky to firefly to fireworks significantly. This development started with the large fairs, the breeding ground for so many aesthetic innovations.

FIGURE 10.4 Windows, Institut du monde arabe (Jean Nouvel), Paris / © 2014 Gernot Böhme.

Things appearing in light

So far, I have discussed three main phenomena of light: cleared space, the space of light, and lights in space, without yet engaging with the relationship of light with things. This approach seemed necessary in order to avoid a traditional prejudice which brings light into a most intimate relationship with the body. This prejudice is closely related to another, that light cannot be seen. That light has an intrinsic relationship with the body is another ancient and still cumbersome prejudice. The Pythagoreans, for example, defined colour as the surface of bodies,[3] because they could apparently not believe in the free existence of coloured light. And even Goethe, the master of a phenomenology of colours, declares light at a certain point in his *Faust* to be dependent. Mephistopheles says:

> ... but a part am I
> Of that division which, at first, was all;
> A portion of that dense obscurity,
> Whose womb brought forth presumptuous Light,

---

[3]As recorded by Aristotle, in De sensu et sensibilibus (1960: 439a30 ff).

That claims precedence o'er his Mother, Night!
But here his struggle must prove ever vain –
Fast linked to Body he must still remain:
He streams from Body; Body he makes bright;
And Body stops him, in his rapid flight;
I hope ere long, with Body, he will sink outright! (Goethe & Talbot, 1835: 76–78)

Now, set free from such prejudices, we can give the relationship of light with things its due appreciation.

The transcendental aspect of light, namely that it is an appearance that causes something to appear, comes properly into effect with things: they appear in light. The Greeks, at the beginning of European culture, found this phenomenon so impressive that it became the paradigm of appearance as such. Things also exist without light, of course, and they can appear for example through sound or smell. Nevertheless, Plato understood the becoming of something, as such, as an appearance in light, as a coming forth out of indeterminacy, as the attainment of contour and concision. The essence of things, for Plato, is the idea they bring to expression, and ἰδέα initially means *look* or *appearance*. The being of things, therefore, is understood via the aspect of their appearance in light.

That things appear in light means, of course, that light always co-appears on things. This is, after all, what we call in common parlance *to see the light*. Here, as already mentioned, darkness as an additional condition for the appearance of things comes into effect. For the appearance of things in light is, properly speaking, a coming forth from darkness. It lasts, as an appearance, only as long as darkness is not completely extinguished. Only in interplay with darkness do things in light have contour, depth and concision. I have already noted that an illuminated room without shadows appears to be almost flat, and that things, too, lose their contours in it. This is important to remember if one wants to avoid battering things with light and to preserve their dignity, significance, and generally the event of their existence as such. This is likely to be of significance particularly in advertising and the presentation of commodities. It is here that the festival of things takes place, and it is not eternal values that matter in this instance but the thing as event, its appearance.

Light on things

This takes me from the appearance of things in light to the light on things. In the interaction with things, light changes and faces us, from the side of things, in a well-nigh endless multiplicity of distinct phenomena. I skip over the realm of colours here, since they have essentially been given adequate treatment in Goethe's *Theory of Colours*. Besides colours, though, there are appearances like brilliance, flickering, dullness, radiance, iridescence, fluorescence and much else. It is well known that these forms of appearance of light depend on the material on which it shines and on its surface character. There is a tendency to take these origins into perspective when characterizing and somehow ordering such phenomena. Phenomenologically, though, it would be correct to determine brilliance, faint shimmer, and iridescence, by comparing them. I will try this below with the phenomena of *brilliance* and *faint shimmer*.

Characteristically, these two terms are not only applied to surfaces but also to lights themselves. Thus, one speaks of brilliant lights on a Christmas tree decoration or of the faint shimmer of stars. These applications, for instance, when one says that a surface glitters or shimmers faintly, express somehow, in the context of things, as well, that one sees light in looking at surfaces. Yet, when I said earlier that light always co-appears in some way in the appearance of things, then this remains usually implicit. We can indeed see things in the light, without actually noticing the light about them. However, in the case of brilliance or faint shimmer, light become explicit about things. That can, in the case of brilliance, go so far that the things disappear behind it again; in the case of faint shimmer, they could blur or lose contours. On the other hand, brilliance can give things stronger contours, as long as it is not too strong; the co-appearance of light then renders the emergence of things palpable. That is why splendour on things enhances them in their dignity, as it were, it makes them appear magnificent and significant. Conversely, faint shimmer effects rather an air of restraint; yet, since it marks the beginning of splendour, as it were, this is elegant restraint or understatement. While I certainly do not want to describe the qualities of light on things in an anthropological manner, those expressions nevertheless make sense, because they are able to express the qualities of impression that things obtain from the light playing on them.

With that, the decisive expression has been mentioned: the light on things is crucially responsible for the way they impress us. When things appear in light, this may initially be still very functional and characterless. It is only through the play of light on things that appearance as such acquires a character: things appear to us in a certain way. This type of light phenomenon is extraordinarily significant. One may well say that, in design, cosmetics or architecture, the deployment of materials is essentially determined by how their surfaces interact with light. The art of surface refinement has been devoted to these qualities since the days of ancient Egypt. The talk of an era of new materiality is certainly apposite: the selection of materials plays an exceedingly important role in design and architecture. Yet, one must not forget that this concerns primarily surfaces, and that their aesthetic significance is constituted properly by their relationship with light.

Lighting

I have essentially divided the light phenomena discussed here into two large groups, which differ with respect to the relationships of light with space and light with things. In concluding, I want to engage in detail with a type of light phenomenon that connects these two groups, as it were, namely so-called lighting. I do not want to associate this term with a technical and practical meaning, according to which one could ask, for instance, how to best illuminate a bathroom. When I say lighting, I mean a light phenomenon in the sense, for example, in which we talk about an evening lighting, that is, something like the glow falling on a scene and, in a way, tinging it or, better put, *tuning* it. A classical basic type of lighting is the red sunrise or sunset, but one also speaks of a festive, dim, cheerful or oppressive lighting. *Lighting* describes a basic type of atmosphere constituted by light. If atmosphere is a tuned space, or an environment that appears to people in a certain way, then the lighting of a space or scene is of decisive importance. Colours, light, distribution of light, intensity, concentration or, conversely, diffusion of light are what endow a space, or a scene, with a certain atmosphere. This is best seen in the practice of stage design, where illumination crucially determines the atmosphere or climate prevalent on stage.

In a sense, as already noted, the phenomenon of illumination is an aggregation of the other two groups of phenomena discussed, namely *light and space* and *light on things*. It is the brightness that fills a space more or less completely and plays on things – it is this interplay that constitutes the phenomenon of lighting.

When ordered by their atmospheric effects, light phenomena again show a spectrum of their own: from moods in weather and seasons (e.g., autumnal lighting and dusk) to synaesthetic characters (like cold or radiant lighting) to a deliberate *mise en scène* (like festive illumination), which then also has a social character. The visibility of light's mood character (or, rather, of our being affected emotionally by light) connects this whole spectrum of light phenomena. Light as atmosphere endows the things and scenes or environments that appear in a particular light with an emotive character. We feel concerned and moved, we are tuned in a particular way by a particular lighting. In *brightness* (*Helle*), we see, and thus light is for us, as sighted beings, of extraordinary, constitutive importance. However, we have to ask whether light as *lighting* may not be even more important, insofar as it allows us to see the world in a particular way and thereby founds our affective participation in the world.

11

The Art of Staging as a Paradigm for an Aesthetics of Atmospheres

FIGURE 11.1 International Motor Show (IAA), Frankfurt / © 2001 Gernot Böhme.

Producing atmospheres

My aesthetics of atmospheres went along with an interest in the stage set from the very beginning. Whereas Hubert Tellenbach still considered atmospheres almost as something naturally given like nest odour (*Nestgeruch*) (1968), and Hermann Schmitz (who proceeded from Rudolf Otto' work) thought of them as emotive powers (1969: § 149), an aesthetic approach would have to foreground their producibility. In scenography, one can speak of a climate being set in scene on stage; so that, for example in radio plays, *Atmo* (short for atmosphere: indeterminate background noises) is deployed to anchor events in German broadcasting. Taking inspiration from practices of producing atmospheres is also inestimably valuable for theory because, in this way, the customarily alleged, quasi-objective status of emotional atmospheres can be justified. Scenography would be meaningless if each theatregoer only perceived something subjective.

Atmosphere – a well-known but extremely vague phenomenon

The term *atmosphere* derives originally from meteorology and designates the pregnant upper layer of air. Only since the eighteenth century has this expression been used metaphorically, namely for moods that are 'in the air' or for the emotional tinge of a space. Today, it is common in all European languages and no longer seems contrived – it is hardly noticed as a metaphor anymore. One speaks of the atmosphere of a conversation, the atmosphere of a landscape or a house, and the atmosphere of a celebration, or an evening, or a season. Yet, the way in which we talk about atmospheres is highly differentiated even in everyday language. An atmosphere is tense, cheerful or serious, oppressive or uplifting, cold or warm. We also talk of the atmosphere of the *petit bourgeoisie*, the atmosphere of the twenties, or the atmosphere of poverty. To bring some order to these examples, one can divide atmospheres into moods, synaesthesia, movement suggestions, or communicative and social-conventional atmospheres. Importantly, when we talk about atmospheres, we designate their *character*. This expression already brings the understanding of atmospheres into close proximity with physiognomy and theatre. The character of an atmosphere is the mode in which it conveys to us, as participating subjects, a disposition. A serious atmosphere tends to make me serious, a cold atmosphere makes me shudder.[1]

---

[1] See my essay, '"*Mir läuft ein Schauer übern ganzen Leib*" – *das Wetter, die Witterungslehre und die Sprache der Gefühle*' (' "A Shudder Runs Through My Whole Body" – Weather, Meteorology and the Language of Feelings', 2007).

The scientific application of the term *atmosphere* is of relatively recent origin. It began in the area of psychiatry, with Hubert Tellenbach's book *Geschmack und Atmosphäre* (Taste and Atmosphere, 1968). Quite close to the olfactory, the term *atmosphere* here means something like the climate of home, or nest odour, that is, a bodily-sensually perceptible sphere of familiarity. Meanwhile, atmospheres have been explored extensively within phenomenology, and they are discussed today in interior design, urban planning, advertising and all areas related to scenography – for example, the background composition in broadcasting, film and television. Generally, it is fair to say that atmospheres are topical wherever something is staged, wherever design matters – and today that means almost everywhere.

The matter-of-factness in talking about and engaging with atmospheres is indeed surprising, given that the phenomenon of *atmosphere* itself is something rather vague, indeterminate or even indeterminable. The reason for this is related to the fact that atmospheres are totalities: they flood out over everything, they tinge the entire world or sight, they let everything appear in a certain light, and they aggregate a multiplicity of impressions into an overall mood. One cannot really talk about the whole, though, certainly not about the whole of the world; speech is analytical and has to adhere to particulars. Further, atmospheres are something like a vista, like the aesthetic quality of a scene. They are the *More* (*Mehr*) about which Adorno speaks in oracles in order to distinguish a work of art from a poor piece of work; or the *Open* (*das Offene*) that, according to Heidegger, affords us the space for something to appear in the first place. From this perspective, there is something irrational about atmospheres, literally, something inexpressible. After all, atmospheres are something utterly subjective. In order to say what they are, or better, to determine their character, one has to expose oneself to them, one has to experience them in one's own overall mood. Without the sentient subject, they are nothing.

And yet, the subject experiences them as something 'out there', as something by which he or she can be assailed or seized as by an alienating power. Are atmospheres something objective then, after all? Atmospheres actually represent a typical phenomenon of the in-between, something between subject and object. This does not make them more tangible as such, given that they do not have a secure ontological position – at least in European culture. Precisely for that reason, though, it is worth approaching them from two sides: from the side of the subjects and from the side of the object, from the aesthetics of reception and from the aesthetics of production.

Aesthetics of reception and production

The understanding of atmospheres as a phenomenon derives from the aesthetic of reception. As poignant forces, atmospheres are given to the subject and tend to put a person into a characteristic mood. Since they tend to drift up from anywhere, as something that would have been called a *je ne sais quoi* in the eighteenth century, they are experienced as numinous – and thereby as irrational.

The matter looks entirely different when approaching atmospheres from the side of an aesthetics of production, which enables us rationally to access the 'inconceivable' (*Unfaßliches*). Scenography, which aims to produce atmospheres, frees atmospheres from the odour of the irrational. Its whole endeavour would be meaningless if atmospheres were purely subjective. For the stage designer has to take a larger audience into account, which is by and large capable of experiencing the atmosphere produced on stage in the same way. The stage set, after all, is intended to provide the atmospheric background for the events on stage, it is meant to tune the audience in on the play and provide the actors with a sounding board for their performances. Scenography, then, shows us in practice that atmospheres are something quasi-objective. What does that mean?

While atmospheres are no things, that is, while they do not exist as entities that remain identical over time, they can nevertheless be recognized as identical by their character, even after an interval. Further, while they are perceived only in subjective experience in each case – as a taste, say, or a smell according to Tellenbach – it is quite possible to talk about them intersubjectively. We can talk to each other about the prevailing atmosphere in a room and that can teach us that intersubjectivity can rely on something other than an identical object. The prevailing scientific way of thinking has conditioned us to assume that intersubjectivity is founded on objectivity, so that the determination of presence and certainty of something are independent of subjective perception and can be delegated to an apparatus. The quasi-objectivity of atmospheres, however, reveals itself in its linguistic communicability. This communicability has some prerequisites, of course: an audience has to a certain degree be homogenous, that is, accustomed to particular modes of perception to experience a stage set in nearly the same way.

Nevertheless, the quasi-objective character of atmospheres persists beyond those culture-specific aspects. It is evident in the fact that atmospheres can be experienced as surprising and sometimes even in contrast with one's own mood. One example is that, in a cheerful mood, I get mixed up with a group of mourners: the prevailing atmosphere can move me to tears. For that, too, the stage set can serve as a practical proof.

Fantastic art/unreliable fabrication

Can atmospheres indeed be produced? The term *making* (*machen*) refers to dealing with material conditions, things, instruments, sound and light.

Atmosphere itself is not a thing, however, but rather a hovering in-between, that is, between things and perceiving subjects. Thus, the making of atmospheres is restricted to the arrangement of the conditions under which an atmosphere can appear. These conditions I call *generators*.

The peculiar character of such a making, which consists not properly in the fabrication of a thing but rather in fixing the conditions under which the phenomenon can appear, can be explained by recourse to Plato's theory of mimesis.[2]

In order to expose the treacherous art of the Sophists, Plato introduces in his dialogue *The Sophist* a division of the pictorial arts (2006: 235e 3–236c 7). He poses a difference between *eikastike techne* (εἰκαστικὴ τέχνη, likeness-making art) and *phantastike techne* (φανταστικὴ τέχνη, fantastic art). The latter is particularly interesting in our context. In the case of *eikastike techne*, mimesis consists of the faithful replication of an original. *Phantastike techne*, by contrast, takes liberties with and deviates from the original because it considers the view point of the spectator and strives to make that which it wants to represent appear in such a way that viewers 'correctly' recognize it. For this distinction, Plato takes his bearings from the practices of the sculptors and architects of his time. Thus, the head of a very large statue was commonly made disproportionally large, lest it seem too small to a viewer. Likewise, the horizontal lines of a temple were slightly curved upwards to prevent the impression of sagging (Lamb & Curtius, 1944). This art of the *phantastike* may not yet be quite what we have in mind concerning the art of producing atmospheres – but it does already contain the decisive moment, namely that the artist's aim is not to produce an object or artwork but the impression the object conveys to the viewer. This is why this art is called *phantastike techne:* it refers to the subject's power of imagination, or *imaginatio*. Closer to our concerns here is the notion of *skenographia* (σκηνογραφία, stage painting), which the Greeks developed already during the fourth century BC. Aristotle in his *Poetics* attributes it to the tragic poet Sophocles (1449a 18, after the Standard Greek Edition by Bekker, e.g., Aristotle, 1968: 8). Classical scholars believe that this is the origin of perspectival painting, an invention usually attributed only to the Renaissance period (Frank, 1962: 20). This, then, led on to geometrical proportion theory (particularly the theorem of intersecting lines) as we know it from Euclid's *Elements*. For in order to create spatial depth in painting, the objects shown – buildings, trees, or humans – have to be perspectivally foreshortened. Thus, scenography is an art that is explicitly oriented towards the subjects' production of ideas, in this case the spectators, in its concrete practices.

---

[2]See Chapter III.2, 'A Theory of the Image', in Böhme (2000b).

It aims not to form objects but rather phenomena. The treatment of objects merely serves the creation of conditions under which these phenomena can appear. This is, however, not possible without the cooperation of the subject, that is, the viewer. Interestingly, Umberto Eco maintains precisely this about all pictorial representation: it does not represent the object but creates the conditions of perception under which the idea of the object can appear for the viewer of the image (Chapter 3.5, 'Critique of Iconism', Eco, 1976). While this may be exaggerated, it is certainly true for impressionist painting, where the aim is not the replication of an object or landscape but the creation of a particular impression or experience in the viewer. The Pointillist techniques provide striking proof of this: the colours the painter wants to be seen are not to be found on the tableau, after all, but 'in space', or in the imagination of the viewer.

The art of the stage set has, of course, long transcended mere scenography. Wagner's operas seem to have provided a special occasion for this, because they required, on the one hand, a fantastic ambiance in any case and, on the other, they were particularly intended to affect feelings, and not only the faculty of the imagination (Schuberth, 1955: 86f, 95f). The breakthrough, however, occurred only with twentieth-century electrical engineering and the control of light and sound.[3] A kind of stage art began to evolve that is no longer limited to designing and furnishing the stage area but capable, on the one hand, of making the stage and the events on it appear in a special light and, on the other, creating an acoustic space that *tunes* the whole. With that, the possibility arose for scenography to leave the stage area and spread into the front of house, or even into space in general. These luminous and sonic spaces are no longer perceived from a distance but experienced immersively. At the same time, this provides the conditions for an expansion of set design into a general art of staging, as it is deployed particularly in the design of discotheques and large events (e.g., at open air festivals or the opening ceremonies of sport events, Larmann, 2007).

Further, the current dominance of light and sound design allows us retrospectively to recognize more precisely what the making of atmospheres, also in more objective areas, consists of. Clearly, that it is not really about views, as the old type of scenography still held but much more about the making of tuned spaces, that is, atmospheres. Thus, the making, insofar as it is about the design and definition of geometrical space and its contents, cannot relate to the concrete properties of space and the things contained in it. Or, better, what matters is not the determinations of things but their

---

[3]Particularly the chapter '*Mehr Licht! – Die Lichtbühne*' ('More Light! – The Light Stage', in Eckert 1998: 106–113).

emanations into space, that is, what they accomplish as generators of atmospheres. Therefore, rather than qualities, I speak of ecstasies,[4] of ways of stepping outside of oneself. The difference between qualities and ecstasies can be illustrated by the contrast between convex and concave: a surface that is concave in relation to the body it encloses is convex in relation to the adjacent space.

Even though the ecstasies of things, that is, their modes of expression, are decisive for design, we are not really used to characterizing things in that way. Instead, in keeping with our ontological tradition, we characterize things according to their matter and form. For our purposes, however, Jakob Böhme's model of things is far more appropriate here: his conception of things is modelled on a musical instrument (1651). Consequently, their bodies are something like the sounding board of an instrument, whose external properties, which he calls signatures, are moods or attunements that are articulated in its expressive forms. And, finally, their sound or *smell* (German: *Ruch*) is characteristic of what things are – that is, how they manifest their essence.

Sound and smell – in my terminology, their ecstasies – determine the atmosphere things emanate. They are also the mode in which things are palpably present in space. And this provides us with another definition of atmosphere: it is the palpable presence of something or someone in space. The ancient Greeks had a beautiful term for this already: *parousia* (παρουσία: presence, arrival, or visit). Thus, according to Aristotle, light is the *parousia* of fire (Aristotle & Shields, 2002: 418b13).

Conclusion: The art of staging

What I have called *phantastike techne*, following Plato, should today probably be called design. After all, we have so far taken our bearings from a prototypical area of design, scenography. However, it is important for our purpose to change the traditional understanding of design as something like *Formgebung* (shaping) or *Gestaltung* (styling).[5] The extraordinary importance of light and

---

[4]See pp. 37ff.

[5]I have clarified this particularly at the Werkbund centenary celebration at the ZKM, Karlsruhe (Böhme, 2008). *Formgebung* und *Gestaltung* are used synonymously for *Design* in German and refer to the creative work on the outer appearance of an object. In the past, particularly at the height of functionalism, these terms were deployed in the place of *Design* to avoid proximity with *Styling*. While *Formgebung* implies a focus on shape or form, *Gestaltung* is principally capable of incorporating emotional, atmospheric and poetic elements, even though this has not been traditionally the case.

FIGURE 11.2 Cathedral of Light (Albert Speer) at NSDAP Reichsparteitag, Nürnberg / © 1936 Unbekannt (Bundesarchiv, Bild 183-1982-1130-502/CC-BY-SA 3.0).

sound, not only in scenography but also in advertising, marketing, urban planning or interior design, already shows how inadequate this understanding is. Instead, one could talk of a practical or, better, poetic phenomenology, since it is about the art of bringing something into appearance. Despite its polemic intent, phenomenologist Hermann Schmitz' term *Eindruckstechnik* (technology of impression) is apt. Schmitz (1999) uses this expression polemically, though, for the propagandist creation of impressions during the Nazi era, which Walter Benjamin termed the *aestheticization of politics* (Benjamin, 1969: 242).

It is perhaps better, then, to talk more generally of an *art of staging*. This allows us, on the one hand, to maintain the connection with the paradigm of scenography. On the other hand, this term identifies the main contemporary purpose for the production of atmospheres: the stage set is itself part of the staging of a drama or an opera. The art of atmospheres is, when it is deployed in the organization of open-air festivals, or the openings of big sport events like the soccer world cup or the Olympic Games, about their staging. The

---

[6]With reference to this term as a characterization of the present state of capitalism, see Böhme (2001c: 69–82).

production of atmospheres in marketing serves the staging of commodities. In the *aesthetic economy*,[6] where commodities serve the satisfaction of elemental needs only to a lesser extent, commodities are primarily appreciated for their staging value: insofar as they help individuals or groups to stage a lifestyle. And, finally, atmosphere functions to stage personalities of political events in democracies, as well (or, better, in media democracies where politics is, after all, performed as in a theatre).

Taken together, these examples show that our current attention to atmospheres within aesthetic theory has its material background in the fact that staging has become a basic feature of our society: the staging of politics, of sport events, of cities, of commodities, and even of ourselves. Choosing the paradigm of the *stage set* for the art of making atmospheres thus reflects the actual theatralization of our life. Theoretically, therefore, there is a lot to be learnt from the paradigm of the stage set, for questions concerning the production of atmospheres generally, and consequently for the art of staging. But there should also much to be learnt practically from the great tradition of scenography. No doubt, this will happen, but one should not expect that there is much to be said about it. Scenography is still passed on in traditional craft modes, through collaboration and imitation in master-apprentice relationships. The leading practical knowledge here is *tacit*, so that it is all the more gratifying to find, in one of the many books concerning the *stage set*, something explicit about the craft. In conclusion, I quote a sample of this type of knowledge about the practice of scenography, taken from a doctoral thesis in philosophy, namely from Robert Kümmerlen's *Zur Ästhetik bühnenräumlicher Prinzipien* (The Aesthetics of Scenographic Principles, 1929).

Kümmerlen writes about the deployment of light on stage and, notably, that it creates an *atmosphere* on stage. He then determines the effect of the light atmosphere further: that the display is mediated by a *characteristic mood*. He mentions *sombre* and *charming* as examples, that is, a synaesthetic and a communicative character. Finally, he even recognizes the in-between status so typical of atmospheres: 'Mere illumination produces an aura between the individual entities on display.' Here is the complete quote:

> The space to be contemplated receives its brightness from illumination; the shapes on stage become visible only through light. By the first function of illumination, the simple provision of light, the atmosphere in which the space is located is created together with brightness, as it were. The light atmosphere, which can be obtained in multiple ways, modulates the space; the shapes on display receive a characteristic mood from the illumination. The space is effective as a whole, the lights rendering the space form a cohesive impression, the space is cast in a uniform light. With the illumination of the whole picture, a 'single feature' is created; a unified

mood emanates from the space, the entire spatial representation is under, for instance, a 'subdued' light. It seems to us that the objects in space 'radiate' in an even light; the space appears 'charming' or 'sombre'. Mere illumination produces an aura between the individual entities on display. The space, rendered in an ethereal impression of brightness, contains a particular mood content. (Kümmerlen, 1929: 36)

12

Church Atmospheres

The numinous and the profanization of church spaces

Writing about the atmosphere of church spaces is not an unexpected challenge for a philosopher, though it is a delicate one. By responding, he pays off a debt of gratitude, as it were, to an origin he had to abandon in order to experience and to think the phenomenon of atmosphere as such. Hermann Schmitz, who first coined *atmosphere* as a philosophical term, relied not only on Ludwig Klages' preparatory work in doing so (see p. 19), but he also drew, quite substantially, on Rudolf Otto's research concerning the numinous (1932). Atmospheres, as expansively diffused feelings, are experienced as poignant forces. This distanced and enlightened, that is, phenomenological description of experiences can also be explained as impressions by divine beings, or as visitations by demons. Accordingly, Hermann Schmitz succeeded in providing a convincing reinterpretation, and consequently also rehabilitation, of the Greek world of gods through his phenomenology of atmospheres (Schmitz, 1969). Mind you, this was a rehabilitation of the Greek world of gods, who, within the frameworks of psychologism, could conversely also be regarded as projections of human emotions: Eris as strife, Ares as militancy, Aphrodite as love, and Zeus as ire. Vis-à-vis such theses about projections, it is the merit of the phenomenology of atmospheres to have showcased the aspect of suffering in such emotions, as well as their trans-subjective character: the experience of an emotion is the affective concernment with something that appears to me from outside, and which I can therefore share with people around me.

It would seem obvious to apply the instruments of a phenomenology of atmospheres to the experiences of impressions made by church spaces as well. Are they not prime examples of the relationship between environmental qualities and dispositions, of tuned spaces, and of quasi-objective feelings? Is one not tempted to proclaim for church spaces, with and against Heraclitus who claimed this for his squalid dwelling: 'This here, too, is full of gods'?

That, however, precisely indicates the venture's delicate nature. Church spaces, after all, belong to institutions that claim authority even over the interpretation of experiences occurring in these spaces or, conversely, attach importance to their design, such that only certain experiences are possible. Thus, even in our times, they show no hesitation in condemning experiences of the numinous in church spaces as relapses into paganism and natural religion (Biéler, 1965). On closer examination, however, what is allowed and intended in church spaces in terms of experiences differs according to denomination and the finer points of the interpretation of dogma. Nevertheless, a kind of fundamental consensus prevails among Christian denominations, which historically goes back to the confrontation with paganism (and which makes Christianity appear strangely enlightened and rationalistic to phenomenologists), namely that churches, as such – with their inventory of altar, crucifix, figures of saints and relics – are actually not at all places of the presence of God. *As such* – and this must be emphasized; according to Christian doctrine, God is, because of what happens in them, particularly the sacraments, present in churches, after all. According to Catholic doctrine, God is present in the Eucharist celebration, that is, the Holy Communion, in the figure of Jesus Christ, according to Jesus' words of the investiture when he offered the bread: 'Take and eat; this is my body' (Matthew 26:26). According to Protestant doctrine, God is present in the figure of Jesus Christ in the community assembly as such, in keeping with Jesus' word: 'where two or three gather in my name, there am I with them' (Matthew 18:20). The churches' interpretative practices seem strange to the phenomenologist because they block all empirical evidence, namely the engagement with the experiences of impressions in church spaces. From an ecclesiastical point of view, there are simply admissible and inadmissible experiences, and this may well explain successive waves of iconoclasm and austerity in design. Impressions that can be experienced in church spaces, even independently of liturgical activities, tend to be perceived as pagan threats. In any event, the phenomenologist, with his aforementioned tendencies towards polytheism, feels expelled.

The churches' dogmatic attitudes stand in remarkable contrast to the actuality of church spaces. For the latter contain a great many characteristic atmospheres, and, over the course of church history, some have even formed that are typical of Christian churches. The churches themselves, through their architects and their collaboration with artists, have actually contributed to the formation of atmospheres. However, it seems like they do not want to recognize the staging of the numinous, which occurs through the production of atmospheres in church spaces. One really has to talk about repression here, considering that key theoretical texts about church architecture comment only on the placement of altar, pulpit and baptismal font and their relationship with the liturgy, or discuss the contrast between centrality and frontality in relation to a particular dogma; a book by the title of *Church Architecture and Liturgy* (Kirchenbau und Gottesdienst, Biéler, 1965) effectively deals only with floor plans. Only very rarely will a historian of ecclesiastical history mention the atmosphere of a church or the aura of a monastery (Norman, 1990). As of the rest, the atmospheric may be assigned a supporting role in the edification of the faithful or the community, at the most. Thus, Paul Brathe, in his book *Theorie des evangelischen Kirchengebäudes* (A Theory of Protestant Church Architecture, 1906: 127f), determines the 'basic mood of the Protestant Christian and the Protestant parish, in their relationship and communion with God', as 'filial trust paired with reverence'. He continues,

already on entering, the church architecture must help awaken this basic mood. It must make entrants feel that they are with the Father – with the Father high above, of course, who became their father only out of mercy. The church, then, must have the basic character of something familiar and heart-warming, yet at the same time not lacking sublimity and solemnity, without which the familiar would tend towards all-too-human coziness. (p. 128)

By comparison, according to Brathe, Catholicism represents God rather as majestic and fearsome, so that 'Catholic church architecture, likewise, has to aspire to a character of solemn greatness and sublimity' (p. 120f). However, such consideration of the characteristic attunement of church spaces is, as said, extremely rare among theorists of church architecture, and one can sense the fear, here, too, that atmospheres might break out of the subsidiary role assigned to them.

Today, a greater impartiality vis-à-vis atmospheres in church spaces might have arisen in ecclesiastic circles. This is certainly linked to a growing ecumenical openness and tolerance concerning dogma, but the main reason is probably a recognition and acceptance of the profane consideration and use of church spaces. It may well be anachronistic to regard church spaces simply as objects of art history even for epochs during which nothing akin to autonomous art existed yet – autonomous, that is, with respect to the religious realm. However, the monuments of church art are (no different from, say, classical Greek temples) given to us and accessible even without the attendant religious practices, after all, and one need not justify this by reference to Hegel, who accorded art a higher stage than religion in the development of objective spirit. Factually, church spaces are considered like art works – in Europe, it is to be expected that the number of tourist visitors of churches will reach or exceed that of religiously motivated church-goers.

FIGURE 12.1 Selexyz book shop inside Dominican Church, Dominikanerkerkstraat, Maastricht / © 2014 Gernot Böhme.

FIGURE 12.2 Selexyz book shop inside Dominican church, Dominikanerkerkstraat, Maastricht / © 2014 Gernot Böhme.

The general question then arises as to which experiences are available to visitors of church spaces independently of their religious affiliation. A great number of church spaces have also already been released from the context of religious practice. This is partially a consequence of historically recurring waves of secularization and partially of the dwindling numbers of church members and the shrinking financial basis of the churches themselves. There are, consequently, many church buildings that have been assigned to a different use, as museums, concert and lecture halls, and even as storehouses or shelters for the homeless. Finally, the churches themselves have opened their spaces to non-liturgical forms of use. Lectures and presentations outside of church services are no longer unthinkable, and art exhibitions are already almost normal in church spaces. Such non-liturgical use of church spaces often relates explicitly to the prevalent atmospheres there; in any event, to take these atmospheres into account cannot be avoided. Therefore, historically, it is now time to thematize the atmospheres of church spaces as such. With that, different aspects will come to the fore from the already mentioned classical instances that preoccupy the theory of church architecture (altar, pulpit, font, rood screen, choir, centrality versus frontality, etc.): namely, the generators of atmospheres. Architectural forms need to be considered with respect to their impressive qualities, particularly their movement suggestions; further, light and twilight, stone, figures and images, the acoustic qualities of a space, colours, materials and insignia of age, and, finally, Christian symbols, of course, which are still effective in profane use or contemplation.

Lastly, it is important to recognize that, with the disintegration of the authority over dogma, the atmospheric unity of church spaces begins to crumble, as it were. That is why, already in the title of this section, atmospheres are referred to in the plural. For this reason, too, the following can only exemplify individual characteristic atmospheres and discuss an arbitrary selection.

Sacred twilight – diaphanous light

Abbot Suger, whose construction work on the abbey church of St. Denis initiated, if not invented, the Gothic style, introduced, in my view, light into church architecture to generate atmospheres. Of course, this occurred within a Christian metaphysics appropriated from neo-Platonism. Here, light was understood as the creative power emanating from God. By contrast with Plato, in whose cave allegory earthly light was but an analogy for the idea of the Good's power of Being, the unified world view of neo-Platonism allowed this power of Being itself to be experienced in light. This is a rare case in which architecturally staged, impressive qualities are interpreted in terms of religious experience (G. Böhme & H. Böhme, 1996: 153ff).

What kind of experience was this, and of what kind was the light mediating such experience? Today, we can re-enact this experience ourselves – if not necessarily in St. Denis, then in many other Gothic churches: this is not light in terms of brightness but light in the sense of appearance or visible radiance. That is, this is a kind of light that is experienced on the basis of darkness, out of holy twilight. Indeed, to be in the dark lies at the basis of this experience of light. We must therefore first question the holy twilight (*heilige Dämmerung*) itself.

Heilige Dämmerung is by now a common German expression for a typically ecclesiastic atmosphere. Is this simply about twilight as it is also experienced in nature, but that is called holy twilight only when it fills church spaces? What is holy about it? It seems to me that it is phenomenologically possible to distinguish between twilight as a natural phenomenon and the holy twilight in church spaces. A way of putting this distinction to the test would be scenographic staging, that is, for example, when the question is how to produce a type of twilight that would be suitable for the *Cathedral* scene in Goethe's Faust.

Crucial for twilight in church spaces is their limitation. Everything here, too, disappears into indeterminate space, yet things do not disappear in an indeterminate expanse as in nature. This is why twilight in church spaces lacks that dangerous moment of getting lost in vastness that during dusk can

FIGURE 12.3 Holy twilight, Münster St. Maria and Markus, Insel Reichenau / © 2006 Gernot Böhme.

contribute to the experience of anxiety. By contrast, holy twilight tends to be enclosing and protecting. On the side of the subject, the character of the holy is matched by the intuition of a secret that twilight harbours. This intuition can, indeed, be stimulated by church insignia and architectural characteristics. However, it seems to me that something like soft light is more likely to articulate twilight in this sense, namely shades of gold and perhaps individual candles. For this intuition and vague expectation, it is important that twilight in church spaces (characteristically delimited in contrast to natural twilight) disappears upwards, as it were. In the high Gothic nave, the columns and buttresses that make twilight dense by their mass at the bottom, where the viewer is, disappear towards the heights, one could say they clear up. And from here, from the upper clerestories, light rakes: as sheaves of light, as stripes, and often – this must have been how it was originally in St. Denis – as bursts of colour.

Characteristically, this type of light and its atmosphere appear in the dark, or on the background of darkness, and, further, its radiance is without source. It gathers up the expectation forming in twilight and leads it upwards. To a Christian, this upward lift may well convey an experience of redemption. Significantly, a related phenomenon in nature is called God's finger in the German vernacular; the expression designates a radiant glow that becomes visible between dark thunderclouds covering the sun. Precisely because the source is not visible, it can be intuited as transcendental: the view itself transcends the light, following the shaft towards its source.

Conversely, radiance in the dark conveys the experience of creation through light. The light shafts lift single objects out of the twilight, sometimes grazing and sometimes directly illuminating. They act as a principle of individuation (*principium individuationis*).

While holy twilight can also exist by itself, diaphanous light appears only in a dusky atmosphere. It articulates and provides direction, it creates zones of light and redeems individuals who experience the atmosphere, as well as individual objects, from being lost in the indeterminate.

Silence and the sublime

Silence and the sublime characterize many church spaces but certainly not all – much depends on the building style here. Further, for silence and the sublime to be effective, several boundary conditions have to be met. This is most often the case when a church is located in the midst of the urban bustle, like, for example, Cologne Cathedral. For both, silence and sublimity, are in themselves contrast experiences and therefore best articulated through ingression, that is, through experiencing the contrast when entering from a different atmosphere.

FIGURE 12.4 Oberfeld in snow, Darmstadt / © 2005 Gernot Böhme.

One is thus almost struck dead by the silence on entering Cologne Cathedral; or, better put, one can feel oneself entering silence as if walking into a wall of fog. Only when lingering on in the cathedral does one notice that this silence is not at all soundlessness. Rather, the silence raises above the muffled murmur through which the big city is present here, too, whereas sounds outside are manifold, individual and meaningful – a ruptured concert.

Just as silence receives the visitor entering the cathedral in a potent density, so the vast nave pulls the view upwards. Just as silence contrasts with the hearing of individual sounds, so this view contrasts with the fixed gaze on individual objects and signals. Only when the view does not get caught somewhere, can the sublime be experienced in this space. Despite what Kant thought, a confrontation with absolute magnitude is not required in any sense for the experience of the sublime. Rather, a detachment from human scale given in the human body suffices.

The pre-Kantian, classical eighteenth-century theory of the sublime held that its experience is one of ambivalence, that is, of simultaneous pleasure and displeasure. Kant moralized this experience, so to speak, and resolved the ambivalence by making the subject rise above sensibility. For him, therefore, objects proper are not sublime, whether they be mountains or pyramids, but the subject him- or herself.[1] By contrast, experiences in church spaces

---

[1]See Böhme (1999b), particularly the chapter 'Pyramids and Mountains' (*Pyramiden und Berge*).

show that the sublime is primarily experienced in one's own body (*primär eine Erfahrung am eigenen Leibe*). Together, the dissolution of the fixed gaze and the movement impression (*Bewegungsanmutung*, see p. 49) of the architecture cause bodily awareness to slide into infinity. Important in this context is that it is precisely this slipping that allows one to feel one's own limits and thereby the smallness of one's body. Feelings alternate between slipping into infinity and being thrown back upon one's body. They thus create the ambivalence that belongs to being affected by the sublime. If this were not the case, that is, if bodily awareness indeed disappeared into infinity, one would not sense sublimity but the so-called oceanic feeling. To sense the sublime – in this case of the church space – contrast is required: the simultaneous sensing of one's own presence in space, that is, one's lost, disoriented presence, in an over-large space. This ambivalence in sensing the sublime links that feeling to the experience of silence. For the latter, too, articulates itself particularly well when it is simultaneously an experience of one's own presence. Silence is always articulated through individual sounds (e.g., the evening's silence through a dog's barking in the distance). In the church space, though, silence is most intensively articulated by one's own footsteps. As with the sublime, the experience of silence is then connected with the sensing of one's own lostness in space.

Admittedly, sublimity and silence are atmospheres that can occur separately from each other. This can be seen by the fact that a sublime atmosphere in church spaces can be augmented by music, particularly by organ music. Nevertheless, because they appear to the subject in the same ambivalent manner, sublimity and silence often enter an intimate connection in church spaces. Their invitation to disappear into the expanse of space simultaneously throws the subject back on his or her small and limited presence.

Stone and space

Stone can afford a very special spatial experience in churches. This phenomenon needs to be defined precisely since stone, as a material, imprints its synaesthetic characteristics on an atmosphere just as other materials do. Atmospheres, moreover, are always spatial phenomena. Yet, in the case of church spaces in which stone and space enter into a special relationship – one thinks above all of Romanesque and Gothic churches – it is not about an indeterminate spatiality, into which atmospheres are poured, but about a particular, well-composed space: space as *spatium*. Limitation, contour, direction and an encompassing volume are all part of it.

Not all types of church are able to convey this kind of spatial experience. To the contrary, some church styles even have a tendency to dissolve space, as a firmly composed and limited order. This starts already during the Gothic period, after all, with the dissolution of walls, the striving for airy heights, the disappearance of the encompassing volume. Down below, however, where people stand or walk, the experience of space as *spatium* is preserved by the columns' bulkiness and the thickness of the stone blocks. In Baroque churches, by comparison, space in the sense of *spatium* disappears behind plaster, together with stone. In its stead, stucco and imagery take over, and a Baroque church, it has been correctly observed, can no longer be discussed purely as architecture:

> What seems to be structural may be manufactured in stucco. Distinctions between the elements of the building, so important to the Renaissance architect, are deliberately confused, so that walls undulate and spaces flow into one another; *putti* fly out from capitals and pediments to lead lives of their own; frescoes continue the architecture into fictitious depths; painted figures emerge into three dimensions; angels hover without apparent support. (Norman, 1990: 196)

When it remains visible, though, stone exudes volume and radiates firmness and calm. This character is reinforced by well-composed blocks, the kit-set style of the Romanesque, and the load of columns and vaults remains sensible and understandable. This is particularly the case in crypts, where the load character of vaults can become almost pressing. By contrast, in the Gothic style one has to say the management of lines with their movement suggestions withdraw the loads (which vaults also imply, of course) from direct perception. On the other hand, in both the Gothic and Romanesque styles, floors form a unity with walls and columns. In this way, stone becomes a totality of spatial experience. In ruins, one can observe how particularly the dissolution of the floor, sometimes more than the lack of a roof, makes the feeling of being inside a building vanish. In an era when sealing is regarded as inferior, it is difficult to articulate adequately the degree to which the creation of solid floors is constitutive of the organization of human spaces. However, walking through Dubrovnik or North Italian cities, one can comprehend this understanding of building empathetically. Stone produces the sense of urbanity, the feeling of being in a completely humanly ordered place: these cities are entirely encompassed by stone floors and walls. In such spaces, one is seized by a kind of primitive human pride, that is, not only by a feeling of security and order, but also by one of rising above nature.

Strangely, the term *oikodome* (οἰκοδομή, edification) figured quite early, already in biblical texts, not so much in the sense of individual uplifting but in the sense of community formation (1 Corinthians 14:26). Even though the original community's meeting place did not matter for community formation as such, the secure house nevertheless became in this way a metaphor for *church*, a term in which both, the house of God and the community, have today become indistinguishable. Church spaces, in which an austere fit-out makes architecture appear in rough stone, in particular, church order remains preserved as a spatial order. By way of boundaries and thresholds, through hiding and revealing, by means of orientations and hierarchies of places in space, as well as through distance and bulk, stone creates space in the sense of *spatium*. These church spaces, more than others, therefore hold so much fascination for profane use.

Genius loci

Today, profane use makes it necessary, but also possible, to speak of the atmosphere of church spaces. However important atmospheres might have been in the building and fit out of churches and their liturgical use, they were treated as something marginal to the situation, whose acknowledgement was prevented by something almost like a taboo. Even if we can thematize the atmospheres of church spaces today by tracing the relationships between environmental qualities and dispositions, without touching on taboo zones, an element has so far nevertheless been missing which makes the theme appear delicate from yet another angle: church spaces remain church spaces, after all, even without liturgical use. Profanization will in most cases remain incomplete. What is it that makes their *genius loci* stay on in church spaces,[2] even in profane use?

It seems to me that phenomenology is able to render account of this fact without recourse to mystical and animist instances. That is because there are, among the generators which determine the characters of atmospheres, not only synaesthesia and movement suggestions but indeed also conventional elements such as signs and symbols. Again, the comparison with the art of scenography is instructive here. Not only will holy twilight be deployed in the staging of a church space in the theatre, but a crucifix will also be mounted somewhere and, for example, hints of Gothic arches and the sound of organ music will be provided in the background.

The crucifix, of course, is clearly a religious symbol and is likely, just like other inscriptions and images with Christian content that are left in church spaces, to convey a church-like atmosphere to them. More interesting, perhaps, are Gothic arches and the organ music. A. W. N. Pugin's opinion, that the Gothic

---

[2]Christian Norberg-Schulz (1979) reintroduced the term *genius loci* into architecture. Robert Joseph Kozljanic (2004) then provided a comprehensive history of this concept.

architectural style is the Christian style as such, may be excessive, yet the Gothic is nevertheless primarily regarded as the style of churches – to the extent even that something church-like seems to adhere to profane buildings in the Gothic style as well. In that sense, certain architectural elements of style do shape the character of atmospheres. A similar convention has developed for organ music. Originally, the organ may well have also been a profane instrument (Brathe, 1906: 182f), yet today it is almost impossible to avoid a church-like character in the profane use of organ music.

In summary, church spaces retain the historical conditioning stemming from liturgical use even when they become profane. Certain insignia, like religious symbols, stylistic features, frescoes and inscriptions, continue to shape the character of these spaces as church-like. Profane use has to take this into account, and that is actually what organizers of art exhibitions, concerts, and lectures do. They anticipate, for instance, that visitors will enter these spaces with a certain awe, a readiness for contemplation and, if I can put it that way, an expectation of transcendence. The latter arises above all because church spaces retain their seclusion from worldly activities: they are used and experienced as special places. As venues for cultural events, particularly for concerts, but also, regrettably, for lectures, they become places of art in the form of secular religion. Church spaces even have a particular attraction for the visual arts – due, of course, to the fact that visual artists can relate their works to an already existing atmosphere, with which they can then play through contrast, augmentation or modification. In this way, they may regain the very aura they lost with modernism. If, according to Benjamin's analysis (2008), this loss occurred in the transition from cult value to exhibition value, then at least a whiff of cult value may be re-imparted to the works of visual art when they participate in the atmosphere of church spaces.

Afterword

Atmospheres to Think About

Atmospheres are the subject matter of productive work in a number of fields, also of reflection on a range of topics. Among the domains of inquiry Böhme has investigated, I'll note four that hold great promise for continued study and creativity: matters of method, of disciplinarity, social sense, and philosophical anthropology.

Phenomenology, in the writings of Husserl, Heidegger and Merleau-Ponty, was less a philosophical doctrine – one that supposedly privileges personal experience – than a philosophical *method*, a style of thought that does not seek to explain or analyse the world in the manner of the natural sciences but to *describe* phenomena as they give themselves to experience. Renewing this project, Böhme's study awakens the *amor mundi* each of us feels, so that we can, with him, (re)discover the ecstasies of things, their expressions, resonances, and performances. The task is not simple, as Le Corbusier observed: 'We must always say what we see, but above all and more difficult, we must always see what we see' (1999: iii).

Seeing in this sense would seem to be celebrated in works of art. But which arts? Each of them equally, though differently? Since the withering of the composite work of art in the nineteenth century, we comfortably speak of the arts in their relative isolation: pure painting, pure music, pure architecture, and so on. Böhme's book does not seek to overcome this plurality with a centralizing concept of art as such; instead, he demonstrates the actuality of rather unexpected conjunctions: plastic acoustics, musical chromatics, dramatic climates, and cinematic promenades – not as metaphors but concrete phenomena.

Sense such as this would not be for you or me alone, it would also be for us. Untimely as the claim may seem, atmospheres, for Böhme, are matters of common concern, moods are apprehended intersubjectively. Aesthetic experience is not only personal, and dispositions can be shared. This 'new aesthetic' elaborates an *ethics* of atmosphere production, according to which human interests intermingle with the beautiful. This thesis is particularly relevant today, when appetites for striking images are so hungry.

Perhaps the most challenging question arising from the book concerns the connections between the pre-reflective sense of atmospheres and other kinds of apprehension; more simply, how felt space can give rise to thought. The question must be asked because what is felt is also, perforce, subject to consideration. The varied spaces of eighteenth-century gardens, for example, not only gave rise to distinct moods but also to characteristic expressions, typical of one or another genre, and to legible emblems – *ideas rendered palpably apparent*. Atmospheres, then, form the background for more explicit perceptions and more intelligible articulations, background in the double sense of where a figure comes from, its history, and the supporting surround for something worth thinking about.

With this book before us, we can pursue the many correlations between practical relevance and aesthetic pleasure, the most decisive of which today is the atmosphere's intellectual substance, for what Paul Ricoeur (1967) once said of symbols must surely be true of atmospheres, that when well contrived they give rise to thought.

Professor David Leatherbarrow,
Chair of the Graduate Group in Architecture, Penn Design,
University of Pennsylvania

References

Adorno, T. W. (1982). *Prisms* (S. Weber & S. Weber, Trans.). Cambridge, MA: MIT Press.

Adorno, T. W., Adorno, G., Tiedemann, R., & Hullot-Kentor, R. (2002). *Aesthetic theory* (R. Hullot-Kentor, Trans.). London: Continuum.

Aristotle. (1968). *Poetics (Introduction, commentary and appendixes by Donald William Lucas)*. Oxford: Clarendon Press.

Aristotle, & Shields, C. J. (2002). *Aristotle: De anima: Books II and III (with passages from book I)* (D. W. Hamlyn, Trans.). Oxford: Clarendon Press.

Aristotle, Gigon, O., & Bekker, I. (1960). *Aristotelis Opera ex recensione Immanuelis Bekkeri: editit Academia Regia Birussica*. Berdini: W. de Gruyter.

Austin, J. L. (1962). *How to do things with words*. Oxford: Clarendon Press.

Bachmann, U., & Hochschule für Gestaltung und Kunst Zürich, HGKZ, FarbLichLabor. (2006). *Colours between light and darkness = Farben zwischen Licht und Dunkelheit*. Basel: Verlag Niggli.

Barthes, R. (1977). The grain of the voice (S. Heath, Trans.). In *Image-Music-Text* (pp. 179–189). London: Fontana.

Benjamin, W. (1969). The work of art in the age of mechanical reproduction. In H. Arendt (Ed.), *Illuminations* (pp. 217–251). New York: Schocken.

Benjamin, W. (2008). The work of art in the age of its technological reproducibility: Second version (E. Jephcott, R. Livingstone, H. Eiland, & Others, Trans.). In M. W. Jennings, B. Doherty, & T. Y. Levin (Eds.), *The work of art in the age of its technological reproducibility, and other writings on media* (pp. 19–55). Cambridge, MA: Harvard University Press.

Bertsch, G. C., Hedler, E., & Dietz, M. (1994). *SED: Schönes Einheits Design = Stunning eastern design = Savoir eviter le design*. Cologne: Taschen Verlag.

Biéler, A. (1965). *Kirchbau und Gottesdienst*. Neukirchen-Vluyn: Neukirchener Verlag.

Böhme, G. (1986). Kants Begriff der Materie in seiner Schrift 'Metaphysische Anfangsgründe der Naturwissenschaft'. In *Philosophieren mit Kant* (pp. 173–196). Frankfurt a. M.: Suhrkamp.

Böhme, G. (1989). Jacob Böhme (1575-1624). In G. Böhme (Ed.), *Klassiker der Naturphilosophie* (pp. 158–170). München: Beck.

Böhme, G. (1991). Über Synästhesien – On synaesthesiae. *Daidalos, 41*, 28–36.

Böhme, G. (1993a). Atmosphere as the fundamental concept of a new aesthetics. *Thesis Eleven, 36*(1), 113–126.

Böhme, G. (1993b). Index over de aestetiske exempler i Kants 'Kritik der Urteilskraft'. *Kritik (Kopenhagen), 105*, 79–80.

Böhme, G. (1995a). *Atmosphäre: Essays zur neuen Ästhetik* (Vol. 927). Frankfurt am Main: Suhrkamp.

Böhme, G. (1995b). *Briefe an meine Töchter*. Frankfurt am Main: Insel Verlag.

Böhme, G. (1995c). Staged materiality. *Daidalos, 56*, 36–43.

Böhme, G. (1998a). *Anmutungen: über das Atmosphärische*. Ostfildern vor Stuttgart: Edition Tertium.

Böhme, G. (1998b). The atmosphere of a city. *Issues in Contemporary Culture and Aesthetics, 7*, 5–13.

Böhme, G. (1998c). Brief an einen japanischen Freund über das Zwischen. In T. Ogawa (Ed.), *Interkulturelle Philosophie und Phänomenologie in Japan* (pp. 233–239). München: Iuridicum Verlag.

Böhme, G. (1999a). *Für eine ökologische Naturästhetik*. Frankfurt am Main: Suhrkamp.

Böhme, G. (1999b). *Kants Kritik der Urteilskraft in neuer Sicht*. Frankfurt am Main: Suhrkamp.

Böhme, G. (2000a). Acoustic atmospheres. A contribution to the study of ecological aesthetics. *Soundscape, 1*(1), 14–18.

Böhme, G. (2000b). *Platons theoretische Philosophie*. Stuttgart: J.B. Metzler.

Böhme, G. (2001a). *Aisthetik. Vorlesungen über Ästhetik als allgemeine Wahrnehmungslehre [Aisthetik. Lectures on Aesthetics as a Common Theory of Perception]*. München: Wilhelm Fink Verlag.

Böhme, G. (2001b). *Einführung in die Philosophie: Weltweisheit, Lebensform, Wissenschaft*. Frankfurt am Main: Suhrkamp.

Böhme, G. (2001c). Zur Kritik der ästhetischen Ökonomie. *Zeitschrift fur Kritische Theorie, 7*(12), 69–82.

Böhme, G. (2003). Contribution to the critique of aesthetic economy (Zur Kritik der ästhetischen Ökonomie). *Thesis Eleven, 73*(May), 71–82.

Böhme, G. (2004). Atmospheres: the connection between music and architecture beyond physics. In N. Baltzer & K. W. Forster (Eds.), *Metamorph, Katalog 9. International Architecture Exhibition* (Vol. 3: Focus). Venezia: Marsilio.

Böhme, G. (2005a). Atmosphere as the subject matter of architecture. In P. Ursprung (Ed.), *Herzog & de Meuron. Natural History*. Baden: Lars Müller Publishers.

Böhme, G. (2005b). Was wird aus dem Subjekt? Selbstkultivierung nach Kant. In I. Kaplow (Ed.), *Nach Kant: Erbe und Kritik* (pp. 1–16). Münster: Lit.

Böhme, G. (2007). ,Mir läuft ein Schauer übern ganzen Leib' – das Wetter, die Witterungslehre und die Sprache der Gefühle ['A shudder runs through my whole body' – weather, meteorology and the language of feelings]. In W. Frick, J. Golz, A. Meier, & E. Zehm (Eds.), *Goethe-Jahrbuch* (Vol. 124, pp. 133–141). Göttingen: Wallstein Verlag.

Böhme, G. (2008a). Die Atmosphäre. In M. Andritzky (Ed.), *Von der guten Form zum guten Leben: 100 Jahre Werkbund* (pp. 107–114). Frankfurt am Main: Anabas-Verlag.

Böhme, G. (2008b). Atmosphären in der Architektur [Atmospheres in Architecture]. In O. Bartels (Ed.), *Metropole* (Vol. 2, pp. 52–67). Berlin: Jovis.

Böhme, G. (2009). Phänomenologie des Lichts [The phenomenology of light]. In J. Turrell & U. Sinnreich (Eds.), *James Turrell – Geometrie des Lichts [Geometry of light]. Zentrum für Internationale Lichtkunst Unna. Exhibition catalogue with text by Gernot Böhme, Julian Heynen, and Agostino de Rosa* (pp. 69–82). Ostfildern: Hatje Cantz Verlag.

Böhme, G. (2010a). The concept of body as the nature we ourselves are. *The Journal of Speculative Philosophy, 24*(3), 224–238.

Böhme, G. (2010b). On beauty. *The Nordic Journal of Aesthetics, 39,* 22–33.

Böhme, G. (2013). *Atmosphäre: essays zur neuen Ästhetik.* Frankfurt am Main: Suhrkamp Verlag.

Böhme, G. (2014). Flanieren in der Postmoderne. In A. Denk & U. Schröder (Eds.), *Stadt der Räume: Interdisziplinäre Uberlegungen zu Räumen der Stadt* (pp. 11–18). Tübingen: Wasmuth.

Böhme, G. (2016). *Ästhetischer Kapitalismus.* Berlin: Suhrkamp Verlag.

Böhme, J. (1651). *Signatura rerum, or the signature of all things: shewing the sign, and signification of the severall forms and shapes in the creation (scanned Duke University Libraries, hosted by Princeton Theological Commons)* (J. Ellistone, Trans.). London: John Macock.

Böhme, G., & Böhme, H. (1996). *Feuer, Wasser, Erde, Luft: eine Kulturgeschichte der Elemente.* München: Beck.

Böhme, H., & Böhme, G. (2010). *Das Andere der Vernunft: zur Entwicklung von Rationalitätsstrukturen am Beispiel Kants.* Frankfurt am Main: Suhrkamp.

Böhme, G., Chakraborty, R. N., & Weiler, F. (1994). *Migration und Ausländerfeindlichkeit* (Vol. 86). Darmstadt: Wissenschaftliche Buchgesellschaft.

Bollnow, O. F. (2010). *Mensch und Raum.* Stuttgart: Kohlhammer.

Boswell, A. (2014). Fractured atmospherics. *Interstices: Journal of Architecture and Related Arts,* 36–46.

Brathe, P. (1906). *Theorie des evangelischen Kirchengebäudes: Ein ergänzendes Kapitel zur evangelischen Liturgik.* Stuttgart: Steinkopf.

Brown, B. (2015). *Other things.* Chicago, IL: The University of Chicago Press.

Campbell, J. (1972). *Myths to live by.* New York: Viking Press.

Cramer, F., & Kaempfer, W. (1992). *Die Natur der Schönheit: Zur Dynamik der schönen Formen.* Frankfurt am Main: Insel Verlag.

Dahlhaus, C. (1982). *Esthetics of music.* New York: Cambridge University Press.

Descartes, R. (1985). *The philosophical writings of descartes* (J. Cottingham, R. Stoothoff, & D. Murdoch, Trans. Vol. 1). New York: Cambridge University Press.

Diaconu, M. (2014). The sky around our bodies: Climate and atmospheric perception. In A. Michaels, & C. Wulf (Eds.), *Exploring the senses: South Asian and European perspectives on rituals and performativity* (pp. 317–337). New Delhi: Routledge.

Durth, W. (1988). *Die Inszenierung der Alltagswelt: Zur Kritik der Stadtgestaltung.* Braunschweig: Vieweg.

Duve, T. d. (1996). *Kant after Duchamp.* Cambridge, MA: MIT Press.

Eberle, M. (1980). *Individuum und Landschaft: zur Entstehung und Entwicklung der Landschaftsmalerei.* Giessen: Anabas-Verlag.

Eckert, N. (1998). *Das Bühnenbild im 20. Jahrhundert.* Berlin: Henschel.

Eco, U. (1968). *La struttura assente.* Milano: Bompiani.

Eco, U. (1972). Introduction to a semiotics of iconic signs. *Versus, 2*(1), 1–15.

Eco, U. (1976). *A theory of semiotics.* Bloomington: Indiana University Press.

Endell, A., & David, H. (1995). *Vom Sehen: Texte 1896–1925 über Architektur, Formkunst und 'Die Schönheit der grossen Stadt'.* Basel: Birkhäuser.

Forssman, E. (1975). *Die Kunstgeschichte und die Trivialkunst: vorgetragen am 27. April 1974.* Heidelberg: Winter.

Frank, E. (1962). *Plato und die sogenannten Pythagoreer: ein Kapitel aus der Geschichte des griechischen Geistes*. Darmstadt: Wissenschaftliche Buchgesellschaft.

Giedion, S. (1967). *Space, time and architecture: the growth of a new tradition*. Cambridge, MA: Harvard University Press.

Goethe, J. W. v., & Eastlake, C. L. (1840). *Goethe's theory of colours; with notes by Charles Lock Eastlake* (C. L. Eastlake, Trans.). London: John Murray.

Goethe, J. W. v., & Talbot, R. (1835). *Part the first of Goethe's Faust*. London: Smith, Elder, and Co.

Gombrich, E. H. (1969). *Art and illusion: a study in the psychology of pictorial representation*. Princeton, NJ: Princeton University Press.

Gombrich, E. H. (1972). The mask and the face: the perception of physiognomic likeness in life and in art. In E. H. Gombrich, J. Hochberg, & M. Black (Eds.), *Art, perception and reality* (pp. 1–46). Baltimore, MD: JHU Press.

Goodman, N. (1968). *Languages of art*. Indianapolis, IN: The Bobbs-Merrill Company, Inc.

Grimm Brothers. (n.d.). *Fairy Tales*, translated by Margaret Hunt (from Grimm's Household Tales. London: G. Bell, 1884). Retrieved from http://germanstories .vcu.edu/grimm/jorinde_e.html

Habermas, J. (2014). *Theorie des kommunikativen Handelns*. Frankfurt am Main: Suhrkamp.

Haraway, D. (1991). *Simians, cyborgs, and women: the reinvention of nature*. New York: Routledge.

Haug, W. F. (1986). *Critique of commodity aesthetics: appearance, sexuality, and advertising in capitalist society* (R. Bock, Trans.). Minneapolis: University of Minnesota Press.

Hegel, G. W. F. (1975). *Aesthetics: lectures on fine art. Vols 1–2* (T. M. Knox, Trans.). Oxford: Clarendon Press.

Heidegger, M. (2010). *Being and time. Revised and with a Foreword by Dennis J. Schrnid* (J. Stambaugh, Trans.). Albany, NY: SUNY Press.

Hejduk, J. (1985). *Mask of Medusa: works 1947–1983*. New York: Rizzoli.

Hirschfeld, C. C. L. (2001). *Theory of garden art* (L. B. Parshall, Trans.). Philadelphia: University of Pennsylvania Press.

Hosokawa, S. (1984). The walkman effect. *Popular music, 4* (Performers and Audiences), 165–180.

Huppertz, M. (2000). *Schizophrene Krisen*. Bern: Huber.

Jencks, C. A. (1987). *The Language of Post-Modern Architecture* (5th edn). New York: Rizzoli.

Julmi, C. (2015). *Atmosphären in Organisationen: wie Gefühle das Zusammenleben in Organisationen beherrschen* (Vol. 10). Bochum/Freiburg: Projekt Verlag.

Jung, H. J. (1979). *Heinrich Stillings Jugend*. Stuttgart: P. Reclam.

Kant, I., & Walker, N. (2007). *Critique of judgement* (J. C. Meredith, Trans.). Oxford: Oxford University Press.

Kimura, B., & Weinmayr, E. (1995). *Zwischen Mensch und Mensch: Strukturen japanischer Subjektivität*. Darmstadt: Wissenschaftliche Buchgesellschaft.

Klages, L. (1970). *Grundlegung der Wissenschaft vom Ausdruck*. Bonn: Bouvier.

Klages, L. (2001). *Vom kosmogonischen Eros*. Bonn: Bouvier.

Klages, L., & Schröder, H. E. (2000). *Der Geist als Widersacher der Seele*. Bonn: Bouvier.

Kozljanic, R. J. (2004). *Der Geist eines Ortes: Kulturgeschichte und Phänomenologie des Genius Loci*. München: Albunea Verlag.

Kümmerlen, R. (1929). *Zur Ästhetik bühnenräumlicher Prinzipien*. Ludwigsburg: Schmoll & Häußermann.

Küppers, B.-O. (1993). Die ästhetischen Dimensionen natürlicher Komplexität. In W. Welsch (Ed.), *Die Aktualität des Ästhetischen* (pp. 247–277). München: Fink.

La Mettrie, J. O. d. (2011). *L'homme-machine: texte intégral [Reproduction en Fac-similé]*. Paris: Avenir des sciences.

La Motte-Haber, H. d. (2004). *Handbuch der systematischen Musikwissenschaft*. Laaber: Laaber.

Lamb, C., & Curtius, L. (1944). *Die Tempel von Paestum*. Leipzig: Insel-Verlag.

Larmann, R. (2007). *Stage design*. Köln: Daab.

Latham, A. (1999). The power of distraction: distraction, tactility, and habit in the work of Walter Benjamin. *Environment and Planning D, 17*, 451–474.

Le Corbusier. (1999). *Le Corbusier talks with students*. New York: Princeton Architectural Press.

MacIntyre, J. (1982). *Der Geist in den Wassern: ein Buch zu Ehren des Bewußtseins der Wale und Delphine*. Frankfurt am Main: Zweitausendeins.

Marcuse, H. (2011). *Eros and civilization*. Retrieved from http://solomon.soth .alexanderstreet.com.ezproxy.aut.ac.nz/cgi-bin/asp/philo/soth/documentidx .pl?sourceid=S10023165

Mersch, D. (2002). *Was sich zeigt: Materialität, Präsenz, Ereignis*. München: Fink.

Mersch, D. (2007). An-Ruf und Ant-Wort. In U. v. Arnswald, & J. Kertscher (Eds.), *Hermeneutik und die Grenzen der Sprache: Hermeneutik, Sprachphilosophie, Anthropologie* (pp. 187–212). Berlin: Parerga.

Morton, T. (2007). *Ecology without nature: rethinking environmental aesthetics*. Cambridge, MA: Harvard University Press.

Newton, I., Hall, A. R., & Hall, M. B. (1962). *Unpublished scientific papers of Isaac Newton; a selection from the Portsmouth collection in the University Library, Cambridge*. Cambridge: Cambridge University Press.

Norberg-Schulz, C. (1975). *Meaning in Western architecture*. New York: Praeger.

Norberg-Schulz, C. (1979). *Genius loci: towards a phenomenology of architecture*. New York: Rizzoli.

Norman, E. R. (1990). *The house of God: church architecture, style, and history*. New York: Thames and Hudson.

Novalis. (2005). *The novices of sais* (R. Manheim, Trans.). New York: Archipelago Books.

Novalis & Stoljar, M. M. (1997). *Philosophical writings*. Albany: State University of New York Press.

Novalis, Kamnitzer, E., & Helmstatt, G. v. (1929). *Fragmente*. Dresden: Wolfgang Jess.

Otto, R. (1932). *Das Gefühl des Überweltlichen. Sensus numinis. [With plates.]*. München: Beck.

Paulitsch, M. (1989). *Moderne Holzwerkstoffe: Grundlagen, Technologie, Anwendungen*. Berlin: Springer.

Plato. (n.d.). Greater Hippias I (translated by Benjamin Jowett). Retrieved from http://www.hermes-press.com/greater_hippias.htm

Plato, & Benardete, S. (2006). *The being of the beautiful: Plato's Theaetetus, Sophist, and Statesman* (S. Benardete, Trans.). Chicago, IL: University of Chicago Press.

Plato, Ferrari, G. R. F., & Griffith, T. (2000). *The republic.* Cambridge, UK: Cambridge University Press.

Portmann, A. (1961). *Animals as social beings.* New York: Harper & Row.

Raff, T. (2008). *Die Sprache der Materialien: Anleitung zu einer Ikonologie der Werkstoffe.* Münster: Waxmann.

Redner, H. (1994). *A New Science of Representation. Towards an Integrated Theory of Representation in Science, Politics and Art.* Boulder, CO: Westview Press.

Reichel, P. (1991). *Der schöne Schein des Dritten Reiches: Faszination und Gewalt des Faschismus.* München: C. Hanser.

Ricoeur, P. (1967). *The symbolism of evil.* New York: Harper & Row.

Riedel, F. (2015). Music as atmosphere. Lines of becoming in congregational worship. *Lebenswelt. Aesthetics and Philosophy of Experience, 6,* 80–111.

Riegl, A. (1985). *Late Roman art industry* (R. Winkes, Trans.). Roma: G. Bretschneider.

Rowe, C. (1976). Character and composition. In *The mathematics of the ideal villa, and other essays* (pp. 59–88). Cambridge, MA: MIT Press.

Scelsi, G., Hirayama, M., Krieger, U., Grözinger, J., & Neffe, R. (2007). *Canti del Capricorno.* Retrieved from http://www.naxosmusiclibrary.com

Schafer, R. M. (2010). *Die Ordnung der Klänge: eine Kulturgeschichte des Hörens.* Mainz: Schott.

Schiller, F. (2004). *On the aesthetic education of man* (R. Snell, Trans.). Mineola: Dover Publications.

Schivelbusch, W. (1988). *Disenchanted night: the industrialization of light in the nineteenth century.* Berkeley: University of California Press.

Schmarsow, A. (2001). *Barock und Rokoko: das Malerische in der Architektur: eine kritische Auseinandersetzung.* Berlin: Mann.

Schmitz, H. (1964). *System der Philosophie. Bd. III.1 Der leibliche Raum.* Bonn: Bouvier.

Schmitz, H. (1965). *System der Philosophie. Bd. II.1 Der Leib.* Bonn: Bouvier.

Schmitz, H. (1969). *System der Philosophie. Bd. III.2 Der Gefühlsraum.* Bonn: Bouvier.

Schmitz, H. (1977). *System der Philosophie. Bd III.4. Das Göttliche und der Raum.* Bonn: Bouvier.

Schmitz, H. (1978). *System der Philosophie. Bd. III.5 Die Wahrnehmung.* Bonn: Bouvier.

Schmitz, H. (1990). *Der unerschöpfliche Gegenstand: Grundzüge der Philosophie.* Bonn: Bouvier.

Schmitz, H. (1999). *Adolf Hitler in der Geschichte.* Bonn: Bouvier.

Schmitz, H. (2002). Hermann Schmitz, The 'New Phenomenology'. In A.-T. Tymieniecka (Ed.), *Phenomenology world-wide: foundations, expanding dynamisms, life-engagements: a guide for research and study* (pp. 491–493). Dordrecht: Kluwer Academic Publishers.

Schnell, R. (1993). City Lights. Zur medialen Interdiskursivität der großen Stadt [City Lights. On the Medial Discursiveness of Big Cities]. In J. Fürnkäs, P. Richter, R. Schnell, & S. Yoshijima (Eds.), *Das Verstehen von Hören und Sehen. Aspekte der Medienästhetik [Understanding Hearing and Seeing. Aspects of Media Aesthetics]*. Bielefeld: Aisthesis Verlag.

Schuberth, O. (1955). *Das Bühnenbild: Geschichte, Gestalt, Technik*. München: Callwey.

Shariatmadari, D. (2015). Swarms, floods and marauders: the toxic metaphors of the migration debate. *theguardian*. Retrieved from http://www.theguardian .com/commentisfree/2015/aug/10/migration-debate-metaphors-swarms -floods-marauders-migrants

Spitz, R. A. (1950). Psychosomatic epidemic of infancy and preventive psychiatry. *Psyche-Zeitschrift für Psychoanalyse und ihre Anwendungen, 4*(1), 17–30.

Staemmler, F.-M. (2007). On macaque monkeys, players and clairvoyants: some new ideas for a Gestalt therapeutic conscept of empathy. *Studies in Gestalt Therapie–Dialogical Bridges, 1*(2), 43–63.

Stillman, J. M. (1960). *The story of alchemy and early chemistry (the story of early chemistry)*. New York: Dover Publications.

Ströker, E. (1987). *Investigations in philosophy of space*. Athens: Ohio University Press.

Takamura, M. (2011). *Tactility and modernity: the sense of touch in DH Lawrence, Alfred Stieglitz, Walter Benjamin, and Maurice Merleau-Ponty*. PhD Thesis, Champaign: University of Illinois at Urbana-Champaign.

Tellenbach, H. (1968). *Geschmack und Atmosphäre. Medien menschlichen Elementarkontaktes (Taste and Atmosphere. Media of elementary human contact)*. Salzburg: Otto Müller Verlag.

von Goethe, J. W. (1840). *Goethe's theory of colours: translated from the German by Charles Lock Eastlake*. London: John Murray.

Waldenfels, B. (2006). Das Lautwerden der Stimme. In D. Kolesch, & S. Krämer (Eds.), *Stimme: Annäherung an ein Phänomen* (pp. 191–210). Frankfurt am Main: Suhrkamp.

Westerkamp, H. (1988). *Listening and soundmaking a study of music-as-environment*. M.A. Thesis, Vancouver: Simon Frazer University.

Wölfflin, H. (1914). *Die klassische Kunst. Eine Einführung in die italienische Renaissance*. München: F. Bruckmann.

Wölfflin, H. (1952). *Classic art: an introduction to the Italian Renaissance* (P. Murray & L. Murray, Trans.). London: Phaidon.

Wright, F. L. (1972). *A testament*. New York: Avon.

Zajonc, A. (1993). *Catching the light: the entwined history of light and mind*. New York: Bantam Books.

Zumthor, P. (1998). *Thinking architecture*. Baden: Lars Müller Publishers.

Index